ADVANCING WORD 2000

FOR WINDOWS

CAROL MCKENZIE & PAT BRYDEN

Learn to pass advanced level exams

- RSA Text Processing Stage III Part 1
- RSA Word Processing Stage III Part 2
- RSA Document Presentation Stage III Part 2

Heinemann Educational Publishers,
Halley Court, Jordan Hill, Oxford OX2 8EJ
A division of Reed Educational & Professional Publishing Ltd

Heinemann is a registered trademark of Reed Educational & Professional Publishing Limited

OXFORD MELBOURNE AUCKLAND JOHANNESBURG BLANTYRE GABORONE IBADAN
PORTSMOUTH NH (USA) CHICAGO

First published 2000
2004 2003 2002 2001 2000
10 9 8 7 6 5 4 3 2 1

A catalogue record for this book is available from the British Library on request.

ISBN 0 435 45433 1

Cover designed by Sarah Garbett

Typeset by TechType, Abingdon, Oxon

Printed and bound in Great Britain by Thomson Litho Ltd, East Kilbride, Scotland

Screen shots reprinted with permission from Microsoft Corporation

Acknowledgements
We would like to thank our respective families for their encouragement and support while writing this book.

Carol McKenzie and Pat Bryden

Tel: 01865 888058 www.heinemann.co.uk

CONTENTS

OCR/RSA TEXT PROCESSING SCHEMES

The Royal Society of Arts Examinations Board has merged and been renamed OCR (Oxford, Cambridge and RSA Examinations). Qualifications formerly certificated by RSA are now awarded through OCR. For the purposes of this series of textbooks, the acronym OCR/RSA will be used for brevity and clarity.

The Suite of Text Processing exams offered by OCR/RSA covers Stages I, II and III. The overall aim of these modular awards is to meet the business document production and presentation requirements of the discerning employer and to give candidates the opportunity to demonstrate competence in text processing skills to the level demanded for NVQ Administration. Specific mapping of performance criteria, range, and knowledge and understanding is given in the OCR/RSA scheme documents. An example of the mapping of OCR/RSA Stage III Text Processing Part 1 to NVQ Administration Level 3 is given below:

Element	Performance Criteria			Range									Knowledge and Understanding						
13.2/14.2/15.2	2	3	7		1	3	8	9	10	5	6	7		1	2	3	4	5	7	8

Stage I indicates the candidate has sufficient knowledge or skill to begin employment, although further study would be beneficial.

Stage II shows a sound understanding of and competence in the subject and a recommendation for employment. It also suggests that someone who holds such a certificate may well benefit from advanced studies.

Stage III indicates an all-round knowledge and understanding of the subject and, in the practical skills, a very high degree of proficiency.

At each stage, there is a *Part 1* examination which assesses the core skills at that stage. A selection of *Part 2* examinations assesses skills in more specific applications such as word processing, typewriting and audio-transcription.

There is a Text Processing Diploma at Stages II and III; this has been designed to recognise all-round achievement in text processing. The following modules, which contribute to the Stage III Diploma, are covered in this book:
* Stage III Text Processing Part 1
* Stage III Word Processing Part 2
* Stage III Document Presentation Part 2

The diploma is awarded to candidates who demonstrate competence in Text Processing *Part 1* and three *Part 2* examinations at the same stage. Additional modules include specialist applications of text processing, for example:
* typewriting
* shorthand transcription, and
* audio-transcription.

ABOUT THIS BOOK

This book has been written as a continuation text to *Introducing Word 2000* and *Extending Word 2000* by the same authors. It has been designed as a progressive course and is suitable for use in the classroom, in an open-learning workshop or as a private study aid.

This book has been produced to assist people who wish to gain advanced level accreditation through the OCR/RSA's Text Processing Schemes, using the Microsoft Word 2000 software package. It is anticipated that users will be familiar with the QWERTY keyboard and have basic competence in using computer hardware.

Units 1–5 are designed for students preparing to take advanced examinations such as OCR/RSA Stage III Text Processing Part 1. These units are also suitable for the revision of text processing skills, without taking an examination.

Units 6–10 are designed for students preparing to take intermediate examinations such as OCR/RSA Stage III Word Processing Part 2. These units are also suitable for students who wish to learn how to prepare multi-page documents, more complex tables and text in 'newspaper columns' without taking an examination.

Units 11–16 are designed for students preparing to take the OCR/RSA Stage III Document Presentation Part 2 examination. These units are also suitable for students who wish to extend their knowledge and skills to include advanced presentation skills without taking an examination.

A brief outline of the examination and examination practice for each stage of learning are included in Units 5, 10 and 16.

Format of the book

Printout checks for all exercises are given at the back of the book (pages 176–216). Use them to check your work.

The Progress Review Checklist (pages 164–165) helps you keep a record of progress, noting the number of errors made. If completed at the end of each working session, this checklist can be referred to quickly, in order to locate the unit to be worked on next.

When completing the exercises, command boxes for Word 2000 functions are given when appropriate. Instruction is given on how to carry out the required function. The commands explain keyboard, mouse and menu operation.

The Glossary of Commands (pages 166–175) provides a comprehensive, alphabetically-listed quick reference for all the Word 2000 commands introduced in the book. The commands are shown for keyboard, mouse and menu users. Shortcut keys are included because many students prefer to use these methods, as they become more familiar with the program.

All exercise material is to be completed in Times New Roman point size 12 unless indicated otherwise.

Working through a unit

1   When you see this symbol, read all the information before you begin. You may also need to refer back to this information as you carry out the exercises.

2   When you see this symbol, carry out the exercises, following the numbered steps, eg 1.1, 1.2.

3   Use Word 2000's spelling and grammar tool to check your document. Proofread the document carefully yourself – the spelling tool does not find every error.

4   Use the Print Preview facility to check your document is going to be correct when printed. If it is, save your work on to your floppy disk (usually in A Drive) or into an appropriate directory. Then print your work.

5   Compare your document with the printout checks at the back of the book (pages 176–216). (If you are using this book in class, your tutor may also wish to check your work.) Correct any errors you find in your work and print the documents again if required.

6   Complete your Progress Review Checklist. Then exit from Word 2000 or begin work on the next unit (as appropriate).

Do not delete files from your disk – you may need them later!

UNIT 1 DOCUMENT FORMATTING, PAGE NUMBERING AND FOOTNOTES

By the end of Unit 1 you should have revised many intermediate formatting techniques. You should also have learnt how to:

◎ start page numbering from a given page number
◎ change the appearance of header and footer text
◎ insert footnotes to appear at the foot of the page.

The techniques for revision listed below are included in Exercise 1A and also in Exercise 2A in the next unit. If you have problems with any of the techniques then you should go back to *Extending Word 2000*. If you do not have access to a copy of the book, you can refer to the alphabetical glossary in this book (pages 166–175) or ask your tutor to explain anything you are unsure about.

◎ Spelling and grammar, indenting text, setting margins, correction signs, consistency of presentation, page numbering, multi-page documents.
◎ Locating information from another document.
◎ Headers and footers.
◎ Enumeration/bulleted points.
◎ Document line length.

Note: The following types of errors are *not indicated* in the draft at Stage III. It is up to you to notice them and to correct them:

◎ Typographical errors.
◎ Spelling errors.
◎ Errors of agreement.
◎ Punctuation errors, including apostrophes.

Word 2000's spelling and grammar checks will give you some help in correcting these but you should always proofread the text through very carefully yourself, as the spelling and grammar check will not pick up every mistake.

Exercise 1A

1.1   Open a new document and key in the following text. Format the document as follows:

◎   Single line spacing, except where indicated otherwise.
◎   Ragged (unjustified) right margin.
◎   Document line length of 13 cm.
◎   Insert a header **CREATIVE PASTIMES** at top right of each page.
◎   Number the pages at the bottom right of each page.

The glossary will remind you of any commands you are not sure of.

THE ART OF DECOUPAGE ← centre and bold

If you are looking for an interesting artistic hobby which is not too difficult to learn and won't break the bank, perhaps decoupage is for you. Many of us admire the design work and paintings produced by others but feel we cannot ourselves make anything of worth. Decoupage demands only patience!

[B]

No special equipment or tools are needed for decoupage projects. This fact makes it ideal as a new hobby which will not prove to be too expensive as many pastimes do. The average household already contains most of the materials and tools you will need to begin.

Copy to [A]

A beginner's kit should comprise:

1. Small scissors or scalpel
2. Large scissors
3. A natural sponge
4. Soft rags
5. Brushes
6. Finger bowl and water
7. Wallpaper paste
8. Coloured pencils and paints

You will probably find most of these items in a cupboard or in your decorating kit.

PROJECTS ← Please make all side headings like this one

You can use your new skills to decorate picture frames, boxes, vases and bowls. If you are really ambitious, you could make an attractive room screen or decorate the top of a coffee table. After practising on small objects to begin with, you will soon come up with other, larger projects!

Please move to [B]

Decoupage Through The Ages — CAPS

(from the French découper - to cut out)

Decoupage became very popular during the 15th century when German furniture was being decorated with elaborate borders simulating 'tarsia' work. The work was so skilfully executed that it was difficult, from a distance, to distinguish it from the complicated wood inlay work which it reproduced. The name *arte povera* was given to the use of cut-outs to decorate Venetian furniture with chinoiserie figures in the style of Oriental lacquer ware. This work is now far from the reach of the poor – it fetches very high prices at auction.

(the poor man's art)

European gentlewomen of the ~~eighteenth~~ 18th century incorporated decoupage into their (sometimes very impressive) repertoire of artistic pursuits.

Together with music, painting and needlework, decoupage gave them an opportunity to create some excellent works. They did not ~~simple~~ amuse simply themselves ~~or keep themselves busy~~; their work provides us (still) with many excellent pieces.

The skill declined in popularity at the beginning of the twentieth century but is now enjoying a revival. This renewed interest has been helped by the advent of the photocopier and the invention of special varnishes.

In the mid 19th century with the mass production of Victorian scrap sheets (collections of colourful images), decoupage became widespread and no longer confined to the gentry. The whole family would be involved in a project such as the production of a scrap screen for the nursery. Work carried out in this way is often rather haphazard as if the main aim of the ~~venture~~ project had ✓ been to cover every spare inch of the available space rather than to plan and prepare a work of artistic merit. *However, the value of the work to those involved was probably of a personal domestic, rather than aesthetic, nature.*

[A] ———————— Decoupage Today

Nowadays

The basic motifs or designs are of 2 types. Some people use special black-and-white printed designs and apply colour using pencils, inks or paints. Others prefer to use printed designs from wrapping paper, wallpaper, cards and magazines. The latter method follows the Victorian tradition of scrapsheets, whilst the former mimics the Venetian (italics) *arte povera and allows more scope for individual creativity.*

1.2 Use the spelling and grammar tool to check your work, and proofread it yourself as well. Make sure the format of the document conforms to the instructions given earlier. Save the document under the filename **EX1A** and print one copy. Check your printout with the printout at the back of the book. If you find any errors, correct them and print the document again, if necessary.

Number pages from a given page number

You have already learnt how to insert page numbering in Word 2000 and how to select the position, alignment and format of the page number. Word 2000 automatically numbers the pages using the number indicated in the status bar at the bottom of the document window.

For some documents, it may be necessary to start page numbering with a number other than 1, for example, if several introductory pages are to be inserted before the main text of the document. There are two methods of setting up this function in Word 2000.

Insert method	View header and footer method
Select: **Page Numbers** from the **Insert** menu Select from the **Position** and **Alignment** options as appropriate Click: **Format**	Select: **Header and Footer** from the **View** menu Click: The 🖼 **Format Page Number** icon on the Header and Footer Tool Bar

The **Page Number Format** dialogue box is displayed on screen (Figure 1.1).

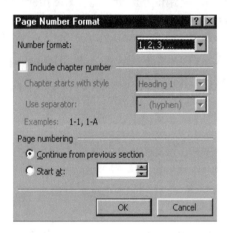

Figure 1.1 Page Number Format dialogue box

◎   Click: **Start at** in the **Page Numbering** section (black dot is displayed)
◎   Key in or select in spin box: The page number you want your document to start from
◎   Click: **OK**

Note: If necessary, you may also change the format of the page number in the **Number Format** dialogue box, selecting Arabic numbers (1, 2, 3), Roman numerals (I, II, III) or letters (a, b, c).

Change the appearance of headers and footers

You have already learnt how to insert headers and footers to appear on each page of a document and how to select the position and alignment of the text. You may be required to change the font, font size or format of the header/footer text to make it easily distinguishable from the body text of the document.

Select: **Header and Footer** from the **View** menu
Key in: Header or footer text
Select: The text
Select: **Font** from the **Format** menu
Select: The required format from: **Font, Font Style, Size, Underline, Colour and Effects**

The **Preview** box displays the text formatted as it will appear in the document:

Click: **OK** to confirm selections
Click: **Close** to close the Header dialogue box

Note: Page numbers are included in the header or footer text box. You may wish to change the appearance of the page number at the same time as you change the header or footer text.

Select: The page number
Select: The required format from: **Font, Font Style, Size, Underline, Colour and Effects** from the **Format, Font** menu as above

 ## Footnotes

Footnotes are used to explain in more depth, or provide references for, a particular point made within the body of the document text. A footnote comprises two linked parts:

1   A footnote symbol, such as a * or a superscripted character, eg [1] is placed as a reference mark in the body of the text next to the word, figure or phrase which needs further explanation.

2   The same symbol is repeated later in the document with the explanatory text.

Note: A superscripted character is printed slightly above the standard line, eg 8.5^2. An example of a footnote is given in Figure 1.2.

> The special discount price for bulk orders[1] applies during the winter quarter[2] only.
>
> 1   Quantities of ten or more
> 2   December-February

Figure 1.2 A footnote

Note: There is no space before the footnote reference mark in the body of the text. There should be at least one space between the footnote character and the explanatory text.

You can insert footnotes manually, using keyboard symbols or superscripted characters. Or you can use Word 2000's automatic footnote command which automatically numbers footnote marks or allows you to create your own custom marks. With this latter method, Word 2000 will automatically renumber the footnote reference marks if you add, delete or move any of them. The automatic method is not difficult to learn and, when you have mastered it, you will find it is more effective than the manual method.

Insert a footnote using Word 2000's footnote command
To enter the footnote reference marker in the text
Position the pointer: Immediately after the last character of the word, figure or phrase requiring a footnote.

Keyboard	Mouse and menu
Press: **Alt + Ctrl + F** (this command bypasses the dialogue box shown in Figure 1.3 and uses default settings. To customise footnotes, use the mouse/ menu method)	Select: **Footnote** from the **Insert** menu

The **Footnote and Endnote** dialogue box is displayed on screen (Figure 1.3).

Figure 1.3 Footnote and Endnote dialogue box

Select: **Footnote** in the **Insert** section
Select: **AutoNumber** in the **Numbering** section to number the footnote(s) automatically
Click on: **OK**

Customise the footnote marker as a symbol
Select: **Custom mark** in the Numbering section
Click on: **Symbol**
Select: **Symbol** from the choice displayed (select another font if required from the Font drop-down menu)
Click on: **OK** twice

Modify the layout of a footnote
Click: **Options, All Footnotes**

◎   **Place at**: allows you to choose the position of the explanatory text – immediately **Beneath** text or at the **Bottom of page**
◎   **Number format**: allows you to select a different footnote display format, eg **a, b, c** or **i, ii, iii**
◎   **Start at**: allows you to specify from which character you want the footnote numbering to start
◎   **Numbering**: allows you to specify the printing of footnotes at different locations in the document

Click on: **OK** to confirm selections

Enter the footnote explanatory text

When you exit the Footnote and Endnote dialogue box, Word 2000 automatically prompts you to enter the explanatory text at the bottom of the page (or other specified location in the document). Word 2000 automatically leaves space after the footnote number or symbol.

Key in: The explanatory text
Click: In the main document to leave the footnote and return to the main document

View footnotes whilst working on the main document text

Double-click: The footnote reference mark in the text

Note: In Normal view, the footnotes appear in the Footnotes panel; in Print Layout view, the footnotes appear at the location they will be printed in the document.

Move or delete a footnote

Use normal cut and paste methods.

Format a footnote

Select: The explanatory text
Use normal text formatting commands, eg bold, italic, font size, etc.

Remove the note separator

You may find that Word 2000 inserts a short horizontal line above the footnotes in your document. OCR/RSA examinations do not require this separating line. However, you will not be penalised if you leave it in. You can remove it, in Normal view, as follows:

Select: **Normal** from the **View** menu
Select: **Footnotes** from the **View** menu
Select: **All Footnotes** in the **Footnotes** drop-down menu
Click: **Footnote Separator** in the **Footnotes** panel drop-down menu
Select: The separator line
Press: **Delete**
Click: Close to return to the main document text

Insert a footnote using the manual entry method
To insert the footnote reference marker in the text

You can use superscript characters or keyboard symbols for the foonote reference marker.

Position the pointer: Immediately after the last character of the word, figure or phrase requiring a footnote

Keyboard	Mouse and menu
Press: **Ctrl + Shift + Plus sign (+)** to change the font to superscript Key in: The footnote character (number, letter or symbol) Press: **Ctrl + Spacebar** to revert to normal text	Select: **Font** from the **Format** menu Select: The **Font** tab Click: The **Superscript** option in the **Effects** section to change the font to superscript Click: **OK** Key in: The footnote character (number, letter or symbol)

Keyboard	Mouse and menu
	Select: **Font** from the **Format** menu Select: The **Font** tab Click: The **Superscript** option in the **Effects** section to revert to normal text Click: **OK**

Enter the footnote explanatory text

Position the insertion pointer: Where you want the explanatory text to appear – usually at the bottom of the page (footnote) or at the end of the document (endnote)

Key in: The same footnote character that was used as a footnote reference mark (in the footnote section, this does not have to be in superscript)

Leave at least one clear space between the reference mark and the footnote explanatory text

Key in: The explanatory text

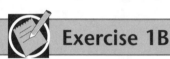

Exercise 1B

1.3   Open the document **EX1A** if it is not already on screen. Save as **EX1B**. Make the following changes to the document format:

◎   Change the header font to Courier New in font size 10.

◎   Change the header alignment to left alignment.

◎   Change the page numbering to start from Page 4.

◎   Add a footer at the left in Times New Roman, font size 8, italic: *Your name*.

1.4   Referring back to the instructions on footnotes, insert a footnote reference marker in the form of an asterisk after the words **small scissors** in the numbered list on the first page of **EX1A** as shown below:

> 1   Small scissors* or scalpel
> 2   Large scissors
> 3   A natural sponge

1.5   Insert the following text as the explanatory footnote (relating to the asterisk you have just inserted) to appear at the foot of the first page:

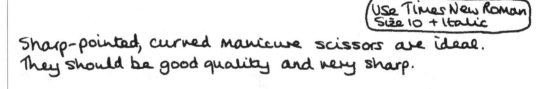

Use Times New Roman Size 10 + Italic

Sharp-pointed, curved manicure scissors are ideal. They should be good quality and very sharp.

1.6   Add the following information at the end of the section referring to **PROJECTS**:

> It may be necessary to prepare the surface you are going to decorate and so you may find that sandpaper, primer, scrapers and paint stripper will be required. It is always worth spending time to prepare the wood or metal correctly to ensure a good final finish.

1.7 Add the following information at the end of the paragraph headed **DECOUPAGE TODAY**:

> Whatever the level of yr artistic ability, you should be able to produce an item to be proud of.

1.8 Use the spelling and grammar tool to check your work, and proofread it yourself as well. Ensure the page break is sensibly positioned and that the document takes up only 2 pages. *You may find it necessary to reduce the top and/or bottom margins to do this.* Resave the document under the same filename (**EX1B**). Print one copy.

1.9 Check your printout with the printout at the back of the book. If you find any errors, correct them and print the document again, if necessary.

 Exercise 1C

1.10 Open the document saved as **EX1B** if it is not already on screen. Save as **EX1C**. Make the following changes to the document format:

- ◎ Change the header format to *Arial* in font size *10* and add <u>underline</u>.
- ◎ Change the header alignment to *centred*.
- ◎ Change the page numbering to start from *Page 1* and centre the page number.
- ◎ Change the document line length to *14 cm*.
- ◎ Change the text alignment to *fully justified* (except for the centred main heading).

1.11 Delete the existing footnote reference marker and footnote text.

1.12 Add the following footnote reference markers and footnote text to the paragraph headed **DECOUPAGE THROUGH THE AGES** as shown below. Ensure the footnotes appear on the same page as the footnote reference.

DECOUPAGE THROUGH THE AGES

Decoupage (from the French découper – to cut out) became very popular during the 15th century when German furniture was being decorated with elaborate borders simulating 'tarsia' work. The work was so skilfully executed that it was difficult, from a distance, to distinguish it from the complicated wood inlay work[1] which it reproduced.

The name *arte povera* (the poor man's art) was given to the use of cut-outs to decorate Venetian furniture with chinoiserie[2] figures in the style of Oriental lacquer[3] ware. This work is now far from the reach of the poor – it fetches very high prices at auction.

1 Use of different woods to form a design
2 Influenced by Chinese art
3 Type of varnish giving a very smooth, glassy coating

Retain footnote style – TNR size 10, italic

1.13 Change the numbered list on the first page to a bulleted list, using the bullet symbol shown below:

❏ Small scissors or scalpel
❏ Large scissors
❏ A natural sponge

1.14 Check your work carefully, ensuring the formatting changes have been made and new footnotes added. Resave the document and print one copy.

1.15 Exit the program if you have finished working or continue straight on to the next unit.

UNIT 2 TEXT FORMATTING, SPELLING, GRAMMAR AND SPECIALISED TEXT

By the end of Unit 2 you should have revised more of the formatting techniques you learnt in *Extending Word 2000* – the second book in this series. You should also have learnt how to:

◎ use AutoCorrect for specialised text
◎ identify and correct errors in the use of apostrophes
◎ identify and correct spelling errors
◎ expand additional abbreviations
◎ interpret additional correction signs
◎ key in specialised text, including symbols, fractions, superscript and subscript.

 ## Proofreading text

One of the main differences between Stage II work and Stage III work is that errors which were indicated for correction at Stage II will *not* be indicated at Stage III. You need to be much more vigilant in checking *all* text whether this is recalled text, manuscript text or keyed in by you.

Typescript containing typographical errors
In the Stage III examinations, you will be expected to carry out complex proofreading, text editing and formatting. Text editing may involve correcting any mistakes made in previous printouts. Watch out for uncorrected spelling errors and transposition errors. Remember, the errors in the draft will *not* be circled for you to correct – you must find them yourself.

Typescript containing spelling errors
Remember, Word 2000 can help you with spelling because it has a built-in spelling and grammar check tool which checks as you type for spelling and grammar errors. Word 2000 will identify a spelling error with a red wavy line and a grammatical error with a green wavy line. However, you must also proofread the text yourself, as Word 2000 will often be unable to check many proper names (eg cities, surnames etc). Also, if you have keyed in the wrong version of a word, eg *their* instead of *there*, Spellcheck will not detect this as both versions are spelt correctly. In the OCR/RSA Stage III examination you will be expected to be able to spell a list of additional words.

Specialist text or frequently used words or names
Only *you* can tell if you have copied names of people or places, or specialist vocabulary, correctly and if a piece of information you were asked to find is correct. If Word 2000 queries a word which you know to be correct, you can ignore Word 2000's prompt to change it. If you are going to use an unusual word fairly frequently then you can add it to the Spellcheck dictionary.

Sometimes, to help you, an author may write unusual words in capitals in the margin and put a dashed line around the word. This is to indicate the correct spelling of the word only – you are not

VYRNWY

CHOLERA

required to key in the word in capitals or to put a dashed line around it! You will find examples of this technique in Exercise 2B.

 ## AutoCorrect

As you type, you may already have noticed that Word 2000 automatically corrects some commonly misspelled words such as *teh* instead of *the* or *adn* instead of *and*. If there is a word you often mistype or misspell, you can add it to Word 2000's list of automatic corrections.

AutoCorrect

Select: **Tools**, **AutoCorrect** from the menu
Ensure the **Replace Text As You Type** check box is ticked
In the **Replace** box, key in: The word you often mistype/misspell, eg unusaul
Key in: The correct spelling of the word in the **With** box, eg unusual
Click: **Add**
Click: **OK**

Word 2000 will also make the following corrections automatically:

◎ Change the second capital letter to a lower-case letter if you accidentally type two capital letters at the beginning of a word.
◎ Capitalise the first letter at the beginning of a sentence.
◎ Capitalise the first letter of the days of the week.
◎ Reverse accidental usage of the cAPS lOCK key.

 ## Exercise 2A

2.1   As you may already have realised, a good use of AutoCorrect is for replacing shortened versions of words which you find particularly difficult to spell. When you key in the shortened version, Word 2000 will automatically replace it with the correct spelling for you. When working with specialist vocabulary, this feature can be a great help. Select **AutoCorrect** from the **Tools** menu. Enter the short version under **Replace:** and the full version, correctly spelt, under **With:**

Replace:	With:
BY CON	BY CONSENT it is hereby ordered:
address all	address all communications for the court to: The Chief Clerk
TMJ	temporo-mandibular joint
Hb	Haemoglobin
oxy	oxyhaemoglobin
Coton	Cotoneaster racemiflorus
phys	physiology

2.2   To test your AutoCorrect entries, with a clear screen, key in the following, pressing the return key between each line:

> BY CON that the Petitioner and the Respondent
> Address all at the County Court
> The TMJ is the only freely movable joint in the head
> Hb combines with oxygen to form oxyhaemoglobin
> Coton var nummularius is also called Wild Cotoneaster
> The study of the function of the human body is phys

If you have followed the instructions correctly for AutoCorrect, Word should automatically have converted your entries to appear on screen as:

> BY CONSENT it is hereby ordered: that the Petitioner and the Respondent
> Address all communications for the court to: The Chief Clerk at the County Court
> The temporo-mandibular joint is the only freely movable joint in the head
> Haemoglobin combines with oxygen to form oxyhaemoglobin
> Cotoneaster racemiflorus var nummularius is also called Wild Cotoneaster
> The study of the function of the human body is physiology

Note: AutoCorrect will only insert replacement entries exactly as they were entered. You would not, for instance, be able automatically to substitute the word 'physiological' instead of 'physiology'. You would either have to key in the whole word correctly, or edit the AutoCorrect entry as appropriate.

2.3   Close the file without saving ready for the next exercise.

Apostrophes

In OCR/RSA Stage III examinations, you will be expected to know when to use an apostrophe and where it should be positioned in the word it relates to. One use of the apostrophe is where it indicates that a letter (or letters) have been left out, eg:

didn't	*(did not)*	aren't	*(are not)*
he'd	*(he had)*	we're	*(we are)*

2.4   Starting a new file, key in the following sentences, shortening the words underlined and putting the apostrophe in the correct place:

> The local residents <u>did not</u> know that <u>they would</u> have to visit the local
> Council office to see the plans. They <u>were not</u> pleased to find that the builders
> <u>had not</u> taken the trouble to consider local feelings. <u>They are</u> to make a protest
> through their local Councillor as they <u>do not</u> think that the proposed
> development is appropriate. <u>They have</u> carried out research and <u>they will</u> take
> their findings along to the meeting.

Leave this work on the screen. Save the document using the filename **EX2A**, but do not close or print the file yet.

Possession

Apostrophes are also used to show possession – that something 'belongs' to someone or something, eg:

Jon's car	*(the car belonging to Jon)*
The writer's opinion	*(the opinion of the writer)*
Next year's holiday	*(the holiday for next year)*
The team's work	*(the work of the team)*

If the word ends in 'ss', an apostrophe is added but there is no extra 's', eg:

The glass' rim	*(the rim of the glass)*

If there is more than one 'possessor', the apostrophe goes after the 's', eg:

The writers' editor	*(the editor of the writers)*
The students' tutor	*(the tutor of the students)*
The glasses' contents	*(the contents of the glasses)*

2.5 Key in the following sentences below the previous exercise, rearranging the underlined words and inserting the apostrophes in the correct places:

> The <u>auditorium of the theatre</u> was full for the <u>last performance of the play</u>.
> The <u>review of the critics</u> had been excellent, praising <u>the flair of the designer</u>
> and the <u>enthusiasm of the cast</u>. The audience waited in anticipation as the
> lights dimmed and the <u>instruments of the orchestra</u> began to produce the music
> which had become familiar to so many people.

Resave the document using the same filename. Leave it on the screen. Do not print it yet.

Its and it's

In speech, 'its' can mean 'it is' (or 'it has') or 'belonging to it'. An apostrophe is used only when the full phrase of 'it is' (or 'it has') is shortened – the apostrophe shows that a letter has been missed out, eg:

It's dry	*(It is dry)*
It's reputed	*(It is reputed)*
It's your turn	*(It is your turn)*
It's been in my possession	*(It has been in my possession)*

But	The television has its screen broken.
	We will look after its production.
	The town had its economy boosted.

2.6 Key in the following passage, below the previous exercises, inserting apostrophes where necessary:

> This plant grows on chalk downland and its shape is described as squat and
> spiny. However, its also found in pine woods, where its been known to grow
> to tree size. Its native to north-western Europe, Asia and North America,
> where its value is mainly for ornamental purposes. A similar tree grows in the
> Mediterranean where its uses are culinary and its valued for its aperitif and
> digestive properties. Its foliage has a pleasant aromatic scent and its distilled
> to produce an essential oil, when its properties are employed for its alternative
> product – perfume.

2.7 Resave the document using the same filename. Check your work on screen against the printout check at the back of the book. If you are unsure of the reason for the inclusion, position or omission of any of the apostrophes, refer back to the explanations in this unit. If you are working with a tutor, you may wish to discuss apostrophes with him or her too. Correct any errors and print a copy of your work.

Spelling in context

You will be expected to be able to spell correctly the following words, and their derivations where marked * (eg plurals, -ed, -ing, -ment, -tion, -ly, -able, -ible). Additional words for Stage III are shown in bold text:

access*	business*	expense*	recommend*
accommodate*	**cancel***	experience*	responsible*
achieve*	client*	financial*	**satisfactory***
acknowledge*	colleague*	foreign	separate*
advertisement*	committee*	government*	**success***
although	correspondence	inconvenient*	sufficient*
apparent*	definite*	**permanent***	temporary*
appreciate*	develop*	receipt*	through
believe*	discuss*	receive*	**unfortunate***

2.8 Spend a little time making sure you know how to spell all the words listed above correctly – ask someone to test you! Learn four per evening and it will take you no time at all.

Exercise 2B

2.9 Use AutoCorrect to prepare for the document by inserting the following shortened and full versions of words and phrases which will appear in the text:

Replace:	With:
Isambard	Isambard Kingdom Brunel
Vic	Victorian
tech	technology
bact	bacteriology

2.10 Starting with a clear screen, key in the following document, ensuring you correct all spelling and grammar errors, use apostrophes correctly, and correctly reproduce the full versions of the words and phrases inserted into AutoCorrect in 2.9 above.

- ◎ Insert the header <u>The Technological Age</u> to appear on each page.
- ◎ Number all pages.
- ◎ Insert your name in a footer.
- ◎ Use fully justified margins.
- ◎ Use single line spacing unless instructed otherwise.
- ◎ Use a document line length of 12.5 cm.

THE VICTORIANS ← (Centre and bold)

British society & economy had been transformed during the Industrial Revolution and the effects ~~affects~~ of the changes were felt throughout the Empire and the rest of the world.

The Victorians developped sience, invention and engineering skills to an unprecedented level in a relatively short space of time, using technology to improve the quality & life. (Copy to B)

A 'girdle' was placed around the world when telegraphy ~~technology~~ & telephony were invented. Improved communication systems supported the rapid developments in technology. (Move to A)

(double line-spacing)

, Such as Isambard K_ B_ and ~~George~~ Robert Stephenson,

The Victorian age was a time when self-confidence was displayed by the nation. Scientists and engineers were the heroes of the age and their achievements have delivered long-lasting benefits on a large scale. They created wealth through their expertise and the values of enlightenment and democracy accompanied their enterprises. Public enterprise resulted in many magnificent public buildings and several ambitious civil engineering projects were undertaken.

Public Enterprise   ← (use this style for all side headings)

(VYRNWY)

On a grand scale, the Thames Embankment and the Vyrnwy Valley reservoir[1] remind us of the public works which were (out) carried (during the Victorian era)

On a smaller scale, towns and cities benefitted from gas street lighting and a burst of house-building activity. In Newcastle upon Tyne, described as 'the best designed Victorian town in England, 13,000 homes were built ~~between~~ in the first seventy yrs of the 19th century, leaving a permanent testimony of the age, in it's grand buildings. (at least)

PUBLIC HEALTH   (CHOLERA)

Diseases such as cholera, tuberculosis & anthrax claimed very many lives, and often at an early age. During the latter half of the nineteenth century, new work was ~~done~~ carried out in the science of bacteriology[2]. Surgery became less hazardous as antisepsis was promoted and

vaccination against diseases such as anthrax was introduced.
The nursing profession traces its roots to the Victorian era
with it's most famous practitioner, Florence Nightingale,
working to relieve suffering in the Crimea. ⌐CRIMEA⌐

TRANSPORT

(✓) Railways dominated the scene, ~~combining~~ *bringing together* all the acheivements
of the Victorians in one service. Isambard K. Brunel again
demonstrated his tenacity and genius thru his involvement
in ship-building, railways and civil engineering projects.
⌐Locomotives made in the 'manufactories' of Britain
were delivered to South Africa, ⌐India,⌐ ⌐Australia,⌐ Japan &
South America, as well as to most of Europe. A definate
impact was made on the infrastructures of many foriegn
countries. ←

COMMUNICATIONS

⌐A⌐

┌─────────────────────────────┐
│ The Metropolitan Underground │
│ Railway was opened in London │
│ in 1863. │
└─────────────────────────────┘

⌐B⌐

1 Supplying the City of Liverpool.
2 Robert Koch working in Berlin.

2.11 Save the document using the filename **EX2B**. Use the spelling and grammar tool to check your work and proofread it yourself as well. Using the Print Preview facility, check your work with the printout at the back of the book. If you find any errors, correct them and print one copy of the document.

Typescript containing abbreviations

You will be expected to be able to expand the following abbreviations in examinations. You should key in these words in full whenever you see them, unless instructed otherwise. Additional abbreviations for Stage III are shown in bold text.

Note: In the OCR/RSA examinations and when using open punctuation, there are no 'full stops' after the abbreviations.

a/c(s)	account(s)	necy	necessary
approx	approximately	opp(s)	opportunity/ies
appt(s)	**appointment(s)**	org	organisation
cat(s)	catalogue(s)	poss	possible
co(s)	company/ies	ref(s)	reference(s)

dept(s)	department(s)	ref(d)	refer(red)
dr	dear	sec(s)	secretary/ies
gntee(s)	guarantee(s)	temp	temporary
immed	immediate(ly)	sig(s)	signature(s)
info	information	yr(s)	year(s)
mfr(s)	manufacturer(s)	yr(s)	your(s)
misc	miscellaneous		

Some abbreviations should be kept as they are, for example:

etc	eg	ie	NB
PS	plc	Ltd	& (in company names)

Note: Word 2000's spelling check may suggest that some abbreviations such as ie and eg should have full stops, for example i.e. and e.g. In word processing, it is now common practice to omit the full stops in such instances. You can add the abbreviations without full stops to the spelling memory as follows:

Key in: The abbreviations and run the spelling check
When the spellchecker stops on the abbreviation, click: The **Add** button

Word 2000 will then add this to its memory and will not suggest full stops for this abbreviation again.

You will also be expected to key in the following words in full:

◎ Days of the week, eg Wednesday, Thursday.
◎ Months of the year, eg February, September.
◎ Words in addresses, eg Grove, Drive, Crescent.
◎ Complimentary closes, eg Yours faithfully/sincerely.

Typescript containing correction signs

You should already be familiar with basic text correction signs showing amendments required by the author. The following list shows *all* the correction signs you can expect to come across in advanced examinations such as OCR/RSA's Stage III Word Processing Part 1:

Correction sign	Meaning
[or //	Start a new paragraph here
	Run on – join paragraphs or sections of text
⌃ ⌃ (word)	Insert a word (or words) here. The words may be immediately above the insertion sign or circled and joined to the insertion sign by an arrow or line
	Transpose horizontally
	Transpose vertically
⌢	Close up – ie don't leave a space

Leave a space – ie split the words at this point

Move to the right

Move to the left

 Let it be. Key in or retain the word(s) with the dashed underline and the circled tick next to it (them)

 ## Inserting additional text into an existing document

Text authors often require additional information to be incorporated into a document while it is being prepared or after it has been printed. In the OCR/RSA Stage III Text Processing Part 1 examination, the invigilator will simulate this by giving two additional pieces of information to candidates between 15 and 20 minutes after the start of the examination. In the examination, as you would at work, make sure that you have paper and pen ready to take down this information when it is given. Make sure you insert the additional information in the correct positions. There will be gaps in the text to indicate these positions.

Working with specialised text

Stage III examinations include work likely to be given to a senior word processor operator and may also be concerned with topics of a specialist business or technical nature. It is very important you reproduce the text correctly, checking all text is correctly spelt and that technical material is accurately keyed in. At work, if you are not sure of the correct spelling or interpretation, you should always ask for help and then make a note of any information which may crop up again in other pieces of work – so you do not need to ask the same question again.

Adding characters not available on the keyboard

You may be required to reproduce symbols such as

◎   fractions, eg $^1/_4$ $1^1/_2$ $6^3/_4$
◎   accented letters, eg à é ñ ä

Fractions
Word 2000 automatically creates common fractions such as $^1/_4$, $^1/_2$, $^3/_4$ as you key in the numbers with the oblique stroke (solidus) between them: for example if you key in 1/4 Word 2000 will convert this to $^1/_4$. Some other fractions such as 1/3 and 2/5 are not automatically converted in this way but are available by using the **Insert Symbol** function and selecting a font style which contains the fraction you require. You will learn about this function later in this unit.

Fractions (using superscript and subscript)

Some fractions are not available as symbols but can be reproduced by the use of superscript and subscript. Examples are $^2/_7$, $^1/_{52}$ and $^4/_{12}$ – representing 2 days, 1 week and 4 months respectively in medical 'shorthand'. Follow the instructions below to insert fractions not available as symbols.

Keyboard	Mouse and menu
Press: **Ctrl + Shift + Plus sign (+)** Key in: The first number (numerator), eg **1**	Select: **Font** from the **Format** menu Click: **Superscript** in the **Effects** box (✓ in box) Click: **OK** Key in: The first number (numerator), eg **1**

The number will be reduced in size and raised above the typing line.

Revert to normal text:

Keyboard	Mouse and menu
Press: **Ctrl + Spacebar** Key in: / (the solidus) Press: **Ctrl + =** (equal sign) Key in: The second number (denominator), eg **52**	Select: **Format, Font** as above Click: **Superscript** in the **Effects** box (no ✓ in box) Click: **OK** Key in: / (the solidus) Select: **Format, Font** as above Click: **Subscript** in the **Effects** box (✓ in box) Click: **OK** Key in: The second number (denominator), eg **52**

The number will be reduced in size and lowered below the typing line.

Revert to normal text:

Keyboard	Mouse and menu
Press: **Ctrl + Spacebar**	Select: **Format, Font** as above Click: **Superscript** in the **Effects** box (no ✓ in box) Click: **OK**

Accented letters

You may be required to key in text containing words from other languages and it is vital these are accurately reproduced. Many languages use accents to indicate pronunciation and you must note these carefully and reproduce them. You can access accented letters by using the **Insert Symbol** function and selecting a font style which contains the accented letter you require. For example:

Ç, Î, à, ö, ē, é, ñ, Ø, ý, ĝ, Æ, ę, Û

Insert Symbol function

Select: **Symbol** from the **Insert** drop-down menu
Select: **Symbols** tab in the dialogue box
Select: **(normal text)** in the **Font** box

The **Symbol** dialogue box is displayed on screen (Figure 2.1).

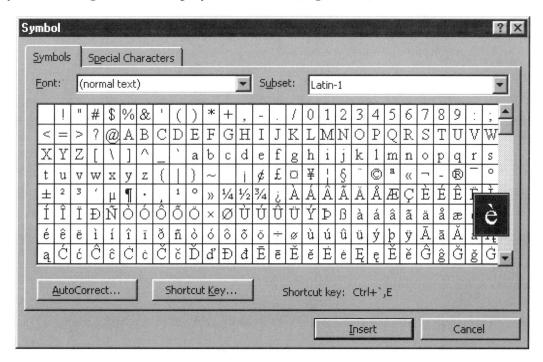

Figure 2.1 Symbol dialogue box

In Figure 2.1, the lower-case letter è with a grave accent has been selected by clicking on the character. This allows you to check this is the character you wish to use. The shortcut (combination) keys you could use to reproduce the same character are also displayed.

Click: **Insert** to select this character and insert it into the text
Click: **Close** to return to the document

Shortcut keys
As you saw in the Symbol dialogue box, you can also apply accents to text in other languages using the **combination keys** function (ie pressing two or more keys simultaneously).

Figure 2.2 shows the keys to be used to reproduce accented letters. (This table can be found in the Help menu under 'Insert an international character by using a shortcut key'. You could print a copy to keep for reference.)

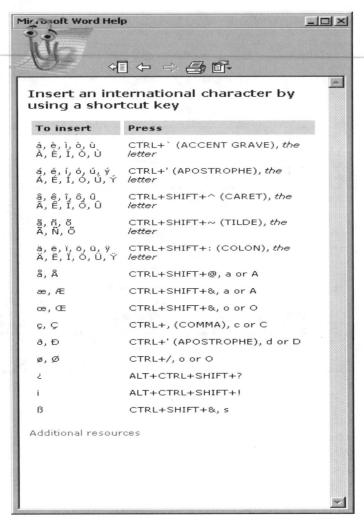

Figure 2.2 Insert an international character by using a shortcut key

For example, when keying in the word *fricassée*, to produce the é:

Press **Ctrl + '** (apostrophe)
Press: **e**

To insert an accent with an upper-case letter:

Press: The key combination
Press: **Shift** + the letter

For example, when keying in the word *NOËL*, to produce the Ë:

Press: **Ctrl + Shift + :** (colon)
Press: **Shift + E**

Other symbols

Note: You will find many other useful symbols such as ticks, fractions, arrows etc by investigating the different fonts in the Symbol dialogue box.

Some examples are:

$$\$ \ ¥ \ § \ © \ ϒ \ ‰ \ ♥ \ ✔ \ ④ \ ⤕ \ ♣ \ \&$$

Experiment with these when you have some spare time. However, remember to confine your use of some of the more unusual symbols to your own work – do not use them in examinations!

2.12 Note the following information which will be needed for Exercise 2D:

The paper used by Röntgen was barium platinocyanide.

Sir John Brown's factory was called Atlas Works.

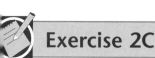

Exercise 2C

2.13 Referring to the instructions on inserting symbols, key in the following text which is to accompany diagrams, copying the symbols exactly as shown. Use superscript/subscript for raised/lowered characters.

$A_1B = A_1B_1 = C_2B_2 = C_3B_3 = C_4B_4$
Invar expansion coefficient = $< 1 \times 10^{-6}$ per °C
Elinvar expansion coefficient = 8×10^{-6} per °C
The device is indexed through 30° or $^1/_{12}$ of a circle
If a_A and a_B were equal in value, then a_R would be zero as cos (180/2) = 0
SI is an abbreviation of Système International d'Unités
$y = 3.29x + 13.97$
Gauge accuracy can be taken as ±10%
Exchange rates – ¥197.25/US$1.635/NZ$2.6025/£1.00

2.14 Check your work very carefully against the book and correct any errors. Save your work using the file name **EX2C** and print one copy.

Exercise 2D

2.15 Open the document **EX2B** if it is not already on screen. Save as **EX2D**. Make the following changes to the document format:

- ◎ Change the document line length to 13.5 cm.
- ◎ Change the document alignment to left justification.
- ◎ Change the header alignment to right alignment.
- ◎ Change the third paragraph to single line spacing.

2.16 Add the following text to the document as the third paragraph under the heading *Public Health*. Copy the text as shown; do not correct the spelling.

←——Professor Wilhelm Conrad Röntgen of Würzburg discovered, almost by accident, the effect of light on a piece of _____ paper. After further investigation and research this discovery became what we now call X-rays.

The Illustrated London News in April 1986 reported that the Duke and Duchess of York (later to become King George V and Queen Mary) had had their hands 'photographed' using X-rays and gave the additional comment that 'the Röntgen ray is no respecter of persons, and gives a touch of homeliness to the most illustrious anatomy'.

(Indent at left and right)

2.17 Add the following text to the document immediately before the last paragraph:

The new technology made it poss for mfrs to develop new devices and improve old ones in preparation for warfare. The late 19th century was a critical time for the developement of naval warfare in the armouring of ships. Sir John Brown of Sheffield was a pioneer mfr of steel using the method introduced by Henry Bessemer.

He was concerned, like many others at the time, that the French were producing an armoured battleship. *(Please refer to information at 2.12)*

In his manufacturing base, _____↓_____, he made rolled armourplate to a thickness of 4½ inches, which he felt would be stronger than the hammered plate of the French ship.

Competition between the British, French and Italians in the development of naval guns culminated in the Italian ship 'Duilio' carrying 100-ton 17.7 inch muzzle loaders, making them 50 per cent more powerful than the British guns. The 100-ton guns were in fact produced by William Armstrong³ of Elswick.

Making way for progress

Although the aims of the Victorian entrepreneurs were usually altruistic, the railway companies caused the demolition of workers housing as they forged their way into London. The princely sum of 1s 6d (7½p) compensation was paid towards the cost of their moving to other accommodation.

Parliament insisted that a special train be put on for the workers to travel to their places of work from their new lodgings *in the suburbs* and this was called the Workmen's Penny Train, the fare being 1d per journey.

PERSONAL TRANSPORT

The boneshaker, or vélocipède as it was known in France, was developed by Michaux in Paris and improved on an earlier model – the Laufmaschine - made by Drais in 1817. The bicycle was to prove a most useful and enjoyable method of transport for many years, *until the motor car monopolised the roads.*

³ *A solicitor turned engineer in later life*

2.18 Use the spelling and grammar tool to check your work, and proofread it yourself as well. If you find any errors, correct them. Resave the document and print one copy.

2.19 Exit the program if you have finished working, or continue straight on to the next unit.

UNIT 3 PRODUCING BUSINESS DOCUMENTS

By the end of Unit 3 you should have learnt how to:

◎ produce a business letter and a memorandum on preprinted forms and templates using open punctuation and fully blocked style, with postdating and enclosure marks for multiple enclosures

◎ confirm facts by locating information from another document and including it where indicated.

Note: Although Word 2000 has an in-built Letter Wizard facility, it is not entirely suitable for OCR/RSA examination purposes.

In the OCR/RSA Stage III Text Processing Part 1 examination you will be expected to produce a business letter and a memorandum either by printing onto a preprinted form, or by using a template file. You will have already learnt most of the requirements at Stages I and II, but some details are repeated here as a reminder and for ease of reference.

Preprinted forms or template files

As in Stages I and II, in the Stage III examination you will be asked to print business documents using either a preprinted form or a template file stored on the computer. Refer back to either of the first two books of this series if you need to refresh your memory on this topic.

Multiple enclosures

In the Stage III examination you should check the text carefully to see if there is more than one enclosure. If there is only one enclosure, indicate this by keying in **Enc** at the end of the letter or memo. If there is more than one enclosure you must key in **Encs**. Failure to indicate multiple enclosures will result in penalties.

Page numbering

Second and subsequent pages of a letter or memo must be numbered.

Postdating

You should always date a letter or a memo with the date of typing, unless there is a specific instruction to do otherwise. There may be occasions when you need to postdate a business document – check the instructions carefully and enter the appropriate date.

Confirming facts

You will be asked to insert information that can be found in one document into another. (At work you would be expected to consult paper files, computer databases etc.) Take notice of the text you are keying in. This way it will be easier to locate and select the correct piece of information to make your document accurate.

Routing of copies

It is normal practice for the sender to keep one copy of a letter or memo for reference. Additional copies may be required for other people and this is usually indicated at the foot of the document, eg:

Top and 2 copies please. One file copy and one for Sue Thompson. Indicate routing.

The routing indication is inserted at the bottom of the document (under any enclosure mark), eg:

Copy: **Sue Thompson**
       File

When all the copies of the document have been printed, it is normal practice to indicate the destination of each copy by ticking, or underlining in coloured pen, or by using a highlighting pen:

Copy: **Sue Thompson**
       File — Top copy – goes to addressee shown at top of the letter or memo

Copy: **Sue Thompson** ✓
       File — First copy – goes to Sue Thompson

Copy: **Sue Thompson**
       File ✓ — Second copy – goes into the file

Memorandum layout

A memorandum (memo) is a document sent 'internally' to convey information to people who work in the same organisation. At the top of the document, it is customary to enter **From** whom the document is being sent, **To** whom it is being sent, and also to include a **Reference**, the **Date** of sending and usually a **subject heading**. There is no complimentary close on a memo.

You should always insert a date, either the date of typing or a postdated date if specified. Some people like to sign or initial their memos but this is not necessary. Organisations have different ways of aligning and setting out the items on the memo. Two acceptable versions are shown in the examples in Figure 3.1.

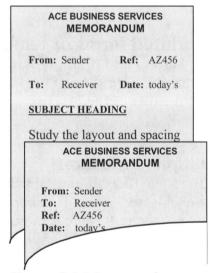

ACE BUSINESS SERVICES
MEMORANDUM

From: Sender   **Ref:** AZ456

To: Receiver   **Date:** today's

SUBJECT HEADING

Study the layout and spacing

ACE BUSINESS SERVICES
MEMORANDUM

From: Sender
To: Receiver
Ref: AZ456
Date: today's

Figure 3.1 Memorandum layouts

Business letter layout

A business letter (Figure 3.2) is written on behalf of an organisation and is printed or keyed in on the organisation's own letterhead. An attractive letterhead gives a good impression of the organisation and contains all relevant details, for example, telephone numbers, e-mail address and web-site addresses. Only the name and address of the addressee (recipient) of the letter have to be keyed in because the sender's details are already printed on the letterhead. The company's letterhead may be stored as a template file (blueprint) on your computer – you can recall it whenever you need to complete a company letter.

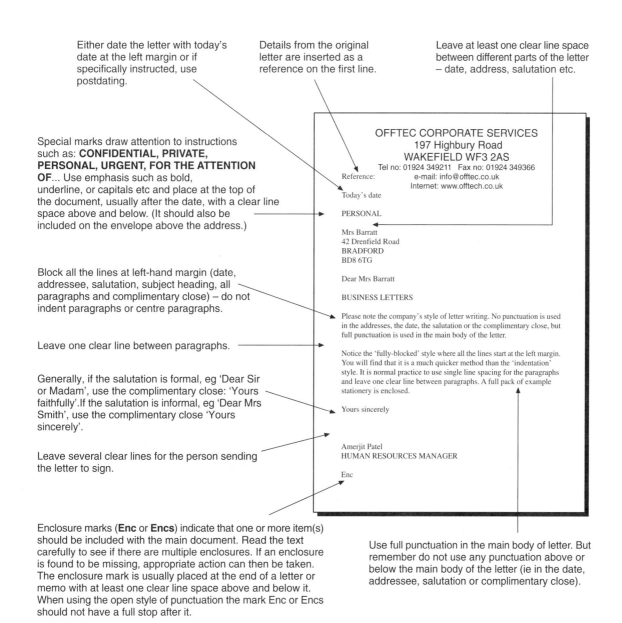

Either date the letter with today's date at the left margin or if specifically instructed, use postdating.

Details from the original letter are inserted as a reference on the first line.

Leave at least one clear line space between different parts of the letter – date, address, salutation etc.

Special marks draw attention to instructions such as: **CONFIDENTIAL, PRIVATE, PERSONAL, URGENT, FOR THE ATTENTION OF**... Use emphasis such as bold, underline, or capitals etc and place at the top of the document, usually after the date, with a clear line space above and below. (It should also be included on the envelope above the address.)

Block all the lines at left-hand margin (date, addressee, salutation, subject heading, all paragraphs and complimentary close) – do not indent paragraphs or centre paragraphs.

Leave one clear line between paragraphs.

Generally, if the salutation is formal, eg 'Dear Sir or Madam', use the complimentary close: 'Yours faithfully'. If the salutation is informal, eg 'Dear Mrs Smith', use the complimentary close 'Yours sincerely'.

Leave several clear lines for the person sending the letter to sign.

Enclosure marks (**Enc** or **Encs**) indicate that one or more item(s) should be included with the main document. Read the text carefully to see if there are multiple enclosures. If an enclosure is found to be missing, appropriate action can then be taken. The enclosure mark is usually placed at the end of a letter or memo with at least one clear line space above and below it. When using the open style of punctuation the mark Enc or Encs should not have a full stop after it.

Use full punctuation in the main body of letter. But remember do not use any punctuation above or below the main body of the letter (ie in the date, addressee, salutation or complimentary close).

Figure 3.2 Business letter layout

Exercise 3A

3.1 Create a standard file for a business memorandum head. You will need to recall this memo template file later in this unit, and in other units of this book. Starting a new file, key in the following text, centring both lines and using the text emphasis indicated. (If the Gill Sans font is not available on your computer, choose another from the Font menu.)

Gill Sans MT
font size 24
bold

Gill Sans MT
font size 18
bold

3.2 Save your document using filename **Memotemplate**. Close the file – you do not need to print at this stage.

3.3 Create a standard file for a business letterhead. You will need to recall this letter template file later in this unit, and in other units of this book. Starting a new file, key in the following text, centring all lines and using the text emphasis indicated:

PANACHE TRADING LTD

67 Firth Road
HUDDERSFIELD
HD12 7GT

Tel no: 01484 489472   Fax no: 01484 489315
Internet: www.panache.co.uk   e-mail: sales@panache.co.uk

Gill Sans MT
font size 24
bold

Gill Sans MT
font size 12

Gill Sans MT
font size 10
italic

3.4 Save your document using filename **Lettertemplate**. Close the file – you do not need to print at this stage.

3.5 Starting with a clear screen, retrieve the **Lettertemplate** file which you saved at step 3.4. Using Times New Roman, font size 12, key in the rest of the letter details, following any specific instructions and correction signs. Remember to expand any abbreviations. Use the spelling and grammar tool to check your work, and proofread it yourself as well. If you find any errors correct them. Save the document under the filename **EX3C** and print one copy.

Mr Austin Phelphs
Buisness Ideas Ltd
43 Lemback Rd
HUDDERSFIELD
HD4 9ST

Please mark the letter URGENT and insert a heading:
LOCAL INDUSTRY INNOVATION FAIR

Dr Mr P___

Thank you for yr recent letter inviting us to participate in a L__I__I__F__, and requesting suggestions and ideas which may contribute to it's success. First of all, may I congratulate you on ~~starting up undertaking~~ piloting this exciting new initiative, which will be a great opp for local cos. I think many cos will greet yr proposal with ~~enthus~~ enthusiasm. ꓕ I have circulated yr letter to all our Heads of Dept to see if other colleagues in our org has any ~~help~~ helpful ideas for the event. —

In the mean time, may I reccomend that we convene a meeting between the various Marketing Managers of ~~the~~ cos ~~who are~~ (interested) in order to brainstorm ideas and develop a time schedule (and) draft plan. ◄

I am enclosing our co cat and ~~buisiness~~ info leaflets which will give you some background details about the orgs' activities and interests. I thought it might be useful for you to have prior sight of them to aid any pre-event publicity measures. Please let me know if you intend to ~~coordinate~~ coordinate such a meeting. Otherwise, perhaps I could make an appt to meet with you seperately to discuss a way forward.

yrs scly
Kim Redknapp
Marketing Manager

use Times New Roman font for the letter text

Exercise 3D

3.6 Starting with a clear screen, retrieve the **Memotemplate** file which you saved at step 3.2. Key in the rest of the memo details, following any specific instructions and correction signs. Remember to expand any abbreviations. Use the spelling and grammar tool to check your work, and proofread it yourself as well. If you find any errors correct them. Save the document under the filename **EX3D** and print one copy.

~~Name~~ From: ____ ⬆ ____ ⬆ , Marketing Manager to Heads of Depts. (please insert name from Exercise 3c)

(use Times New Roman for the memo text)

Ref: KR/009/34

LOCAL INDUSTRY INNOVATION FAIR

(mark the memo PERSONAL)

May I draw yr attention to the attached letter which sets out some proposals for a L_I_I_F_ [A would appreciate it if you could forward yr ideas & suggestions as to how we could benefit ~~in~~ from participating in such an event. –

I believe that the event would provide us with an ideal opp to promote our buisness services to ~~both~~ both prospective (and) current cleints. We would also be able to network with other cos in the area who may be able to ⬆ open up new opps for us thro' sub-contracting arrangements. (in working with me)

① If their is ~~someone~~ someone who would be interested on this initiative, I would be grateful if you could let me know on yr reply. As you is aware, two of my key staff are on long-term sickness, so even a few hours from you or yr staff would be very much appreciated. It will be necy to have names of people who would be willing to "~~man~~ staff' the event on a rota basis, altho' I am currently awaiting confirmation of dates.

(emphasise this paragraph)

Please could you send yr comments to Sue Bridges, Marketing Officer, by Friday (insert date of ~~first~~ Friday of next week) so that she can co-ordinate them in readiness for my first planning in ~~planned~~ meeting. (when this will take place)

(Top and 2 copies please. One file copy and one for Sue Bridges. Indicate routing)

Exercise 3E

3.7 Starting with a clear screen, retrieve the **Lettertemplate** file which you saved at step 3.4. Key in the rest of the letter details, following any specific instructions and correction signs. Remember to expand any abbreviations. Use the spelling and grammar tool to check your work, and proofread it yourself as well. If you find any errors correct them. Save the document under the filename **EX3E** and print one copy.

Letter to Mrs Fiona Wetherby, 45 Luerton Walk, HUDDERSFIELD, HD5 7HR. Use the heading ORDER CODE REFERENCE : TR77W

Ref OM/SS/87

Dr Mrs W ———

Thank you for yr recent order which we received last week. [Our normal delivery time for orders is within 7 days. Unfortunately, the goods you specified are currently out of stock & there may be a slight delay of approx fourteen days before we are able to undertake delivery. We have placed a special order with our mfr and the goods will be sent to you direct from there own premises. (in order to speed up the process)

This means that this letter will act as yr temp invoice for the following goods ordered on yr a/c:

Quantity	Item description	Price	Invoice no
1	Deluxe filing cabinet	£219.99	7/3769

emphasise in bold

Delivery will be made using the suppliers' own carrier service & should be within 21 days. The carrier will contact you *by telephone* to arrange a suitable delivery time. Your telephone number is shown on our records as 01454 432751. If this has changed, or is incorrect, please contact our Answer Line on Freephone 0800 119 237 asap. (and ask to speak to one of our Customer Service Agents)

If you are unhappy with these arrangements, or dissatisfied with the goods after delivery, you may use the same A — L — F — number —

We will do our best to resolve any problems which may arise.

If you wish to cancell the order, again please use the <u>Freephone (line)</u> Answer and ask to speak to one of our Sales Advisers.

The Answer line is staffed during ~~normal~~ standard office ⊘ hours of 9.00am - 1730pm, Mon to Fri, but you may leave a messages outside office hours on the voice mail and someone will return your call.

We aim to make your purchases with Panache Trading as trouble free as poss. If you have ~~some~~ any further ~~questions~~ queries about our services, please don't hesitate to contact me.

Yrs scly

Dyllis Morgan
Sales Supervisor

 Exercise 3F

3.8   Starting with a clear screen, retrieve the **Memotemplate** file which you saved at step 3.2. Key in the rest of the memo details, following any specific instructions and correction signs. Remember to expand any abbreviations. Use the spelling and grammar tool to check your work, and proofread it yourself as well. If you find any errors correct them. Save the document under the filename **EX3F** and print one copy.

use the same memo layout as Ex 30

Memo to Estelle Deneuve, Customer Services Manager, from Ryllis Morgan, ↑ — ↑

please insert job title from Exercise 3E

Ref: DM/376/21

Top and 2 copies please. One file copy and one for Jim McDonnagh. Indicate routing

I have recieved notification from one of our suppliers' that they is ~~sttting~~ unable to meet any orders from us until (insert date of last Friday of next month)

[I am concerned that corespondance has already gone out to several of our customers advising them that there ~~delt~~ *delay* would only be a 3-week⁺ on there orders. —

this sentence in bold

I would appreciate it, therefore, if you could ~~contact~~ *notify* ✓ these clients immed to explain the further delay and offer our apologies for any inconveneince caused. We are able to offer them a 5% discount against the original purchase price as a finanshial incentive not to cancell their orders.] It would be helpful if you could confirm to our Finance Dept which clients decide to taken up this offer, along with yr letter ref. Our supplier has assured me that outstanding orders will definately be dealt with as a priority so I do not anticipate any further difficulties at this time. However, I have made an appt to meet with them in a fortnight to double check their ~~schedule~~ production. [A list of clients is attached. If necy, you may contact my sec for any other info you need on each customer a/c. Most of those listed are long-standing customers and its' vital that we maintain good relations with them. Should you receive ~~orr~~ any complaints, please notify Jim McDonnaghs' sec so that ~~Jim~~ ~~isable to~~ can ~~handle~~ *deal* with them at a more senior level.

3.9 Exit the program if you have finished working, or continue straight on to the next unit.

UNIT 4 CONSOLIDATION 1

By the end of Unit 4 you should have revised and practised all the techniques and skills needed for the OCR/RSA Stage III Text Processing Part 1 award, and additional techniques and skills which will help you in the workplace and in preparation for the Part 2 award.

Look at your Progress Review Checklist and at your completed exercises to remind yourself of what you have learnt so far and to identify any weaknesses. Then complete the following exercises as revision.

Exercise 4A

4.1 Starting a new document, key in the following text which is later to form part of a larger report. Use an unjustified right margin and insert page numbering at the bottom centre. Double line spacing throughout.

> Header: Occupational Aspects
>
> **STRESS AND ILLNESS** ← Centre, embolden and underline please
>
> (- % - _ % according to statistics)
>
> It is
> ~~Its~~ an alarming fact that the majority of our waking hours is spent working. If working involves being in contact with people we do not particularly like, in a job which we do not enjoy, where little ~~regard is paid to showing~~ appreciation of employee's achievements, and where the financial remuneration is felt to be insufficient, then we become 'stressed' and a reaction of some type is ~~provoked~~. triggered. is shown
>
> we are
> If, in addition to these negative factors at work, we're struggling to pay bills' or having problems with accomodation or in family or social relationships, it's not surprising that a few individuals display severe symptoms of distress. It is
> our
>
> **The pecking order** ← please use this heading style throughout except for main heading
>
> Some authorities beleive that the factor of 'being in control' is vital. Although senior buisiness executives work hard, they do tend to be more in control of their work and the work itself is often varied.
>
> The
> ~~This~~ ability to exercise control over use of time and tasks to be performed during their working day protects them, to some extent, from the effects of stress. Unfortunately,
> this
> ~~the~~ same ability to control there own environment may also give them the opp to exercise control over their 'inferiors' and, when this is perceived to be counter-productive by the 'controllee', adds even more to the stress level of the latter. The manager of a dept therefore should aknowledge and apreciate ~~their~~ responsibility for the health of colleagues in his or her charge. his or her
>
> Move to [A] please

You may have seen a list of life events or/life stress scale.[1] Each life event, ranging

from death of a spouse at the top of the scale (100), and minor law breaking at the

base
✓ bottom of the scale (11), has a score out of 100. This list of life events does/not only

include so-called 'negative' events, such as divorced or being fired but also includes

events which are commonly perceived to be 'positive'. Examples are mariage or

holidays.

Percentages of working hour spent working = 60% - 70%
Insert where appropriate

It is
Its said that an individuals' risk of suffering a stress-related illness is
related to their score on the life events scale during the preivous year.
Approximately 50% of people who exceed 200 on the scale develop
health problems. All most 80 per cent of people who exceed 300 sucumb
to ill health.

on the scale

A

The costs of stress

Individuals suffering the effects of stress can easily identify
the costs in personal terms. Their health, relationships and
ability to enjoy life are adversely affected. However, their is
also enormous cost to commerce, industry & the professions too.

Persons under stress are more accident-prone — another factor
affecting health, and generating costs to the health service,
the employer and the person concerned and their family.

The costs are shown as:

* increases in premature retirements
* premature deaths (increases in)
* higher absence rates
* higher health care costs

Footnote in point size 10 please

1 sometimes called the Holmes Rahe scale after its authors

4.2   Check your work on screen against the printout check at the back of the book. Correct any errors, save as **EX4A** and print a copy of your work.

Exercise 4B

4.3   Open the document you saved as **EX4A** unless it is already on screen and save as **EX4B**. The document is to be incorporated into a larger report. Please make the following format changes so that the styles of the separate parts of the report are consistent:

◎   Use justified margins.

◎   Use a left margin of 4 cm and a right margin of 1.5 cm.

◎   Change the position of the page numbers to the bottom right of the page and start from Page 6.

◎   Change the header text to become footer text in Times New Roman, font size 10, italic style and left-aligned.

◎   Add the following right-aligned header – Modern Times.

◎   Change to single line spacing except where otherwise indicated.

◎   Move the paragraphs headed **Predisposing factors** to come immediately after the main heading and retain double line spacing for these two paragraphs.

4.4   Insert the following text immediately before the last paragraph within **The costs of stress** section:

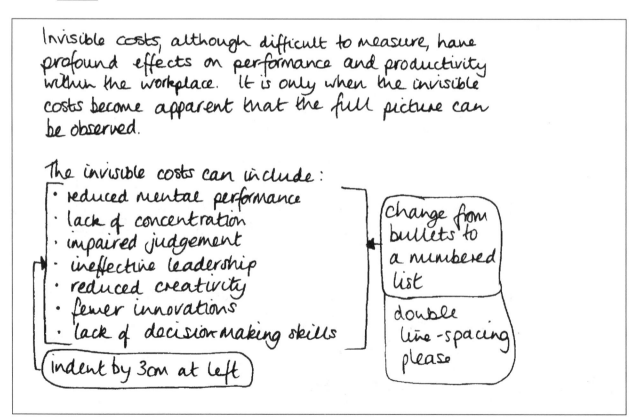

4.5 Add footnotes symbols and footnote text to the section headed **The costs of stress** as shown below:

The costs are shown as:

- increases in premature retirements
- increases in premature deaths
- higher health care costs
- higher absence rates[2]

indent by 3 cm at left and change to a numbered list

Persons under stress are more accident-prone[3] – another factor affecting health, and generating costs to the health service, the employer and the person concerned and their family. *The tendency to have accidents can be related to forgetfulness, anxiety and impaired coordination.*

Retain position after new text at 4.4 and before Highest risk groups

[B]

Footnotes in font size 10

2   *The highest absence rate is found in the transportation and communications industry (8.97%).*

3   *1.6 million accidents happen at work each year.*

Highest risks groups   *Move to [B] above*   *use double line-spacing*

The most stressfull occupations are considered to be nursing, social work, police and teaching. In Nov 1994 a senior social worker won a High Court case for compensation against his employer. The judge said that he should have been given more support.

4.6 Check your work on screen against the printout check at the back of the book. Correct any errors, save as **EX4B** and print a copy of your work. Exit the program if you have finished working or continue straight on to the next unit.

UNIT 5 EXAMINATION PRACTICE 1

By the end of Unit 5 you should have completed a mock examination for the OCR/RSA Stage III Text Processing Part 1 award.

OCR/RSA Stage III Text Processing Part 1

This examination assesses your ability to apply advanced processing and production skills to produce, from handwritten and typewritten draft, a variety of standard business documents. The award demonstrates competence to the level demanded for NVQ Administration Level 3.

The examination lasts for $1^1/_4$ hours and you must complete three documents using a word processor or a typewriter. Printing is done outside this time.

Examinations are carried out in registered centres and are marked by OCR/RSA examiners. The centre will give you instructions regarding stationery.

Letters must be produced on letterheads (either preprinted or template) and memos may be produced on preprinted forms by keying in entry details or by use of a template.

Examination hints

When sitting your examination:

◎   You may use a manual prepared by the centre or by the software manufacturer.
◎   Put your name, centre number and document number on each document.
◎   Check your work very carefully before printing – proofread, spellcheck.
◎   Assemble your printouts in the correct order at the end of the examination.

You are now ready to try a mock examination for Stage III Text Processing Part 1.
Take care and good luck!

The list of assessment criteria for this examination is long and detailed. To be sure you have reached the required standard to be entered for an examination, you need to work through several past papers and have these 'marked' by a tutor or assessor who is qualified and experienced in this field.

Dr Mr Lyness

Letter to Mr R Lyness, 10 Sun St Penworth Hill HUDDERSFIELD HD9 8DW. Our ref TAD/Lyn/S2000. Heading: PEAK WOODWORKING SHOW

My colleague,

Timothy Wardell, has past yr name to me informing me that you are intrested in taking part in the Peak W— S— to be held later this yr. [The Show ~~takes the form~~ consists of demonstrations, exhibitions and sales points]. It is to be held at the Central Exhibition Centre in Darlock Vale. One of the exhibitions will ~~be~~ staged by the Guild of Derbyshire Woodworkers and the other will be a display of work done by the students at Ashsage College.

Bookings are often made 12 months in advance.

Unfortunateley, I cannot confirm a unit booking for you at the moment as all units ~~are~~ have been allocated. However, I ~~have~~ will place yr name on the waiting list and should a unit become available thro' cancellation, I will contact you.

Occasionally, cancellations are made due to illness.

I understand that you would like to take a sales unit to display yr meditation stools.

Please complete the enclosed application form and attach a cheque for £50. Yr check will not be processed until yr booking is confirmed. If you have any further queries, you can contact me by telephone or fax at the numbers given above or by e-mail.

I also enclose 2 complimentary tickets to the Show I hope that you will be able to utilise these or pass them to a friend or colleague who would enjoy the Show.

, worth £5 each

Yrs scly

THOMAS A DARNBOROUGH
Events Sales Administrator

Memo to Timothy Wardell, Human Resource Department, from Thomas A Darnborough, E_ S_ A_ . Ref TAD/Staff/S2000

STAFF OUTINGS TO PANACHE EVENTS

Thank you for passing on Roger Lyness' name to me. I have written to him offering him a place on the sales unit waiting list for the P_ W_ S_ . *Please add name of show*

As we discussed earlier today, I am writing to give you a list of the ~~Shows~~ events due to take place in the forthcoming months which are reasonably local & maybe of interest to members of staff:

.We can offer half-price /entrance to all of the events which we organise. We are unable to offer any further discounts as catering, transport etc are sub-contracted.

ticket

Peak Woodworking Show	Darlock Vale	14/5 Sept
Northern Arts & Crafts Festival	Ilkley	20/21/22 Aug
Beautiful Gardens	Harrogate	6 July
21st Century Living	Derby	13/14 Aug
" " "	Coventry	27/28 Aug
Media Mela	Manchester	21/22 Sept

Indent from left margin by 25mm

I have arranged to have full details of each event sent to you in the next few days so that you can ~~distribute~~ ~~circulate~~ them to staff. Your ~~plan~~ ~~idea~~ plan to encourage participation will (be well accepted), in my opinion, and should increase awareness & interest amongst all depts and branches of the org. Please keep me informed, and let me know if I can be of further assistance.

SELECTING TIMBER ← (centre heading please)

(Please use double line spacing except where indicated)

~~Softwoods~~ Hard woods

There are two main classes of timber: hardwoods and softwoods. Hardwoods are not necessarily 'hard' in nature. They are derived from deciduous, broadleaved trees which shed their leaves in winter and grow in temperate climates. They have open cells which carry moisture thru the tree by ~~conduction~~ OSMOSIS. ✓

If you wish to avoid problems throughout the manufacturing process and with the finished product, you need to take great care in the selection of your raw materials. There are very many factors to be taken into a/c when ~~deciding on~~ choosing your timber or board.

(Inset by 25 mm from left)

(embolden) → SOFTWOODS ← (please use this style for all side headings)

~~On the other hand~~, soft woods are derived from cone-bearing (coniferous) trees with needle-like leaves. The cells are not open and the sap (moisture) passes through the thin, semi-permeable cells walls.

Heartwood

On the end grain, of a section of round wood there is a ~~section~~ area of ~~round wood~~ 'pith' which is the original sapling around which all later growth has occured. As a matter of interest, if the 'heart' is off-center, this is an indication that stress has been applied, perhaps through resisting gravity or prevailing gale-force winds & storms.

Note: knots in softwoods should be no more than ¾ " in diameter

Timber is an expensive material and

Use single line spacing from this point to end of document

You need to be on the look-out for defects when you are purchasing it.

Defects in the wood will have to be cut out, causing wastage.

The following should be avoided:

6   'heartwood' in softwood boards

5   *1*   'waney' edges where the bark and sapwood have been left on

3   *2*   'splits' across the timber caused during felling or compression

4   *3*   'warping' where the board is no longer flat and straight but curved in section

1   *4*   'knots' – except in softwoods if less than _____ in diameter

2   *5*   'shakes' where the timber has splits ~~along the length~~ caused during the drying

out process

[Unfortunately, not all defects are apparent (immed); they ~~come to light~~ *emerge* during manufacture

Converting logs to timber

The main aim is to obtain as much useful timber as poss. However, hardwood planks

should show a ~~specified~~ *peculiar* grain pattern. Hardwood which is to be used for finished

work where the grain is not important, eg on legs and rails, may simply be cut into

boards of ½ in, $^5/_8$ in, or $^7/_8$ in. Where the appearance of the grain is important, cuts

are made carefully, perhaps using tangential ~~or in a~~ *or* radial cuts to produce the

optimum effect.

GRADES OF TIMBER

Grading is carried out according to the visual quality of one face of the board. 'Firsts and Seconds' are boards with one defect-free face. 'No 1 Common and Selects' may have some discolouration or blemishes on the reverse but a good quality face. 'Merchantable' grades are lower in quality

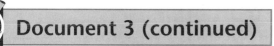

However, ~~beauty~~ interesting textures and patterns can be found in lower grades and, for certain projects, may be ideal.

<u>Sawn timber terminology</u>

Pieces of timber are described according to its size, as follows:

Baulk — a squared log of at least 115 mm square

Batten — softwood often 50mm × 19mm

Board* — hardwood up to 32mm thick

Plank — at least 280mm wide and 50-150mm thick

Slab** — regarded as waste and made from outside of logs

Strip — less than 102mm × 50mm

* sold S/E (square-edged) or W/E (waney-edged)

** useful for covering stacked timber

UNIT 6 ADVANCED WORD PROCESSING

By the end of Unit 6 you will have revised many of the formatting techniques you learnt at the Intermediate level. You should also have learnt how to:

◎ paginate a document following instructions
◎ follow a house style for the production of documents
◎ locate and select information to be included in a document.

The techniques for revision listed below are included in Exercise 1A. Before starting the exercise, refresh your memory if necessary by referring to the glossary (pages 166–175) and ask your tutor to explain anything you are unsure about.

◎ Multi-page documents.
◎ Widows/orphans.
◎ Copy blocks of text.
◎ Move blocks of text.
◎ Sort text in a list.
◎ Search and replace text.
◎ Move around the document – quick methods.

Pagination

In OCR/RSA Stage I and Stage II examinations, you were expected to be able to insert page breaks in documents in sensible places, ensuring a new page is started at a position in the text which did not leave fewer than two lines of text either at the foot of one page or at the top of another (widows and orphans). In Stage III examinations, you will be required to insert page breaks as instructed in the document even if this leaves a lot of space on the page.

Insert page breaks by pressing **Ctrl + ↵ (return/enter)** in the appropriate position.

Following a house style

In the workplace, you may find you are expected to produce documents to a certain format – eg margins, layout, enumeration, fonts etc. This format may differ from what you have learnt in this book or elsewhere. In addition to preprinted letterheads and memos, your place of work may have a logo which appears on all communications. In large organisations, there will be an information or procedures manual setting out the standards required or a template stored on the network. In smaller organisations, you may have to look at previously-prepared documents on file and take note of the style used.

Exercise 6A

6.1 Key in the following article for a staff training manual using the prescribed format as follows:

- ◎ Justified text.
- ◎ Equal left and right margins.
- ◎ Equal top and bottom margins.
- ◎ Times New Roman, font size 12.
- ◎ Single line spacing.
- ◎ Blocked paragraphs.
- ◎ Left-aligned headers using Times New Roman, font size 10.
- ◎ Number all pages at the bottom left.
- ◎ Centre the main heading and use capitals, bold and underline.

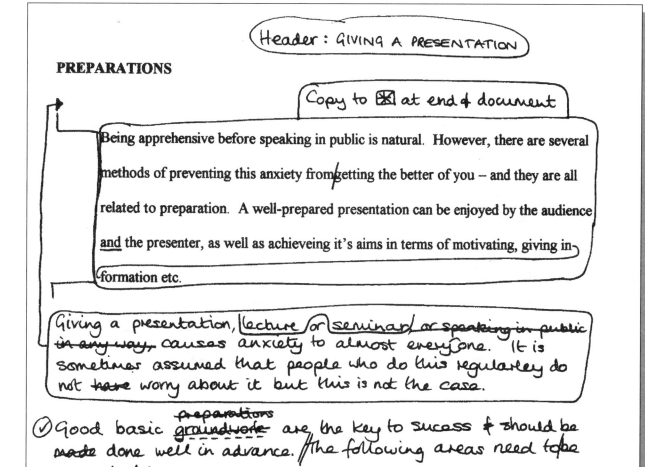

Header: GIVING A PRESENTATION

PREPARATIONS

Copy to ⊠ at end of document

Being apprehensive before speaking in public is natural. However, there are several methods of preventing this anxiety from getting the better of you – and they are all related to preparation. A well-prepared presentation can be enjoyed by the audience and the presenter, as well as acheiveing it's aims in terms of motivating, giving information etc.

Giving a presentation, lecture or seminar or speaking in public in any way, causes anxiety to almost everyone. It is sometimes assumed that people who do this regularley do not have worry about it but this is not the case.

✓ Good basic ~~groundwork~~ preparations are the key to sucess & should be ~~made~~ done well in advance. The following areas need to be researched:

The occasion or event
The location
The audience/listeners

Indent by 2.5 cm from left Margin

Clear info about the occasion can be obtained from coordinators, managers and colleagues. However, it may be necy to ask pertinent questions to get definate facts in this respect. The list below may help:

, even persistent,

Dept/organisation
Organisational objectvies
Formality/dress requirements
Speakers/presenters involved
Programme/order of proceedings
Time allowance and start time
Questions and/or discussion opps

Please sort into alphabetical order and indent list by 25 mm from left Margin

Page 2 starts here
A

Number of delegates/visitors
Expectations of delegats
Prior knowledge and/or skills
Pre-conceptions on the topic(s)
Key figures present likely to be
Poss hostility or opposition to the topic
Pre-existing ~~tensions~~ conflicts between sections within the of/group

Please sort and indent as previous list

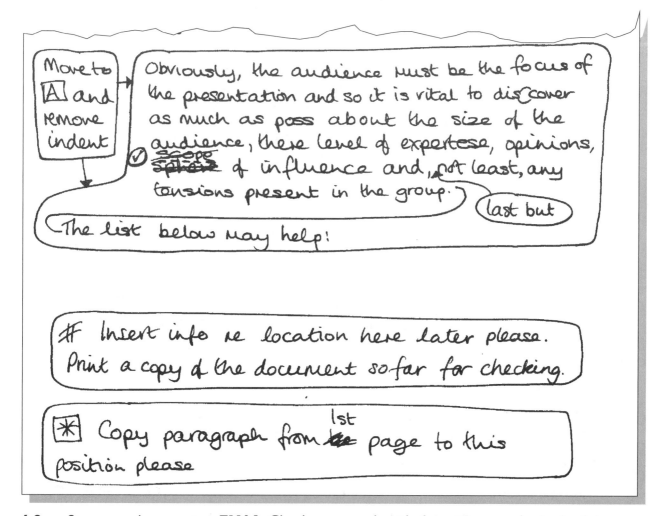

6.2 Save your document as **EX6A**. Check your work with the printout at the back of the book. If you find any errors, correct them and print a copy of your document.

Locating and selecting information

In OCR/RSA examinations, you are often required to insert information which is either contained in the same document, another document or given to you by the invigilator. In the Stage III Text Processing Part 2 examination, the examination paper includes a *resource sheet* which can be detached from the main documents. The resource sheet contains information you will need to produce the documents, together with other information which is not needed. It is up to you to select information which is needed and incorporate it into the documents in the correct positions as instructed.

It will help if you read the document you are working on very carefully so you have an understanding of the topic. It will then be easy for you to extract the required information.

Exercise 6B

6.3 Open the document you saved as **EX6A**. Save it as **EX6B** and make the amendments shown. Refer to the resource sheet to find the necessary information.

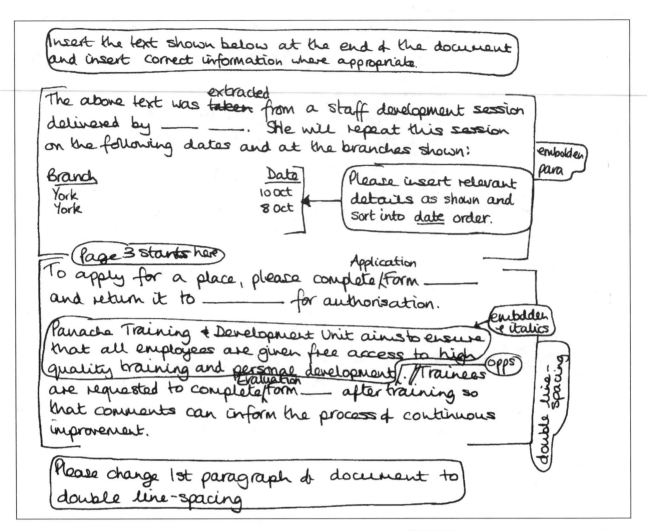

Insert the text shown below at the end of the document and insert correct information where appropriate.

The above text was ~~taken~~ extracted from a staff development session delivered by ___ ___. She will repeat this session on the following dates and at the branches shown:

embolden para

Branch   Date
York   10 oct
York   8 oct

Please insert relevant details as shown and sort into date order.

Page 3 starts here

To apply for a place, please complete Application /Form ___ and return it to ___ for authorisation.

Panache Training & Development Unit aims to ensure that all employees are given free access to high quality training and ~~personal~~ Evaluation development. /Trainees are requested to complete /form ___ after training so that comments can inform the process of continuous improvement.

embolden & italics

Opps

double line-spacing

Please change 1st paragraph of document to double line-spacing

6.4   Insert the following text into the document on screen (**EX6B**) at the point indicated by the symbol # in the manuscript for Exercise 6A:

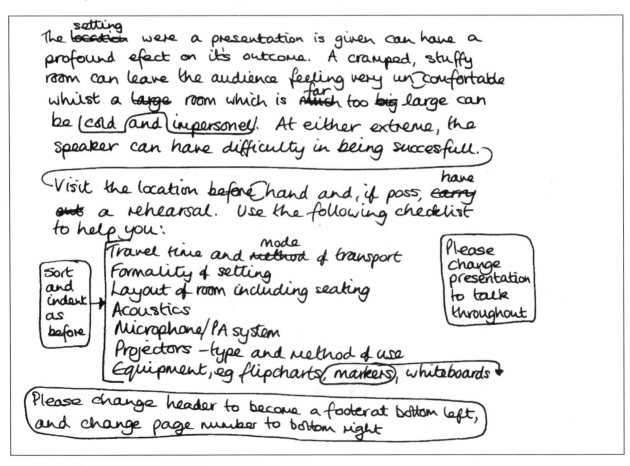

The ~~location~~ setting were a presentation is given can have a profound efect on it's outcome. A cramped, stuffy room can leave the audience feeling very un comfortable whilst a ~~large~~ room which is ~~much~~ far too ~~big~~ large can be cold and impersonel. At either extreme, the speaker can have difficulty in being succesfull.

Visit the location ~~before~~ hand and, if poss, ~~carry out~~ have a rehearsal. Use the following checklist to help you:

Sort and indent as before

Travel time and ~~method~~ mode of transport
Formality of setting
Layout of room including seating
Acoustics
Microphone/PA system
Projectors - type and method of use
Equipment, eg flipcharts, markers, whiteboards

Please change presentation to talk throughout

Please change header to become a footer at bottom left, and change page number to bottom right

6.5 Check your work with the printout check of the back of the book. If you find any errors, correct them. Resave the document and print one copy.

Working in a specialist environment

If you are working in a specialist environment, such as legal or medical, you may find it is still the custom in your organisation to do the following:

◎ Use the word *Re:* before the subject heading on letters and memos. For example:

Re: Sale of property at 48 Park Close
Re: Eleanor MARRIOTT, DOB 1.1.2000

◎ Have letters signed on behalf of the organisation but without identifying the signatory by name and designation. For example:

Yours faithfully
SYON, LEICESTER & CO

(No signatory name)
(No designation of signatory)

The reference at the top of the letter will usually identify the person who is dealing with the matter. For example:

Our ref: AKL/CLR/14748

This matter is being dealt with by A K Leicester

Exercise 6C

6.6 Open the document stored as **Lettertemplate**, save as **EX6C** and change the alignment and format of the printed heading as shown below:

◎ Change the left margin to 3 cm and the right margin to 2 cm.
◎ Change the alignment to right aligned.
◎ Put the telephone number, e-mail address etc on separate lines.

The printed heading should now look like this:

PANACHE TRADING LTD

67 Firth Road
HUDDERSFIELD
HD12 7GT

Tel no: 01484 489472
Fax no: 01484 489315
Internet: www.panache.co.uk
e-mail: sales@panache.co.uk

6.7   Key in the following letter, keeping to the following house style:

◎   Fully blocked style with open punctuation.

◎   Left-aligned/ragged right margin.

◎   Times New Roman, font size 12.

◎   Subject heading: initial capitals, bold and underscore; font size 12.

◎   Reference: author's initials/wp operator's initials (you)/T&D/Ext 346.

◎   Complimentary close:

Yours faithfully
PANACHE TRADING LTD

4 clear lines for signature

Amanda Murray-Leith
TRAINING & DEVELOPMENT OFFICER

◎   Enclosures:
Indicate multiple enclosures and their nature:
Enclosures: *list enclosures*

Our ref AM-L/etc

Mr J P Astley
Sovereign Business Solutions
(add address)

Dr Mr A—

Training & Development on Payroll Package

I am writing to give you further info on the above subject as requested. Details of staff development sessions within the P— Group is circulated to all heads of units and depts (Monthly). Proposals for new initiatives are made on form ____ which is available on the Panache intranet. I believe that you have already developed a proposal with one of our Training Officers.

Info is also displayed on all noticeboards throughout the org and in the weekly Staff Newsletter.

Branches in ___, ___ and ___ have custom-built training accomodation with computer terminals, and you are welcome to visit any or all of these sites prior to delivering the training sessions. A new facility in ___ will be ready for use in ____.

As you will see from the enclosed schedule, in order to support the introduction of the new system which is to be installed initially at the Huddersfield site, training will be held on ___ and ___. This particular development is mandatory for all personnel and payroll units staff. Unit managers from other branches will be expected to attend. I enclose the draft proposal form for your attention. Please contact me within the next week so that we can finalise plans.
Yrs ffly

Boxed instructions (top right):

Please put Panache in bold wherever it appears.

Refer to Resource Sheet for information.

Ensure letter fits on one page by adjusting margins.

6.8 Check your work with the printout check of the back of the book. If you find any errors, correct them. Save as **EX6C** and print one copy. Exit from the program if you have finished working or continue straight on to the next unit.

PANACHE GROUP STAFF NEWSLETTER

A weekly publication for all employees of the Panache Group. Please contact the Publicity Unit if you would like to contribute.

TRAINING & DEVELOPMENT UPDATE

As the new training block in Derby nears completion, we would like to take this opportunity to remind all employees of the facilities which are available within the organisation. The Midland Boulevard block will be ready for use in 3 months time and applications are invited for the position of Unit Manager.

BRANCH	SITE	ACCOMMODATION	UNIT MANAGER
Huddersfield	Firth Road	1 Seminar Room 3 Training Rooms 1 Computer Room	Louisa Weston
Manchester	Moss Hill Lane	3 Training Rooms 1 Computer Room	Elaine Cross
York	Victoria Way West	2 Training Rooms 1 Computer Room	Vikram Syal
Derby	Midland Boulevard	3 Training Rooms 1 Computer Room	To be appointed

COURSES FOR YOUR DEVELOPMENT

The following courses are to be offered during the coming months.

COURSE	BRANCH	DATES	PRESENTER
Giving a talk	Manchester	7 September and 8 November	Louisa Weston
Giving a talk	York	8 October and 10 October	Louisa Weston
Giving a talk	Huddersfield	12 October and 10 November	Louisa Weston
Payroll system*	Huddersfield	13/14 October and 11/12 November	James Astley
E-mail and intranet	Huddersfield	13 November	Elaine Cross
E-mail and intranet	Manchester	10 November	Elaine Cross
Customer Service	York	2/3 December	Vikram Syal
Customer Service	Manchester	5/6 December	Vikram Syal

* Training sessions will be delivered by specialist staff from **Sovereign Business Solutions,** 26 Waverley Road, BRADFORD, BD5 2SM.

A GENTLE REMINDER

If you would like to attend any of the above sessions, please do not contact the T & D Unit direct. Obtain the appropriate form and discuss your wishes with your Head of Unit, whose authorisation will be required before the application can be processed. Forms to be used for Training & Development purposes are shown below.

PURPOSE	CODE	PURPOSE	CODE
Course Proposal	TDPR1/1	Application to attend	TDAP1/2
Course Approval	TDPR1/3	Course Planner	TDCP1/4
Course Evaluation	TDEV1/5	Resource Request	TDRR1/6

UNIT 7 ADVANCED TEXT FORMATTING

By the end of Unit 7 you should have revised some of the formatting techniques you learnt at Intermediate level. You should also have learnt how to:

◎ change font, font size and type of emphasis
◎ allocate space horizontally and vertically within a document
◎ format text in newspaper-type columns for the whole document and for a section of a document
◎ copy text from one document to another using the Window option on the Menu Bar.

Changing the font (typeface), font size and type of emphasis

The use of different fonts and font sizes is an effective way of emphasising text in a document. Throughout your work in this book, the main font you have used has been Times New Roman in font size 12. You should know how to increase and decrease the font size and you may have discovered that a range of other font styles is available to you.

Examples

This sentence is shown in Times New Roman font size 14 and italics
`This sentence is shown in Courier New font size 10 and bold`
<u>This sentence is shown in Arial font size 14 and underlined</u>
<u>This sentence is shown in Arial font size 12, underlined and highlighted</u>
`THIS SENTENCE IS SHOWN IN COURIER NEW FONT SIZE 12 AND ALL CAPS`
`THIS SENTENCE IS SHOWN IN COURIER NEW FONT SIZE 12 AND SMALL CAPS`

In OCR/RSA Stage III Word Processing Part 2 examinations, you will be asked to change the font style (typeface) and/or the 'pitch' (font size) for a portion of text.

View fonts

In Word 2000, you can see the fonts available to you as they will appear when printed. This is a very useful feature which allows you to select appropriate fonts quickly.

When you click on the **Font** button on the Formatting Tool Bar, you will see a drop-down list of fonts (Figure 7.1). Fonts which you have used recently will be shown at the top of the list above a double horizontal line. Below this line, you will find an alphabetical list of the fonts you can choose with each font name shown in its font style.

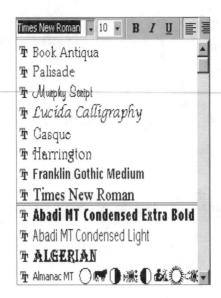

Figure 7.1 An example of a Font list

If you cannot view the drop-down font list:

Select: **Toolbars** from the **View** menu
Click: **Customize**
Click: **Options**
Click: To insert a ✓ in the **List font names in their font** check box
Click: **Close**

 Format fonts

Dialogue box method	
Keyboard	**Mouse**
Press: **Ctrl + D** Select: The **Font** tab	Select: **Font** from the **Format** menu Select: The **Font** tab
The **Font** dialogue box is displayed on screen (Figure 7.2). 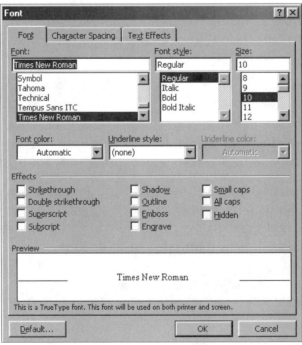 **Figure 7.2** Font dialogue box	

The Preview box shows the font which is currently selected in its style. Select from the options shown below to format the font for selected portions of text:

Select: The font you require from the **Font** list
Select: The font style you require from the **Font style**, **Underline** or **Font Color** boxes
Select: The font size you require from the **Size** list
Select: The effect you require from the **Effects** list
View: Your selection in the **Preview** box

Keyboard shortcut/mouse method		
Format/emphasis	**Keyboard**	**Mouse**
Bold	Press: **Ctrl + B**	Click: Bold **B** button
Italics	Press: **Ctrl + I**	Click: *Italics* **I** button
<u>Underline</u>	Press: **Ctrl + U**	Click: <u>U</u>nderline **U** button
Colour		Click: **Font color** **A** ▾ button
Change font	Press: **Ctrl + Shift + F**	Click: **Font** Times New Roman ▾ button
	Press: Cursor keys to select a font from the list	Select: A font from the drop-down list
Change font size	Press: **Ctrl + Shift + P**	Click: **Font Size** 12 ▾ button
	Press: Cursor keys to select a size from the list	Select: A point size from the list
next larger point size: **next smaller point size:**	Press: **Ctrl +]** or **Ctrl + Shift + >** Press: **Ctrl + [** or **Ctrl + Shift + <**	
Remove emphasis (back to plain text)	Select: The text to change back Press: **Ctrl + Spacebar**	Select: The text to change back Click: Appropriate button again *or* Select: **Normal** in the **Style** box on the **Formatting Tool Bar**
Change case *Options:* Sentence case lower case UPPER CASE	Select: The text to be changed Press: **Shift + F3** until the required formatting is displayed	Select: The text to be changed Select: **Change case** from the **Format** menu Click: The required case in the **Change Case** dialogue box Click: **OK**
Change to all capitals	Select: The text to be changed Press: **Ctrl + Shift + A** Repeat: The command to reverse the action	Select: The text to be changed Select: **Font** from **Format** menu Click: **All caps** in **Effects** section *or* Select: **Change Case** from the **Format** menu Select: **UPPERCASE**
Change to small capitals	Select: The text to be changed Press: **Ctrl + Shift + K** Repeat: The command to reverse the action	Select: The text to be changed Select: **Font** from **Format** menu Click: **Small caps** in **Effects** section
Highlight text (you can only highlight existing text)		Select: The text to be changed Click: **Highlight** ✎ ▾ button

Format text while keying in

Click: The appropriate command button (eg click on the **B** button to switch bold text on)
Key in: The text
Click: The appropriate command button again to switch the emphasis off

Format existing text

Select: The text to be changed
Click: The appropriate command button

Margin alignment

Alignment	Keyboard	Mouse
Centre text (between left/right margins)	Press: **Ctrl + E**	Click: **Centre** button
Align to left (ragged right margin)	Press: **Ctrl + L**	Click: **Align Left** button
Fully justify (justified left and right margins)	Press: **Ctrl + J**	Click: **Justify** button
Align to right (ragged left margin)	Press: **Ctrl + R**	Click: **Align Right** button

Line spacing

Keyboard	Mouse
Press: **Ctrl + 1** (single line spacing)	Select: **Paragraph** from the **Format** menu
Press: **Ctrl + 2** (double line spacing)	Select: **Indents and Spacing, Line Spacing**
Press: **Ctrl + 0** (to add or delete a line space)	Select: The appropriate line spacing from the drop-down menu

Consistency of presentation (fonts)

It is very important to ensure the text is presented consistently throughout a document. You should not be tempted to use too many different fonts within a document as this will usually look unprofessional. It is normal practice to use the same font, font size and type of emphasis for specific parts of a document (eg main text, headings, footnotes etc). To make this easier, you can use the **Style** button on the **Formatting Tool Bar** or copy the format from one block of text to another.

Review formatting

To check font and formatting of existing text.

Formatting Information boxes method	Formatting Tool Bar method
Press: **Shift + F1** A **?** is displayed at the side of the mouse pointer Position: The **?** over the text to be reviewed Click: The left mouse button Paragraph Formatting and Font Formatting text advice boxes are displayed on the screen Check: The details shown in the Formatting Information boxes Press: **Shift + F1** again to reverse action	Select: The text to be reviewed Check: The formatting options displayed on **Formatting Tool Bar**, eg font style, font size etc

Use styles

Word 2000 offers a range of predetermined styles where a combination of font, font size and style of emphasis is collectively given a numbered heading style. These are displayed in the Styles drop-down list on the Formatting Tool Bar (Figure 7.3).

Note: The combination of features stored under any one 'heading' may vary from one system to another.

Figure 7.3 Style drop-down menu

Keyboard	Mouse
Select: The text to be formatted to a particular style Press: **Ctrl + Shift + N** (Normal) Press: **Alt + Ctrl + 1** (Heading 1) Press: **Alt + Ctrl + 2** (Heading 2) Press: **Alt + Ctrl + 3** (Heading 3)	Select: The text to be formatted to a particular style Select: The style formatting option required from **Style** drop-down list on the Formatting Tool Bar

Copy formats	
Keyboard	**Mouse**
Position the cursor: In the block of text displaying the required format Press: **Ctrl + Shift + C** Select: The block of text where the required format is needed (the **Format Painter** brush symbol is displayed) Press: **Ctrl + Shift + V**	Position the cursor: In the block of text displaying required format Click: **Format Painter** on the Standard Tool Bar Position the Format Painter brush symbol: In the block of text where the format is required Click: The left mouse button

7.1 Referring to the instructions 'Formatting fonts' above, experiment with the different fonts available to you by reproducing the following text, ensuring each line is shown in the font style and size given, and that you use the instructions given to obtain the desired effects:

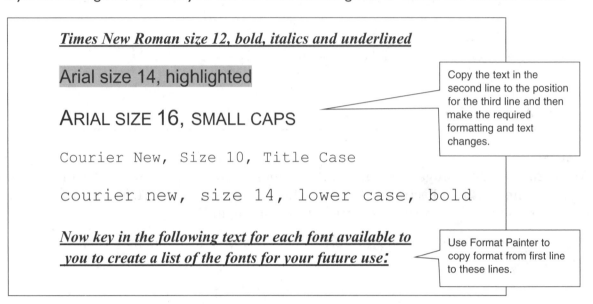

<u>Times New Roman size 12, bold, italics and underlined</u>

Arial size 14, highlighted

Copy the text in the second line to the position for the third line and then make the required formatting and text changes.

ARIAL SIZE 16, SMALL CAPS

Courier New, Size 10, Title Case

courier new, size 14, lower case, bold

<u>Now key in the following text for each font available to you to create a list of the fonts for your future use</u>:

Use Format Painter to copy format from first line to these lines.

7.2 Key in a line of text for a selection of the fonts which is available to you on your system, as follows:

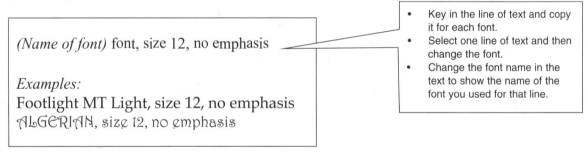

(Name of font) font, size 12, no emphasis

- Key in the line of text and copy it for each font.
- Select one line of text and then change the font.
- Change the font name in the text to show the name of the font you used for that line.

Examples:
Footlight MT Light, size 12, no emphasis
ALGERIAN, size 12, no emphasis

7.3 Print a copy of your work from Exercise 7A if you wish to keep it for reference. Close the file without saving.

Exercise 7B

7.4 Open the document you saved as **EX4B** and save as **EX7B**. Referring to instructions 'Formatting fonts' and 'Copy formats' above, make the following font formatting changes to the document:

◎ Change the header text to 'Work in the 21st century' and to Arial font size 10.
◎ Change the footer text to Arial font size 8 italic.
◎ Increase the font size of the main heading **STRESS AND ILLNESS** by 2 points.
◎ Change all other headings to Times New Roman, font size 14, bold.

- ◎ Reduce the font size for the numbered items under the **The costs of stress** section to 10 point.
- ◎ Change the third and fourth paragraphs of the document ('It is an alarming … to … symptoms of distress') to italic.
- ◎ Repaginate the document sensibly.

7.5 Check your work on screen against the printout check at the back of the book. Before printing, review the text formatting by referring to the instructions 'Review formatting' above. Correct any errors, save as **EX7B** and print a copy of your work.

Exercise 7C

7.6 Starting a new document, and referring to the instructions in 'Use styles' and 'Consistency of presentation' above, key in the following notice using the styles shown:

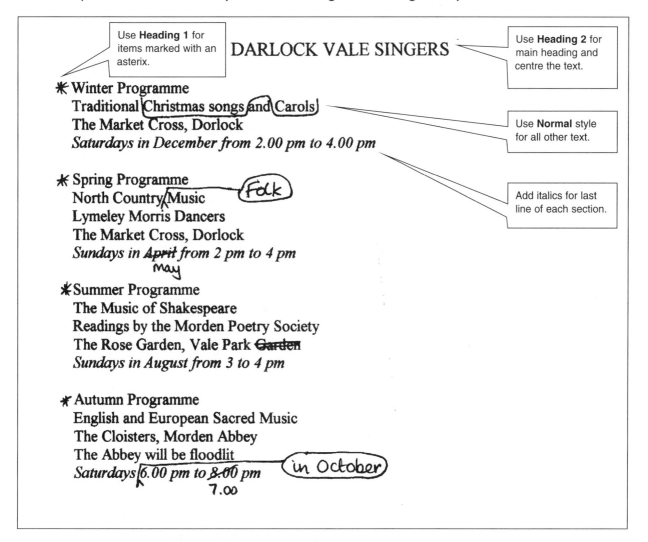

7.7 Save your work as **EX7C** and print one copy. A version of the document is shown at Exercise 7E but your document may not look the same as the prestored styles may be different on your system. You should check you have keyed in the text correctly though.

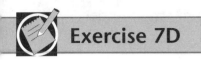
7.8 Key in the following notice using fonts, font sizes and styles of emphasis of your own choice to create an eye-catching display:

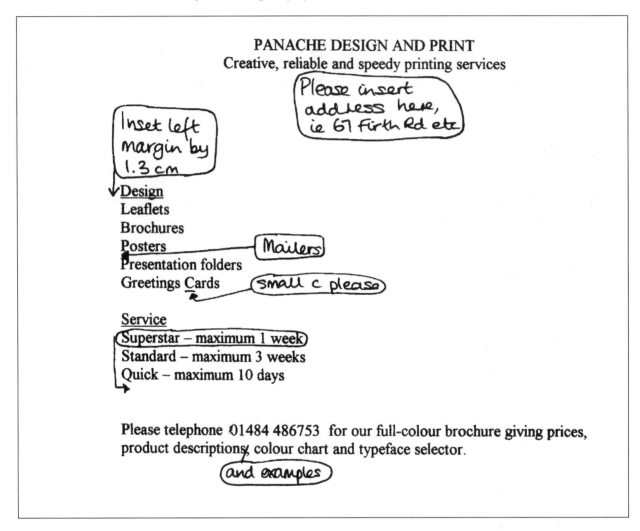

7.9 Save the document using the filename **EX7D** and print one copy. Compare your document with the printout check at the back of the book and correct any errors.

Allocate space

You may be required to leave space within a document for the later insertion of a picture or diagram. In OCR/RSA examinations the measurement required is usually given in centimetres. In the Stage III Word Processing Part 2 examination, you will be given the minimum and maximum horizontal and vertical dimensions of the space to be left.

Allocate a horizontal space from the left or right margin
Note: It is easiest to do this is after the whole document has been keyed in.

Using indent markers on ruler	Using the Format, Paragraph menu
Select: The block of text which is to be positioned at the side of the space *or* Place the cursor: Immediately before the first character of the block of text Move: The **Left Indent** or **Right Indent** marker to the required position on the horizontal ruler	Position the insertion pointer: Immediately before the first character of the text to be indented Select: **Format, Paragraph, Indents and Spacing** from the menu bar In the **Indentation** box, key in: The measurement required in the **Left** or **Right** boxes
Note: It may be necessary to move the indent marker back to the left margin at the required point in the text.	Word 2000 will accept the measurement in centimetres, inches or points, and will then convert this into the unit of measurement currently in use (usually centimetres).

Allocate a vertical space across the full typing line

It is easiest to do this after the whole document has been keyed in.

Delete: Any space already present before the first line of the text to come after the space
Position the insertion pointer: Immediately before the first character of the text to come after the space
Select: **Format, Paragraph, Indents and Spacing** from the menu bar
In the **Before** box, key in: The measurement required. Word 2000 will accept the measurement in centimetres, inches or points, and will then convert this into the unit of measurement currently in use (usually centimetres)

Allocate a rectangular space using a text box

The use of a text box without a line around it allows precise measurements to be used for the required space. This can be done during or after keying in.

If the Drawing Tool Bar is not already on screen:

Select: **View, Tool Bars, Drawing**

The **Drawing** Tool Bar is displayed on screen (Figure 7.4).

Figure 7.4 Drawing Tool Bar

Click: The ⊞ **Text Box** button on the Drawing Tool Bar
Click: Anywhere in the document – a text box will appear on screen
Select: **Text Box** from the **Format** menu (the text box must be selected for this option to be available)
Click: The **Size** tab

In the Size and rotate section:

Key in: The required **measurements** for **Height** and **Width**
Click: The **Colors and Lines** tab

In the Line section:

Select: **No line**
Click: The **Layout** tab

In the Layout style section:

Select: **Square**

Click: **OK**

Drag: The **Text Box** to the required position in the document

Position: The text box very carefully. If the required space is to be measured from the left margin, you must line up the left-hand side of the text box exactly with the left margin of the text

The document text should now wrap around the box leaving a space of the required dimensions. You should use a ruler to double-check the space allocation dimensions when you have printed out your document.

Exercise 7E

7.10 Open the document you saved as **EX7C** and save as **EX7E**. Referring to the instructions 'Allocate a horizontal space from the left or right margin' and 'Allocate a vertical space across the full typing line' above, allocate spaces in the document as shown below.

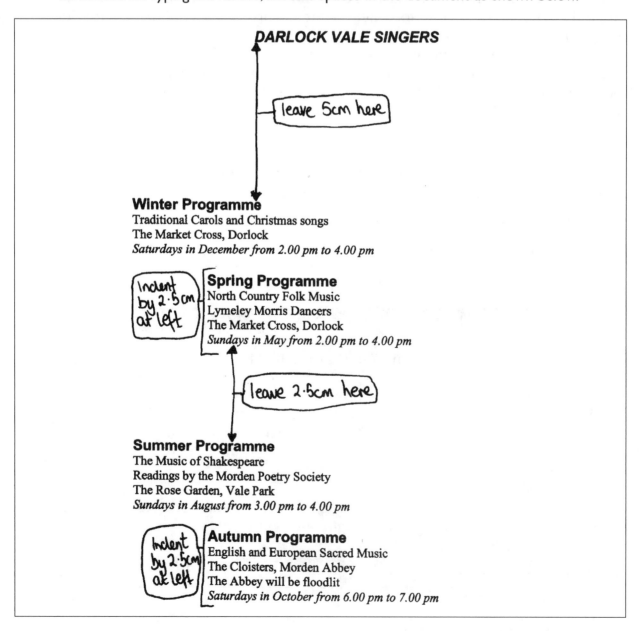

7.11 Resave the document and print one copy. Compare your document with the exercise above to confirm the proportions of the allocated spaces. Remember that your printout may not show the same styles. Use a ruler to double-check you have used the correct space allocations.

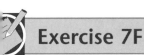

Exercise 7F

7.12 Open the document you saved as **EX7C** and save as **EX7F**. Referring to the instructions 'Allocate a rectangular space using a text box', allocate spaces in the form of unruled text boxes in the document as shown below:

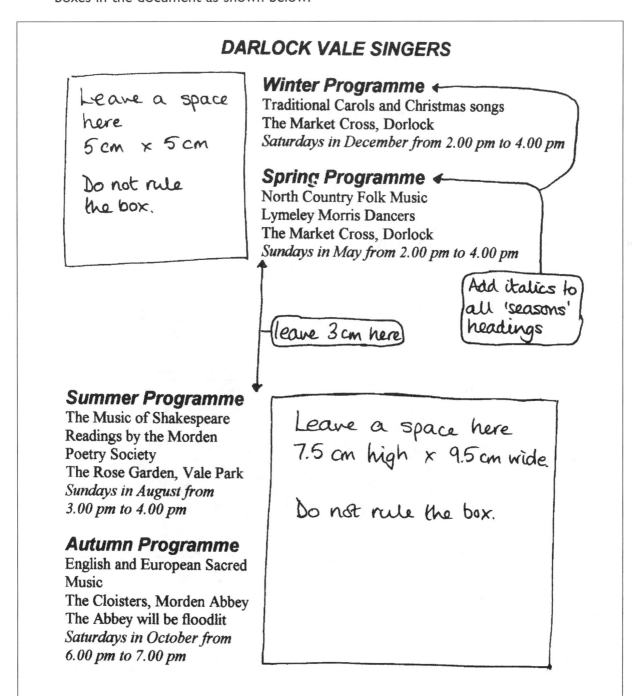

7.13 Resave the document and print one copy. Compare your document with the preceding exercise to confirm the proportions of the allocated spaces. Remember that your printout may not show the same styles. Use a ruler to double-check you have used the correct space allocations.

Newspaper columns

A newspaper column format is often used to make a document easier to read and less formal in layout. This is often used for leaflets, newsletters and bulletins.

In the OCR/RSA Stage III Word Processing Part 2 examination, you will be required to display one document in a two-column format throughout. In the OCR/RSA Stage III Document Presentation Part 2, you will be required to display one section of a document only in two-column format.

Format columns for the whole document

Click: The ▦ **Columns** button on the Standard Tool Bar

Drag: The cursor across the grid to select the required number of columns

Your document will be displayed in Print Layout view

or

Select: **Columns** from the **Format** menu

The **Columns** dialogue box is displayed on screen (Figure 7.5).

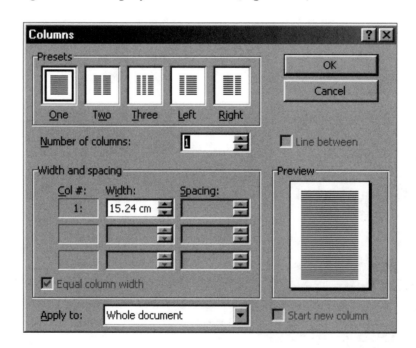

Figure 7.5 Columns dialogue box

Select: The required number of columns in the **Presets** section of the **Columns** dialogue box.

or

Key in: The required number in **Number of columns** section

Check: Your selected column display format in the **Preview** box
Click: **OK**

Your document will be displayed in Print Layout view.

Format columns for a specific section of a document

Select: The section of text which is to be changed to a multi-column format
Click: The ▤ **Columns** button on the Standard Tool Bar
Select: The number of columns required from the grid *or*
Select: **Columns** from the **Format** menu
Select: The required number of columns in **Presets** section of the **Columns** dialogue box *or*
Key in: The required number in **Number of columns** section
Check: Your selected column display format in the **Preview** box
Check: That the **Apply to** box shows **Selected text**
Click: **OK**

Insert a column break to force text into the next column

Position the cursor: Where you want the new column to begin
Select: **Break** from the **Insert** menu
Click: **Column break**

The text will move to the top of the next column.

Change the column widths

Check: That you are in **Print Layout** view (select **Print Layout** from the **View** menu) and that the horizontal ruler is displayed (select **Ruler** from the **View** menu)

Move: The left and/or right column markers on the horizontal ruler to the required position (note the separate margin markers for each column)

OR

Select: **Column** from the **Format** menu
Specify: Measurements for each column width and the spacing between columns in the width and spacing section
Click: **OK**

Note: If 'equal column width' box in the dialogue box is ticked, you cannot change column widths individually.

Insert vertical lines between columns

Check: That you are in **Print Layout** view (select **Print Layout** from the **View** menu)
Position the cursor: In the column section where a line is to be added
Select: **Columns** from the **Format** menu
Click on: The **Line between** box so that it is ticked
Click: **OK**

Remove column formatting

Check: That you are in **Page Layout** view (select **Page Layout** from the **View** menu)
Position the cursor: In the column section to be formatted

Click: The ▦ **Columns** button on Standard Tool Bar
Drag: To select one column *or*
Select: **Columns** under the **Format** menu
Select: **One** column in **Presets** section *or*
Key in: **1** in **Number of columns** section
Check: Your selection in the **Preview** box
Click: **OK**

 ## Exercise 7G

7.14 Starting a new document, key in the following text displaying the whole document in a two-column newspaper column format, and using Arial font in size 12.

PANACHE PERSONAL INVESTMENTS

Most of us would like to become wealthy overnight, or at least increase our buying power considerably. Our chances of winning the lottery or 'coming up on the pools' are very slim, but we carry on trying because we say 'someone ~~wins, why not me?~~' has to win.

At first site, investing in shares and stocks may seem less exciting than taking a [interesting &] chance but it can be extremely profitable. Property, works or art, gold and precious jewels stones have all been considered to be good stores of wealth in the past, but, as our societies values have changed, these may have become less predictable investments. Investing in the stock market is not as complex as it seems. Like all other institutions, it has its own jargon but the principles are reasonably simple.

Panache Investments, a branch of the P_____ T_____ Ltd Group of cos, have [Please refer to letterhead for full company name] designed a series of one-day seminars, conveniently timed on Saturdays, for would-be investors.

The Seminar programme aims to take the mystery our of the investment industry and make it accessable & , more importantly, profitable, for people who have always been interested but never felt able to take the plunge.

Just as no one house, job or car is right for everyone, so no one investment plan is appropriate ~~correct~~ for all potential investors. Our values differ and we have differing needs according to our age, occupation, life-style etc.   The degree to which we are prepared to risk our hard-earned cash is an important factor. The P_____ Investment Seminars could help you to decide on a strategy which is right for yr circumstances and with which you feel comfortable.

Unlike most other Seminars, the Panache programme is not linked to a financial institution and therefore does not promote particular products nor rec comission. [and anticipating the result,] The short-lived 'high' experienced with taking a gamble is not for everyone. If you would prefer researched facts and supported decision-making, the Panache Seminars may be just what you have been waiting for. Don't wait any longer – start making yr fortune now! [emphasise last sentence please]

7.15 Save as **EX7G** and print one copy. Check your work with the printout at the back of the book. If you find any errors, correct them and print the document again, if necessary.

Exercise 7H

7.16 Open the document you saved earlier as **EX7C** and save as **EX7H**. Insert the following text as indicated. Format the document as follows:

◎ Referring to the instructions in 'Format columns for the whole document' above, change the whole document to a two-column newspaper column layout.

◎ Use the same style formats for headings and body text as in Exercise 7C.

◎ Use justified margins for the second column only.

◎ Insert a column break immediately before the section headed **Public Collection** so that this section starts the second column.

Please insert the following text after the Autumn Programme section

Public Collection

All proceeds to the Lymeley Hall Hospice. *Please* Telephone the Sec *of the D V Singers* on 01234-2687419 for further details.

Membership

Participating members of the Singers come from all walks of life and most live within a 15-mile radius of Dorlock Vale. Meetings and rehearsals take place in 'The Red Rose' at Dorlock on Thurs evenings throughout the yr except during local school holidays.

New members are always welcome. If you are interested, please contact the Sec or just come along to the Function Room at the The Red Rose between 7.30 pm and 9.30 most Thurs. You will be made very welcome. ← *italics please*

7.17 Resave the document and print one copy. Check your work with the printout at the back of the book. If you find any errors, correct them and print the document again, if necessary.

Exercise 7I

7.18 Open the document **EX7H** unless it is already on screen and save as **EX7I**. Referring to the instructions in 'Allocate space' above, leave spaces in the document as shown on the next page. Change to a ragged right margin for the whole document.

Underline heading as shown

DARLOCK VALE SINGERS

Winter Programme

Traditional Carols
and Christmas
songs
The Market Cross,
Dorlock
*Saturdays in
December from
2.00 pm to 4.00 pm*

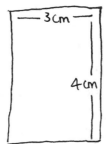

Spring Programme

North Country Folk Music
Lymeley Morris Dancers
The Market Cross, Dorlock
*Sundays in May from 2.00 pm to
4.00 pm*

Summer Programme

The Music of Shakespeare
Readings by the Morden Poetry
Society
The Rose Garden, Vale Park
*Sundays in August from 3.00 pm to
4.00 pm*

Autumn Programme

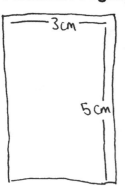

English and
European Sacred
Music
The Cloisters,
Morden Abbey
The Abbey will be
floodlit
*Saturdays in
October from
6.00 pm to
7.00 pm*

Public Collection

All proceeds to the Lymeley Hall
Hospice. Please telephone the
Secretary of the Darlock Vale Singers
on 01234-2687419 for further details.

Membership

Participating
members of the
Singers come from
all walks of life
and most live
within a 15-mile
radius of Dorlock
Vale. Meetings
and rehearsals take
place in 'The Red
Rose' at Dorlock
on Thursday
evenings
throughout the
year except during
local school
holidays.

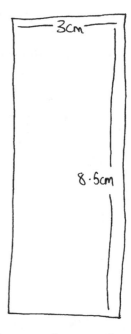

New members are always welcome. If
you are interested, please contact the
Secretary or just come along to the
Function Room at The Red Rose
between 7.30 pm and 9.30 pm most
Thursdays. *You will be made very
welcome.*

*Please insert unruled
rectangular spaces
as shown*

7.19   Resave the document and print one copy. Check your printout with the exercise above.
Use a ruler to double-check the space allocations. If you find any errors, correct them and
print the document again, if necessary.

Exercise 7J

7.20 Open the document you saved earlier as **EX7G** and save as **EX7J**. Referring to the instructions in 'Format columns for a specific section of a document' above, reformat the text as shown below and use a justified right margin:

PANACHE PERSONAL INVESTMENTS

[Centre, embolden & underline]

[Leave a space here 5cm wide and 3cm high. Do not rule the box.]

Most of us would like to become wealthy overnight, or at least increase our buying power considerably. Our chances of winning the lottery or 'coming up on the pools' are very, very slim, but we carry on trying because we think 'someone has to win'.

At first sight, investing in stocks and shares may seem less exciting than taking a chance but it can be extremely interesting and profitable. Property, works of art, gold and precious jewels have all been considered to be good stores of wealth in the past but, as our society's values have changed, these may have become less predictable investments.

Investing in the stock market is not as complex as it seems. Like all other institutions, it has its own jargon but the principles are reasonably simple.

Panache Investments, a branch of the Panache Trading Ltd Group of companies, has designed a series of one-day seminars, conveniently timed on Saturdays, for would-be investors. The Seminar programme aims to take the mystery out of the investment industry and make it accessible and, more importantly, profitable, for people who have always been interested but never felt able to take the plunge.

Just as no one house, job or car is right for everyone, so no one investment plan is appropriate for all potential investors. Our values differ and we have differing needs according to our age, occupation, life-style etc. The degree to which we are prepared to risk our hard-earned cash is an important factor. The Panache Investment Seminars could help you to decide on a strategy which is right for your circumstances and with which you feel comfortable.

[2-column display]

Unlike most other Seminars, the Panache programme is not linked to a financial institution and therefore does not promote particular products nor receive commission. The short-lived 'high' experienced with taking a gamble and anticipating the result, is not for everyone. If you would prefer researched facts and supported decision-making, the Panache Seminars may be just what you have been waiting for. **Don't wait any longer – start making your fortune now!**

[Indent this paragraph by 4cm at right]

7.21 Resave the document and print one copy. Check your printout with the preceding exercise. Use a ruler to double-check the space allocations. If you find any errors, correct them and print the document again, if necessary.

Exercise 7K

7.22 Open the document you saved earlier as **EX7D** and save as **EX7K**. Referring to the instructions in 'Format columns for a specific section of a document' above, reformat the text as shown below. Make sure that the two-column display resembles that shown below by inserting a column break and removing indents if necessary. *Remember that your document will have a different appearance as you added your own fonts and text emphasis.*

PANACHE DESIGN AND PRINT
Creative, reliable and speedy printing services
67 Firth Road
HUDDERSFIELD
HD12 7GT

<u>Design</u>
Leaflets
Brochures
Posters
Mailers
Presentation folders
Greetings cards

<u>Service</u>
Standard – maximum 3 weeks
Quick – maximum 10 days
Superstar – maximum 1 week

2-column format for these lists please

Please telephone 01484 486753 for our full-colour brochure giving prices, product descriptions and examples, colour chart and typeface selector.

Please leave a space here 3cm high and 6 cm wide.
Do not rule the box.

7.23 Resave the document and print one copy. Check your printout with the exercise above. Use a ruler to double-check the space allocations. If you find any errors, correct them and print the document again, if necessary.

Copy text from one document to another

You have already learnt how to copy text from one position to another within the same document. The facility to copy blocks of text from one document to another document is a very useful one in practice. This technique forms part of the OCR/RSA Stage III Word Processing Part 2 examination. The method is very similar to that for copying text within the same document. The additional step is to switch from the source document to the destination document using the **Window** option on the main menu bar, or using the document buttons on the **Task Bar** at the bottom of your screen.

Open the source document(s)

Open all the documents you need to use in the usual way (Word 2000 allows you to have several documents open at one time).

Check all required documents are open – viewing one document at a time

Window option on Main Menu	Document buttons on Task Bar
Select: **Window** from the **Menu bar** The **Window** drop-down menu is displayed on screen (Figure 7.6) **Figure 7.6** Window drop-down menu Check: That all the documents you need are shown on the drop-down menu	Check: That all the documents you need are shown on the Task Bar (each document has a separate button) (Figure 7.7) **Figure 7.7** The Task Bar

---

Check all required documents are open – viewing documents simultaneously

Window option on Main Menu	Task Bar method
Select: **Window** from the **Main menu** Click: **Arrange All** in the Window drop-down menu All open documents are displayed in their own windows.	Position the cursor: Anywhere on the Task Bar except on a document or program button Click: The right mouse button Click: Cascade Windows All open documents are displayed in their own windows in 'cascade' format *or* Click: Tile Windows Horizontally All open documents are displayed in their own windows one above the other on the screen

Window option on Main Menu	Task Bar method
	or
	Click: Tile Windows Vertically
	All open documents are displayed in their own windows side by side on the screen

To reverse the simultaneous viewing facility

Window option on Main Menu	Task Bar method
Click: The ❏ **Maximize** button in the Title Bar of the document you wish to work on The document then becomes the active document and other documents are hidden.	Position the cursor: Anywhere on the Task Bar except on a document or program button Click: The right mouse button Click: **Undo Cascade** *or* **Undo Tile** The document then becomes the active document and other documents are hidden.

Copy text from source document to destination document

Select the text to be copied	
Window option on Main Menu	**Task Bar method**
Position the cursor: In the source document if all documents are arranged in the window The document then becomes the active document; the Title Bar is displayed in blue. Double-click: On the name of the source document on the Window drop-down menu The document then becomes the active document and other documents are hidden.	Position the cursor: In the source document if all documents are arranged in the window The document then becomes the active document; the Title Bar is displayed in blue. Other documents are visible with their Title Bars 'greyed out' *or* Click: The ❏ **Maximize** button in the Title Bar of the document you wish to work on The document then becomes the active document and other documents are hidden.
Select: The text to be copied using the normal selecting and copying techniques	

Switch to destination document

Window option on Main Menu	Task Bar method
Select: **Window** from the **Menu Bar** The **Window** drop-down menu is displayed on screen. Select: The document where you want the text to appear The destination document will become the active document and other documents are hidden.	Position the cursor: In the destination document if all documents are arranged in the window The document then becomes the active document; the Title Bar is displayed in blue. Other documents are visible with their Title Bars 'greyed out' *or* Click: The ❏ **Maximize** button in the Title Bar of the document you wish to copy to The document then becomes the active document and other documents are hidden.

Paste the selected text into the destination document

Window option on Main Menu	Task Bar method
Position the insertion pointer: At the point where you want the copied text to appear Paste: The text into position using the normal pasting techniques	Position the insertion pointer: At the point where you want the copied text to appear Paste: The text into position using the normal pasting techniques *Note*: If text is to be *moved* from one document to another, the 'drag and drop' facility can be used between documents if both source and destination document are arranged in the window.

Switch between documents using shortcut keys

When you have practised using the above methods, you could try using the shortcut keys:

To close the active window:
Press: **Ctrl + W**
To switch to the next window:
Press: **Ctrl + F6**
To switch to the previous window:
Press: **Ctrl + Shift + F6**

Exercise 7L

7.24 Open the following documents and check under the **Window** menu that they are both listed:

◎ **EX7C**

◎ **EX7H**

7.25 Starting with a new document, key in the following document, using a single column format. Copy text from the other open documents and insert as instructed.

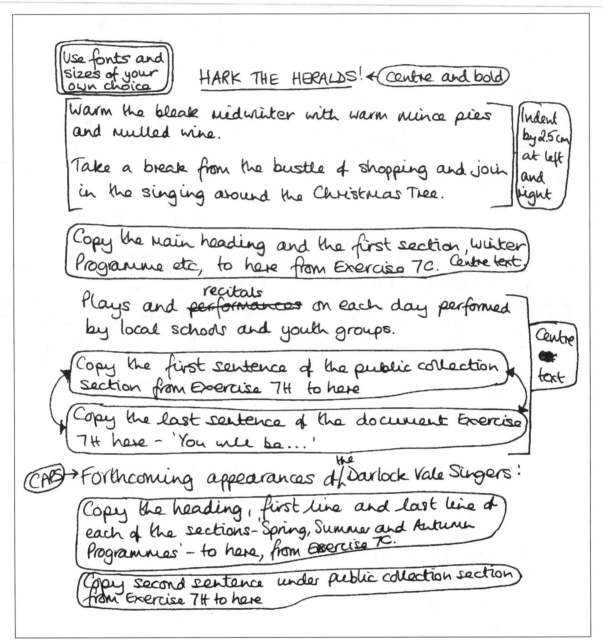

7.26 Save the document using filename **EX7L** and print one copy. Check your work with the printout at the back of the book. If you find any errors, correct them and print the document again, if necessary. Exit the program if you have finished working or continue straight on to the next unit.

UNIT 8 RULED TABLES IN LANDSCAPE FORMAT

By the end of Unit 8 you should have learnt how to:

◎ apply ruling to a table
◎ produce a table in landscape format
◎ produce a table with subdivided and multi-line headings
◎ produce a table using different column layouts in specified sections
◎ set, delete and change the position of different tab settings within a table
◎ complete the table data using a house style reference sheet.

Creating tables

Presenting data in columns is often used within letters, memos and reports to convey information quickly and clearly. Tabulated columns of information are also used for separate tables and accounts. If you align text on screen by pressing the Space Bar it may not line up when you print. It is more accurate to use either Word 2000's table facilities, or use the keyboard Tab key and default tab stops which are positioned at regular points on the ruler line. Word 2000 offers several different methods for producing a table layout. Simple tables may be reproduced using the **Tab** key and ruler tab settings. In the Stage III Part 2 examination, however, you will be asked to key in a complex table layout in landscape format and you will find it easier to use the **Insert Table** and **Tables and Borders** facilities which allow you to organise information on a page using a grid. Some people like to leave equal amounts of space between columns but this is not absolutely necessary. You should leave at least one clear line after the tabulation work before continuing with any further portions of text.

Creating tables using the Tab key
On some keyboards the Tab key is labelled **Tab** and on others shown as ⁕⇥⁕

◎ In Word 2000 the tab settings are normally defaulted (ie previously set) to every 1.27 cm. Each time you press the Tab key you indent the line by 1.27 cm. You can often complete a table satisfactorily using the default tabs.
◎ You may also need to set a tab to apply a different alignment to the table data, ie a left-aligned, right-aligned, centred or decimal tab.

Leave a clear line space between the heading(s) and the information below.

Leave sufficient space between the headings to allow for the longest line of each column.

Use capitals or underlining to emphasise column headings.

NEW STOCK ITEMS

ITEM	CODE	COLOUR	PRICE	UNIT
Gloves	GV/34	black	£1.50	hundred
Gloves	GV/673	grey	£1.20	hundred
Scarf	SF/112	maroon	£2.25	ten
Hat	HT/95	kingfisher	£2.65	ten

Key in the columns in double or single line spacing according to the instructions provided or amount of space available on the page.

The new stock items detailed above are to be added to the winter catalogue before going to press.

Leave at least one clear line after a table before continuing with any further portions of text.

Types of tab settings

Depending on the type of display, you can choose a

◉ **left-aligned tab** (to block entries to the left)
◉ **right-aligned tab** (to block entries to the right)
◉ **decimal tab** (to align decimal numbers at the decimal point)
◉ **centred tab** (to centre each entry around the tab stop).

You can set a combination of different types of tab stops within the document and even on the same line if appropriate. For example:

123	123	123.99	123
12345	12345	12345.99	12345
1	1	1.99	1
↑	↑	↑	↑
Left-aligned tab	*Right-aligned tab*	*Decimal tab*	*Centred tab*

Tabs

To add, delete or change tab stops in Word 2000:

◉ Select all the paragraphs in which you want to edit the settings.
◉ Make your tab stop changes.

Mouse and ruler method	
Add a tab	Click: The **Tab Alignment button** at far left of horizontal ruler until the type of tab alignment you want is displayed: 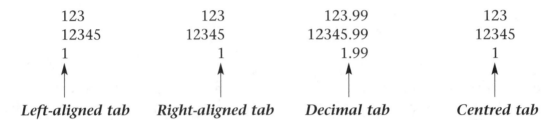
	Left-aligned tab ∟ Decimal tab ⊥
	Right-aligned tab ⅃ Centred tab ⊥
	Click: The mouse pointer on the horizontal ruler at the place where you want to set the tab stop
Delete a tab	Click: The tab marker and drag it off the horizontal ruler
	Release: The mouse button
Move a tab	Click: The tab marker and drag it to the right or left on the horizontal ruler
Change type of alignment	Delete: The tab *then*
	Follow the instructions for adding a tab

Mouse and menu method
Select: All the paragraphs in which you want to add, delete or move tab stops
Select: **Format, Tabs**

The **Tabs** dialogue box is displayed on screen (Figure 8.1).

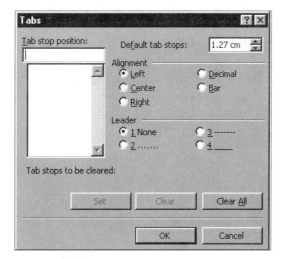

Figure 8.1 Tabs dialogue box

Add a tab (repeat this step for each tab you want to set)	Key in: The required position in the **Tab stop position** box (eg 2.54 cm) Select: The type of tab alignment from the **Alignment** box options (eg Left) Click: **Set** Repeat for next tab stop if appropriate Click: **OK**
Delete a tab	Select: The tab to be deleted from the **Tab stop position** box Click: **Clear**
Delete all tabs	Click: **Clear All**
Move a tab	Delete: The tab *then* Follow the instructions for adding a tab
Change type of tab alignment	Highlight: The tab to be changed in the **Tab stop position** box Select: The new type of tab alignment from the **Alignment** box options Click: **Set**
Reset default tab stops	Select or key in: The distance you want between all tab stops on the horizontal ruler in the **Default tab stops** box (eg 1.27 cm) Click: **OK**

Exercise 8A

8.1 Set tabs to every 1.27 cm if these are not already set by the program default (check the **Format, Tabs** dialogue box). Starting a new file, key in the following exercise (using the default tab settings, press the Tab key to enter the months of the year in the correct positions and before each numerical entry of the table):

```
RETENTION FIGURES FOR BUSINESS STUDIES STUDENTS

Figures indicate percentage retention from September enrolment

                    Nov    Jan    Mar    May    Jul

LEVEL ONE            96     94     94     89     86
LEVEL TWO            99     98     92     91     89
LEVEL THREE         100    100     91     91     90
```

You may retain the abbreviations for the months of the year.

Add underscore separately to each month while keying in or after.

8.2   Press: ↵ (return/enter) several times to leave a gap before the next piece of work.

8.3   Refer back to the instructions given earlier on setting tabs. Clear all tabs and set left-aligned tab stops at **4.5 cm** and **9 cm** only. Check you have set the tab stops in the correct position by pressing the Tab key twice. The cursor should move across the screen to position **4.5 cm** and **9 cm** on your ruler line.

8.4   Key in the main heading and the column headings shown in the next piece of work. Press ↵ (return/enter) so that your cursor is at the left margin.

8.5   Delete the left-aligned tab at **9 cm**. Set a decimal tab at **9.5 cm**. Key in the rest of the columns using the tab key to move between the entries:

```
STAFF ROTA – TUESDAY EVENING ENROLMENT

STAFF NAME            ACTIVITY              TIME

Neil Jarvis          Reception             6.00
Jamil Shah           Open Study Workshop   7.45
Li Tsang             Main Hall             6.45
Sue Longley-Smythe   Main Hall             8.00
```

8.6   Press ↵ (return/enter) several times to leave a gap before the next piece of work.

8.7   Set tab stops for the following exercise in the appropriate places and delete existing tab stops. Use a decimal tab for the first column when required and a right-aligned tab for the third column. Key in the following exercise:

```
INVENTORY ADDITIONS

Cost each (£)    Description           Amount

  1.75          Ringbinders              50
 20.00          Zip disks                20
  0.25          Plastic Pockets         500
  0.80          Tippex                   50
```

8.8   Press ↵ (return/enter) several times to leave a gap before the next piece of work.

8.9   Set the tab stops as appropriate for the column entries below (ie column a = align at left margin, column b = centred, column c = right-aligned, column d = change to decimal after keying in the heading). Then key in the exercise:

NEW ROSES IN STOCK

Description	Category	Quantity	Price (£) each
Aloha	Climbing Rose	5	6.99
New Dawn	Climbing Rose	10	5.99
Sweet memories	Patio Rose	50	4.99

8.10   Save the document using filename **EX8A**. Check your work with the exercises in this unit. If you find any errors, correct them. Resave your work and print one copy.

8.11   Reset the tabs to left aligned every 1.27 cm.

8.12   Clear your screen ready for the next exercise.

Complex table layout in landscape format

Instructions about how to use Word's Table facilities were provided in *Introducing Word 2000* and *Extending Word 2000*, the first two books of this series. If you cannot remember, or don't know how, to use Word 2000's Table facilities, either check with your tutor or consult the earlier books in this series.

In the OCR/RSA Stage III examination you will be required to produce a ruled table using subdivided and multi-line headings. The layout will be more complex than in the Stage II examination, with sections of the table displaying different numbers of columns and/or rows. You will also need to refer to a *resource sheet* – supplied as a separate document – to obtain the data for the table. There may be occasions when you will need to use different tab settings inside the table.

In the Stage III examination, you will be asked to produce the table in landscape format – ie with the longest edge of the paper at the top.

If the table is too large to fit on to the page, remember that you can either reduce the top, bottom, left and right margins, or reduce the font size, or even both.

Apply ruling (borders) to a table
As you have already learnt, Word 2000 automatically produces tables with preruled lines/borders around each cell. Previously, you had to remove the cell lines/borders but for the Stage III examination you should leave the ruling on.

There may be occasions when you want to alter the appearance of ruled cells in the table. To do this:

Select: The cell(s) to which you wish to apply a border, or no border
Click: The **Borders** button on the Formatting Tool Bar
Select: The required border from the choices in the drop-down grid

Set tabs inside a table

Tabs can be set inside a table where you want to specify a particular alignment. This is often useful when you want a column to display decimal figures.

To add, delete or change tab stops in a table:

Select: The column in which you want to edit the tab settings
Make your tab stop changes in the normal way (see earlier in this unit)

To move between tabs in a table:

Press: **Ctrl + Tab**

Note: Pressing the Tab key alone moves to the next row or column.

Exercise 8B

8.13   Starting a new document, reproduce the following table:

◎   Merge cells to produce the required format shown in the table exercise below.

◎   Centre the cell heading **PROJECT MONTHS**.

◎   Left align the **FROM** and **TO** columns.

◎   Centre the **PROJECT TITLE** column.

◎   Centre the cell heading **PROJECT INCOME (£)**.

◎   Insert a decimal tab setting for the rest of the data in the **PROJECT INCOME (£)** column as shown.

◎   Right align the **NET PROFIT** % column.

◎   Adjust column widths as appropriate to improve the presentation.

ANNUAL PROJECT SCHEDULE

PROJECT MONTHS		PROJECT TITLE	PROJECT INCOME (£)	NET PROFIT %
FROM	TO			
February	June	ARIZONA	6,000.00	50%
March	December	KANSAS	35,000.00	48%
April	October	CHICAGO	69,800.00	35%
May	September	TEXAS	139,000.00	40%

8.14   Save the document using the filename **EX8B**. Check your work with the exercise above. If you find any errors, correct them. Resave your document and print one copy.

Change the paper size to landscape orientation

Select: **Page Setup** from the **File** menu (Figure 8.2)
Select: The **Paper Size** tab
Click on: **Landscape** in the **Orientation** box
In the **Apply to** box check that: **Whole document** is shown
Click: **OK**

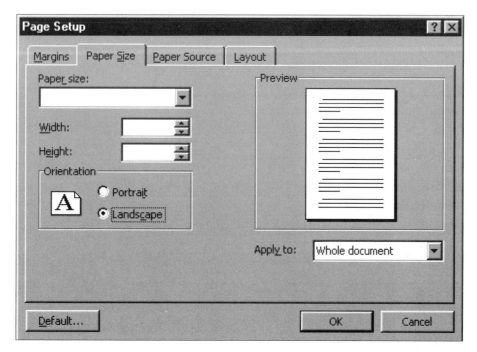

Figure 8.2 Page Setup dialogue box

Note: Check the paper orientation by selecting **Whole Page** from the **Zoom** spin box on the Standard Toolbar. The longer edge of the page should appear at the top. Alternatively, you can use the **Print Preview** facility to view the layout of the page.

Complex table layouts

Word 2000 offers several different methods of producing a complex table layout. Practise the following methods to see which one you feel most comfortable with. Remember, if the table is too large to fit on to the page, you can either reduce the top, bottom, left and right margins, or reduce the font size, or even both. It can be useful to key in each item in the table in a separate row where you need to align text across rows or where you need to sort table items into a particular order.

1 Use the **Insert Table** ▦ facility to design the basic layout of the whole table.

Then, merge the appropriate cells to achieve the correct number of columns and move the column dividers to reposition the column dividers in the bottom section.

2 Use the **Insert Table** ▦ facility to design each section of the table separately, ie produce a separate table for the top section and one for the bottom section.

Then join the two tables by deleting the line space between.

3 Use the **Draw Table** ✎ facility to draw the table layout – this is easiest done in **Whole Page** view:

Draw: The Table outline first
Draw: The row and column dividers
Enter: The data in the usual way
Adjust: The row and column dividers as appropriate

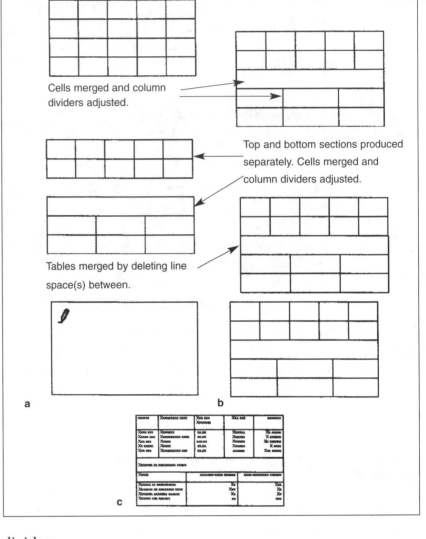

Basic table layout of 5 rows and 5 columns.

Cells merged and column dividers adjusted.

Top and bottom sections produced separately. Cells merged and column dividers adjusted.

Tables merged by deleting line space(s) between.

a

b

c

Exercise 8C

8.15 Starting with a clear screen, follow the instructions 'Change the paper size to landscape orientation' and change the paper size to landscape format. Use the **Print Preview** facility to check the layout of the page is correctly set.

8.16 Study the table layout of the following table carefully. Note that the bottom section of the table contains a different number of columns from the top section, and that the column dividing lines are positioned in different places. Read the section 'Complex table layouts'.

8.17 Reproduce the following table layout using your preferred method of working.

   ◎   Enter the data as shown.
   ◎   Follow the column alignment indicated.

- ◎ Set a decimal tab to enter the data in the **BREAKDOWN COST (£)** column.
- ◎ Using Print Preview, check your work comparing it with the exercise in the unit.

8.18 Save the document using the filename **EX8C**. Check your work on screen with the exercise in this unit. If you find any errors, correct them. Resave your document and print one copy.

MARKETING DEPARTMENT – MONTHLY CLAIMS SHEET – AUGUST

NAME	DATE	DESTINATION	PURPOSE OF JOURNEY	TRAVEL COSTS (£)	SUBSISTENCE COSTS (£)	TOTAL COSTS (£)
Joanna Smith	2 August	Shipley	Client follow-up	4.50	0.00	4.50
Ray Sheard	4 August	Leeds	'New markets' seminar	8.30	2.50	8.80
Monica Daly	4 August	Leeds	'New markets' seminar	8.30	2.50	8.80
Ruth Werner	12 August	Bradford	Meeting with external consultant	2.20	1.00	3.20
Daryl Aines	14 August	Huddersfield	Client follow-up	3.80	0.90	4.70
Sam Barron	21 August	Birmingham	Conference 'Business Ideas'	46.00	5.70	51.70
Jaaya Patel	26 August	Lincoln	Studio workshop	39.00	12.50	51.70

BREAKDOWN OF TRAVEL EXPENSES

TRANSPORT MODE	BREAKDOWN COST (£)	COMMENTS
Car mileage	93.30	Total of 333 miles @ 30 pence per mile
Rail fares	12.60	Cost of day return train fare to Leeds for 2 people
Taxi fares	4.00	To/from Leeds railway station and conference venue
Bus fares	2.20	Local travel only

NOTE: Taxi fares were only used where no other transport was available. Subsistence costs are lower than expected due to refreshments being freely available at most of the conference and seminar venues. Travel costs are slightly higher than estimated due to a change of location for both the Studio workshop and the Business Ideas conference.

8.19 Starting with a clear screen, key in the table shown below. Rule as shown. Save the document using the filename **EX8D**. Check your work with the printout at the back of the book. If you find any errors, correct them and print one copy with the longest edge at the top.

LAMONT LITERARY SOCIETY – SPECIAL SUMMER PROMOTIONS ← (Bold)

CATEGORY	BOOK TITLE	AUTHOR	STANDARD PUBLISHER PRICE(£)	LAMONT SPECIAL OFFER PRICE(£)
Gardening	Water Garden Wonders	Evelyn Harrocks	21.99	15.99
DIY	Make it in a Day	Boris Zavedo	29.99	12.99
Gardening	Heavenly Herbs	Daniel de Courcy	16.99	9.99

Refer to the Resource Sheet for Exercise 8D at the end of this unit to complete all the remaining details of this table. Follow the layout given here.

SUMMER MEMBERSHIP OFFERS

WHAT WE OFFER

Depending on which membership level you select, you can qualify for a further discount on the normal publisher price as shown in the MEMBERSHIP DISCOUNT column. Simply decide on the minimum number of books you wish to be delivered direct to your door each year and take advantage of our great money saving offer.

MEMBERSHIP LEVEL	Minimum Books per Year	MEMBERSHIP Discount
GOLD	12	25%
SILVER	9	20%
BRONZE	6	15%
PLATINUM	3	10%

All membership levels will automatically receive a FREE colour review. (3-monthly)

Exercise 8E

8.20 Starting with a clear screen, key in the table shown below. Rule as shown. Save the document using the filename **EX8E**. Check your work with the printout at the back of the book. If you find any errors, correct them and print one copy with the longest edge at the top.

BRINK ROYD PARK – SUMMER FETE ← *centre + bold*

COMPETITION SCHEDULE

DATE AND TIME		COMPETITION TITLE	ENTRY FEE
Saturday 22 June	11.30 am	Flower arrangement	£2.00
Saturday 22 June	2.30 pm	Art – Landscapes (Water colours/Oils/Acrylics)	£2.56
Saturday 22 June	3.30 pm	Art – Portraits (Water colours/Oils/Acrylics)	£2.50

Refer to the Resource Sheet for Exercise 8E at the end of this unit to complete the rest of this section. Follow the layout shown

ENTRANT APPLICATIONS

COMPETITION TITLE	NAME	ADDRESS	POST CODE	PAYMENT METHOD
Flower arrangement	Soniya Sheraton	2 Valley Way, Halifax	HX1 3TU	Cheque
Art – Portraits (Oils)	Tanya Davies	23 Merton Drive, Halifax	HX3 4BB	Cash
Crafts and Needlework	Alma Thorne	48a Wendle Road, Huddersfield	HD3 7RS	Cheque

Refer to the Resource Sheet for Exercise 8E at the end of this unit to complete the rest of this section. Follow the layout shown.

8.21 Starting with a clear screen, key in the table shown below. Rule as shown. Save the document using the filename **EX8F**. Check your work with the printout at the back of the book. If you find any errors, correct them and print one copy with the longest edge at the top. Exit the program if you have finished working or continue on to the next unit.

Larry's Music and Video Store ← CAPS and bold

STOCK CONTROLLER RESPONSIBILITIES

MEDIUM	STOCK CONTROLLER	STORE LOCATION
Videos	Mike Denbury	Room 418, Racks 1-10, 18-30
CDs	Sharon Balmforth	Room 418, Racks 11-15, Room 417, Racks 2-6
Tapes	Rhonda Jones	Room 417, Racks 1,7-12, Room 419, Racks 1-50
Headphones	Drew Montgomery	Room 418, Racks 16-17
Vinyl	Rhonda Jones	Room 419, Racks 51-65
Miscellaneous	Arshad Ahmed	Room 417, Racks 13-25

ADDITIONAL VIDEO TITLES

TITLE	REF	CATEGORY	PRICE (£) SELL	PURCHASE	NO IN STOCK	STORE LOCATION
Meet Joe Black	43921	12	12.99	6.50	100	418/2
Shakespeare in Love	29117	15	13.99	8.00	12	418/3
Notting Hill	37762	15	12.99	6.50	25	418/29

Refer to the Resource Sheet for Exercise 8F at the end of this unit to complete the rest of the details for this table. Follow the layout shown. ← centre

All new video titles to be added to our website www.larrysvideos.co.uk

Resource sheet for Exercise 8D

CATEGORY	AUTHOR	TITLE	STANDARD PRICE (£)	LAMONT OFFER PRICE (£)
Gardening	Evelyn Horrocks	Water Garden Wonders	21.99	15.99
DIY	Boris Zavedo	Make it in a Day	29.99	12.99
Gardening	Daniel de Courcy	Heavenly Herbs	16.99	9.99
Cookery	Janette Scott	Quick Quisine	18.99	12.99
DIY	Mark Durrit	Rooms for a Change	15.99	10.99
Cookery	Peter Trent-Brown	Lavish Lunches	9.99	7.99
Crafts	Austin Grainger	Modern Metalcraft	8.99	6.99
Travel	Penny Walters	Lakeland Excursions	14.99	12.99
Crafts	Rhia Burns	Patchwork for Pleasure	18.99	14.99

Resource sheet for Exercise 8E

DATE AND TIME		COMPETITION TITLE	FEE
11.30 am	22 June Saturday	Flower arrangement	£2.00
2.30 pm	22 June Saturday	Art – Landscapes (Water colours/Oils/Acrylics)	£2.50
3.00 pm	22 June Saturday	Art – Portraits (Water colours/Oils/Acrylics)	£2.50
3.30 pm	22 June Sat	Art – Still Life (Water colours/Oils/Acrylics)	£2.50
4.30 pm	22 June Sat	Vegetable and Fruit	£2.00
10.00 am	23 June Sunday	Crafts and Needlework	£1.50
12.30 am	23 June Sun	Jams, Pickles and Preserves	£1.50
1.30 pm	23 June Sun	Photography (Colour Section and Black and White Section)	£2.50
2.30 pm	23 June Sun	Poetry/Prose	£2.00

COMPETITION TITLE	PAYMENT METHOD	NAME	ADDRESS	POST CODE
Flower arrangement	Cheque	Sonjya Sheraton	2 Valley Way, Halifax	HX1 3TU
Art –Portraits (Oils)	Cash	Tanya Davies	23 Merton Drive, Halifax	HX3 4BB
Crafts and Needlework	Cheque	Alma Thorne	48a Wendle Road, Huddersfield	HD3 7RS
Jams, Pickles and Preserves	Cash	Edith Vernon	12 Juniper Street, Huddersfield	HD2 8TV
Poetry	Access	Allan Guildford	33 Watmough Street, Halifax	HX2 7HT
Photography (Colour)	Cheque	Miles Mitchell	26 Burns Crescent, Dewsbury	WF13 8BS
Vegetable and Fruit	Cheque	Mary Keene	177 Roxley Road, Huddersfield	HD4 4AC
Art – Still Life (Acrylics)	Barclaycard	Robert Adams	81 Garth Road, Halifax	HX2 9BW
Art – Landscapes (Oils)	Switch	Adeline Roberts	19 Warrington Way, Dewsbury	WF12 7TN

Resource sheet for Exercise 8F

TITLE	REF	NO IN STOCK	CAT	SELL PRICE (£)	PURCHASE PRICE (£)	STORE
Meet Joe Black	43921	100	Twelve	12.99	6.50	418/2
Shakespeare in Love	29117	12	Fifteen	13.99	8.00	418/3
Notting Hill	37762	25	Fifteen	12.99	6.50	418/29
Saving Private Ryan	28117	20	Fifteen	14.99	8.00	418/9
Jack Frost	20199	30	PG	9.99	4.50	418/22
Ransom	36185	16	Eighteen	13.99	7.00	418/19
There's Something About Mary	29935	10	Fifteen	9.99	4.50	418/4
The Full Monty	28137	130	Fifteen	14.99	7.50	418/25
Lost in Space	14339	5	PG	8.99	4.99	418/8
Pulp Fiction	05098	5	Eighteen	13.99	7.00	418/29

UNIT 9 CONSOLIDATION 2

> By the end of Unit 9 you should have revised and practised all the techniques and skills needed for the OCR/RSA Stage III Word Processing Part 2 award, as well as additional techniques and skills which will help you in the workplace.

Look at your Progress Review Checklist and at your completed exercises to remind yourself of what you have learnt so far and to identify any weaknesses. Then complete the following exercises as revision.

Exercise 9A

9.1 Open the file you saved as **EX7G** and save as **EX9A**.

Make the following formatting changes:

◎ Remove the two-column formatting and replace with one-column layout throughout.

◎ Change the font to Times New Roman and the font size to 12.

◎ Change to double line spacing for the whole document apart from where indicated.

9.2 Format and amend the text as shown below:

Please use justified right margin and a document line length of 14 cm. Using font size 10, insert the header LEARN TO BECOME RICHER, and the footer PPIS/Mail/Name of PPI Promotions Manager. Please refer to the Resource Sheet to confirm any details needed to complete the document. Start numbering from Page 5.

Emphasise by increasing font size, adding bold and underline and centre

PANACHE PERSONAL INVESTMENTS

Copy sentence to ✱

Most of us would like to become wealthy overnight, or at least increase our buying power considerably. Our chances of winning the lottery or 'coming up on the pools' are very, very slim, but we carry on trying because we think 'someone has to win'. *every week*

please leave 4cm here

At first sight, investing in stocks and shares may seem less exciting than taking a chance but it can be extremely interesting and profitable. Property, works of art, gold and precious jewels have all been considered to be good stores of wealth in the past but, as our society's values have changed, these may have become less predictable investments.

Networking & time-sharing of holiday properties has not proved to be the money-makers which many entrepreneurs promised by. Fluctuations in the economy have less affect on the share market over a period of time than on disposable income, on which some other investment schemes are based.

Start new page here

Investing in the stock market is not as complex as it seems. Like all other institutions, it has its own jargon but the principles are reasonably simple.

Perhaps you are not ~~witting~~ happy to speculate. Panache P___ I___ will show you how to invest safeley.

Panache Investments, a branch of the Panache Trading Ltd Group of companies, has designed a series of one-day seminars, conveniently timed on Saturdays, for would-be investors. The seminar programme aims to take the mystery out of the investment industry and make it accessible and, more importantly, profitable, for people who ~~have always been~~ are interested but ~~never felt able~~ hesitate to take the plunge.

Just as no one house, job or car is right for everyone, so no one investment plan is appropriate for all potential investors. Our values differ and we have varying ~~differing~~ needs according to our age, occupation, life-style etc. The degree to which we are prepared to risk our hard-earned ~~cash~~ money is an important factor. The Panache Investment Seminars could help you to decide on a ~~strategy~~ plan ✓ which is right for your circumstances and with which you feel comfortable.

In return for a small initial sum of approx £1,5000 per yr & a few hrs a week ~~to begin with,~~ of yr time, you could be earning up to £40,000. If that sounds unbelievable, ~~just~~ simply come along and look at our statistics.

Start new page here

Single line spacing

Unlike most other seminars, the Panache programme is not linked to a financial institution and therefore does not promote particular products nor receive commission. The short-lived 'high' experienced with taking a gamble and anticipating the result, is not for everyone. If you would prefer researched facts and supported decision-making, the Panache Seminars may be just what you have been waiting for. Don't wait any longer – start making your fortune now!

Move this sentence to the very end of the whole document, increase font size and centre.

Please replace Panache Investments with Panache Personal Investments throughout the whole document

9.3 Add the following text to the end of the document, using the same font and font size as the first part. Follow all other formatting and text amendment instructions.

At the seminars, you will learn:

- how to make inflation work for you
- the best time to start investing
- how to obtain your initial funds
- how to estimate risks
- how to avoid extra income tax
- how to choose a reliable company
- how to take full responsibility for your own wealth
- how to avoid the usual ~~beginners~~ pitfalls'

Please indent bulleted list from left margin

The first seminar is free! *Caps and bold*

There is no need to pay out money in advance. You can test the product before you buy it. The hints and skills which you pick up in the first lesson will convince you that you will begin creating wealth and you are on to a winner immediately.

You will be given a simple but effective hand book which will support you through the first few days of your new wealth-creation activities.

Start new page here

Successful investors who started off with Panache Seminars will be present at the first and subsequent seminars to assist you and to confirm the success of the programme.

They will act as your tutors in the beginning and later as your mentors. Quite soon you will be friends and colleagues in this exciting new venture, assisting each other to continue to increase your wealth, and enjoying all the benefits this brings.

Please leave a space here measuring 4 cm wide by 7 cm high. Do not rule.

Single line spacing for these 2 sentences

on the reverse of this booklet

Complete the form to let us know that you are interested. *of seminars*

We will forward full details of the ~~seminar~~ programme to you, together with your preliminary lesson. Details of venues, dates and times are enclosed separately for your reference. It is not obligatory to attend the same venue but the seminars should be attended in order as each one will build on the skills learned in the previous one.

* *Copy sentence from first page to here to make it the next to the last paragraph.*

9.4 Save the document using the filename **EX9A** and print one copy. Check your work with the printout at the back of the book. If you find any errors, correct them and print the document again, if necessary.

Exercise 9B

9.5 Open the file you saved as **EX7D** and save as **EX9B**. Make the following format changes:

◎ Remove the column break previously inserted before **Service** as follows:

    Select: **Normal View**

    Select: The **Section breaks** displayed on the screen

    Select: **Print Layout View** to return to the usual screen display

◎ Remove all indents and centring.

◎ Use a two-column format for the whole document (newspaper style).

◎ Use a justified right margin.

◎ Amend the document as shown below:

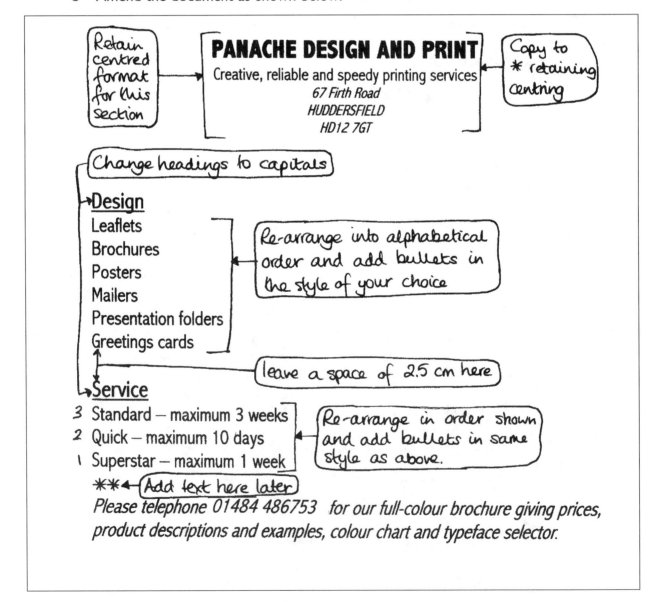

9.6 Add the following text where indicated in Exercise 9B and follow the formatting instructions given:

> Please add the following paragraphs at **. Use a smaller font size for the body text. Retain same font style and size for headings to ensure consistency.

COLOUR PRINTING

Color printing is not as expensive as you may think. We have invested £300,000 or *over* in new technology so that we can supply ~~provide~~ high quality colour work at a reasonable cost. // Selecting colors to give impact to yr stationary and literature without loseing (legibility) and (clarity) can be tricky.

> Start 2nd column here

We will advise you on the best colour combinations and create a selection of samples for you to choose from. (A small charge is made for this service.)

> italic for this sentence please

Photography *(please remember)*

You may supply yr own pictures in print or transparency format, but that the quality must be good. [If you would like our professional photographer to ~~take~~ carry out this work, we would be pleased to arrange this for you.

> Leave a space for a photo here. Space to measure 25 mm x 25 mm. Do not rule the box.

* *Copy name and address from top of document to this position at end of document.*

9.7 Save your work as **EX9B** and print one copy. Compare your document with the printout check at the back of the book and correct any errors.

Exercise 9C

9.8 Key in the following table in landscape format, referring to the resource sheet at the end of this unit for the information you need to complete the table.

9.9 Save your work as **EX9C** and print one copy. Compare your work with the printout at the back of the book. If you find any errors, correct them and print the document again, if necessary. Exit the program if you have finished working or continue straight on to the next unit.

Please key in the table with the longest edge at the top and rule as shown. Sort the items in the first section into date order and the items in the second section into ascending fee (£) order, ie £50 first.

(Put date column before seminar column)

PANASHE INVESTMENT SEMINARS ← (Centre and embolden)

SEMINAR	DATE	CITY	VENUE	TIMES	COORDINATOR
1 Getting Started	2 Jan	Glasgow	Western Hotel	9.30-4.30	Paula Sylvestre
1 — " —	9 Jan	Manchester	Carter Hotel	10.00-5.00	Frances Wood
1 — " —	16 Jan	Hull	Holland Hotel	9.30-4.30	Antony Collins

Please refer to the Resource Sheet and complete all the remaining details from the table. Use the layout shown here; months should be in full.

SEMINAR FEES ← (bold)

SEMINAR	TITLE	DATES	FEE (£)
1	Getting Started	2 Jan, 9 Jan, 16 Jan	£100
2	Moving On	13 Feb, 20 Feb, 27 Feb	£90
3	On the Launchpad	6 Mar, 13 Mar, 20 Mar	£50

(Embolden all column headings)

(Please ensure that the table fits on one page)

PANACHE INVESTMENTS WORKSHOPS

DATE	WORKSHOP	CITY	VENUE	TIMES	COORDINATOR
2 January	1 Getting Started	Glasgow	Western Hotel	9.30 – 4.30	Paula Sylvestre
9 January	1 Getting Started	Manchester	Carter Hotel	10.00 – 5.00	Frances Wood
16 January	1 Getting Started	Hull	Holland Hotel	9.30 – 4.30	Antony Collins
13 February	2 Moving On	Glasgow	Hunter Hall	10.00 – 5.00	Shaheen Kosar
6 March	3 On the Launchpad	Glasgow	Hunter Hall	10.00 – 1.00	Chris Cooke
27 February	2 Moving On	Hull	Holland Hotel	10.00 – 5.00	Antony Collins
20 March	3 On the Launchpad	Hull	Bridge Hotel	10.00 – 1.00	Rodney Lawton
20 February	2 Moving On	Manchester	Irwell Hotel	10.00 – 4.30	Robert Horne
13 March	3 On the Launchpad	Manchester	Carter Hotel	9.30 – 12.30	Karl Hessen

THE PROMOTIONS AND PUBLICITY UNIT

Director:	Jan Vitec
Manager:	Jim Rennie
Administrator:	Kimberley Austin
Graphic designer:	Nicole Temani
Copywriter:	Charles Flowers

UNIT 10 EXAMINATION PRACTICE 2

By the end of Unit 10 you should have completed a mock examination for the OCR/RSA Stage III Word Processing Part 2 award.

OCR/RSA Stage III Word Processing Part 2

This examination assesses your ability to apply advanced processing and production skills to produce a variety of business documents from handwritten draft, typewritten draft and recalled text and also using supplementary information. The award demonstrates competence to the level demanded for NVQ Administration Level 3.

The examination lasts for $1^3/_4$ hours and you must complete four documents using a word processor. Printing is done outside this time.

Examinations are carried out in registered centres and are marked by OCR/RSA examiners. The centre will give you instructions regarding stationery: letters must be produced on letterheads (either preprinted or template) and memos may be produced on preprinted forms, by keying in entry details or by use of a template. The invigilator will give you instructions concerning the recalling of stored files.

Examination hints

When sitting your examination:

◎ you may use a manual prepared by the centre or by the software manufacturer
◎ put your name, centre number and document number on each document
◎ check your work very carefully before printing – proofread, spellcheck
◎ assemble your printouts in the correct order at the end of the examination.

You are now ready to try a mock examination for Stage III Word Processing Part 2. Take care and good luck!

The list of assessment criteria for this examination is long and detailed. To be sure you have reached the required standard to be entered for an examination, you need to work through several past papers and have these marked by a tutor or assessor who is qualified and experienced in this field.

Preliminary task

Key in the following text, expanding abbreviations and making other amendments. This text will be used for Documents 1 and 4 in this unit. Save your work as **UNIT10PRELIMTASK**. Print a copy of this task and check it with the printout check at the back of the book before continuing with the other documents in this unit.

WHERE TO STAY FOR A SHORT BRAKE IN DARLOCK VALE   *[centre and bold]*
A guide to hotels and guesthouses offering week end breaks - Spring and Summer

There is a wide selection of accomodation in this beautiful part of the country, rangeing from modern hotels to rambling farmhouses, from historic ~~country~~ houses to country inns. This info sheet ~~has been designed to~~ *well* provide prospective weekend visitors with a choice of places in which to stay in the Vale. All ~~of~~ the accommodation has been inspected and classified under the National Tourist Authority Triangle Shceme ~~and individual clasifications are given for guidance~~. Several of the hotels has won additional awards for their restaraunts, wine lists or range of beers.

Visitors taking weekend breaks during May and June will be given free Pass to the Past Vouchers allowing up to 50% discounts on admissions charges to museums, art galleries and historic houses in the area. *Please ask for details when booking.*

All acommodation has en-suite bathrooms, colour TV, central heating and tea/coffee-making *[or]* facilities in bedrooms.

A visit to Darlock Vale could include activites such as golfing, fishing, cycling, and horse-riding. Details of locations and organisers are to be found in the <u>Darlock Vale Activites</u> leaflet which can be obtained from local offices of the N_____ T_____ A_____. *[The]* <u>Good Food in Darlock Vale</u> leaflet gives the visitor details of the many excellent restaurants, inns and hotels providing appetising and nourishing meals.

<u>White Wood Farm</u>

Relax in front of a warm log fire, savouring the aroma of farmhouse cooking. The proprietor, Anna Morris, takes great pride in preparing meals from the fresh produce of her kitchen garden. Her bread and cakes have won many prizes at local agri cultural shows. Situated just off the main road from Darlock to Telbridge and convenient for Telbridge Castle.

Glebe Villa ← *(All names of accom to be in this style)*
(by the owner, David Porter)

An early 19th century house approximately ¼ mile from the centre of Claybury on the East Minton road. Decorated in the Victorian style and containing many original features such as the magnificent oak staircase and stained glass windows. A friendly, family atmosphere where children are welcome. Resident's lounge and safe play garden for small children.

<u>The Grove</u>

A detached house in delightful gardens, offering a quiet and secluded haven on the outskirts of Darlock. Panoramic views across the Vale from most bedrooms. Meals taken in south-facing conservatory. A well-stocked library is ~~on hand~~ to all visitors. A non-smoking residence. *Sorry, no ~~pets~~.*   *open*

Recall this document stored as UNIT10PRELIMTASK and amend as shown. Adjust margins to give a line length of 14 cm. Change to double line-spacing (except where indicated) and use full justification. Insert and delete page breaks so that the document prints on 4 pages. Save as UNIT10DOC1 and print one copy.

underline this line

COME

~~WHERE TO STAY~~ FOR A SHORT BREAK IN DARLOCK VALE ←

A guide to ~~hotels and guest houses offering~~ weekend breaks - Spring and Summer

HOTELS & GUEST HOUSES ← *(Caps & bold)*   *West of England*

There is a wide selection of accommodation in this beautiful part of the ~~country~~, ranging from modern hotels to rambling farmhouses, from historic houses to country inns. This information sheet will provide ~~prospective~~ weekend visitors with a choice of places in which to stay in the Vale. All the accommodation has been inspected and classified under the National Tourist Authority *Silver* Triangle Scheme. Several of the hotels have won additional awards for their restaurants, wine lists or range of beers. All accommodation has en-suite bathrooms, colour TV, central heating and tea or coffee-making facilities in rooms.

Many visitors

~~A visit~~ to Darlock Vale *enjoy* ~~could include~~ activities such as golfing, fishing, cycling, and horse-riding. Details of locations and organisers are to be found in the <u>Darlock Vale Activites</u> leaflet which can be obtained from local offices of the National Tourist Authority.

Change typeface and/or font size for these paras

[B] *(Page 2 to start here)*   *(Copy to [A])*

The <u>Good Food in Darlock Vale</u> leaflet gives the visitor details of the many excellent restaurants, inns and hotels providing appetising and nourishing meals *to non-residents*.

(Inset from left & right by 2.5 cm)

Visitors taking weekend breaks during May and June will be given free <u>Pass to the Past</u> Vouchers allowing up to 50% discounts on admissions charges to museums, art galleries and historic houses in the area. Please ask for details when booking. *yr accom.*

(Single line-spacing for all these paras)

White Wood Farm

(Use this style for all property names)

Relax in front of a warm log fire, savouring the aroma of farmhouse cooking. The proprietor, Anna Morris, takes great pride in preparing meals from the fresh produce of her kitchen garden. Her bread and cakes have won many prizes at local agricultural shows. Situated just off the main road from Darlock to Telbridge and convenient for Telbridge Castle.

Glebe Villa

(Parker)

An early 19th century house approximately ¼ mile from the centre of Claybury on the East Minton road. Decorated by the owner, David ~~Porter~~, in the Victorian style and containing many original features such as the magnificent oak staircase and stained glass windows. A friendly, family atmosphere where children are welcome. Residents' lounge and safe play garden for small children.

Insert a header <u>Weekend Breaks</u>, and a footer NTA/DV/WB to appear on every page

(Page 3 to start here)

Lilac

The/Grove

Please change National Tourist Authority to National Tourist Association throughout

A detached house in delightful gardens, offering a quiet and secluded haven on the outskirts of Darlock. Panoramic views across the Vale from most bedrooms. Meals taken in south-facing conservatory. A well-stocked library is open to all visitors. A non-smoking residence. Sorry, no pets. Vegetarian cuisine is offered by the owner, Jayne Green.

3 Nights for the price of 2 ← CAPS & bold   Move to end of document

If you stay on Friday & Sat nights during Sept, you may continue yr break for ~~one~~ an extra night ~~(this)~~ (Sunday) at no extra cost. This offer applies to bed & breakfast bookings at establishments with 2 or 3 Silver Triangles only.   This sentence in italics

SELF-CATERING ← CAPS & bold

If you prefer the informal, relaxed type of break where you can come and go as you please, try one of our self-catering cottages or log cabins. The leaflet Self-Catering in D—V— gives full details.

Move to [B] please   Single line-spacing

The Corn Dolly Inn
Character ~~country~~ village inn dating back to the 17th century where, as you would expect, the walls have been decorated with fine examples of this ancient craft. Superb food, oak beams, patio garden.

Spring Mount Hall
Large, comfortable Georgian House in /quiet village of Mittenford. Antiques and paintings by local artists in public rooms. Award-winning cuisine.

(Page 4 to start here)
Lower Hallburn Farm   , local market
Riverside setting and only 2 miles from Hallburn town, and the site of a Roman villa. Newly-constructed leisure suite with sauna, sunbed, mini-gymnasium and conservatory. Special diets catered for.

32 High St
Georgian town-house in Darlock ~~town~~ centre. Convenient for museums, riverside walks and shops. Wine bar and bistro on ground floor.
[A]

Letter — Top + 2 please. One copy for Sales Dept and one for our file. Indicate routing.

Our ref   LP/Eng/2001

Mr D Parker
Glebe Villa
Insert full address from Resource Sheet

Dr Mr P—

LEISURE AND HEALTH EQUIPMENT

Thank you for yr telephone enquiry regarding our range of equipment. We specialise in the planning and installation of 'Leisure Suites' for small hotels and we have 10 years' experiance in this feild. We purchase equipment and machinery from the best suppliers manufacturers throughout Europe. All products supplied by our co are tested and rigorously meet European standards. // Our service begins with a visit by our Planning and Design Engineers who will discuss yr requirments with you in detail and carry out a full survey of the premises and/or rooms to be adapted.

It has come to my attention that Lower Hallburn Farm near to Darlock, who purchased a range of equipment from us about a yr ago, is only a few miles from Claybury. I have contacted the proprietor, Mr B— O—, and he has kindly agreed to allow you to visit his Hotel and to discuss yr proposals and our services with you. The address and telephone number are as follows: please insert details here from the Resource Sheet

I have pleasure in enclosing our latest cat and price list and I will ask our Sales Dept to telephone you in the near future to follow up yr enquiry.

Yrs ffly

Amelia Byrom
Customer Liaison Unit

Please key in table as shown. Save as UNIT10DOC3 and print one copy, with longest edge at top. Rule as shown.

WEEKEND BREAKS – HOTELS & GUEST HOUSES ~~A BED & BREAKFAST~~

NAME OF HOTEL/GUEST HOUSE	CONTACT NAME	ADDRESS	TEL NO	PRICE PER PERSON (£)
32 High St	Helen Miller	32 High St, Darlock, DV1 8TH	01565-883423	£38.00
Glebe Villa Farm	David Parker	210 East Minton Rd, Claybury, DV8 9FG	01565-874523	£39.00/£75.00
Lower Hallburn ~~Hotel~~ Farm	Ben Oates	North Rd, Hallburn, DV8 6HY	01565-865906	£37.00/£82.00

This section in double line-spacing

Please refer to Resource Sheet for remaining details and follow layout given here.

3 NIGHTS FOR PRICE OF 2 OFFER

NAME OF HOTEL/GUEST HOUSE	TEL NO	SILVER TRIANGLE AWARD	BB PRICE PER PERSON (£)
32 High Street	01565-883423	2	£38.00
Glebe Villa	01565-874523	2	£39.00

This section in single line-spacing

Please right-align this column

Please refer to Resource Sheet and add details of other participating establishments

Embolden all headings please

Recall the heading and first 4 paragraphs of the document stored as UNIT10PRELIMTASK and amend as shown. Display the whole document in 2 columns (newspaper style). Save as UNIT10DOC4 and print one copy.

WHERE TO STAY ~~FOR A~~ SHORT BREAK**S** IN DARLOCK VALE
~~A guide to Hotels and guest houses offering weekend breaks~~ Spring and Summer

The
~~There is a wide~~ selection of accommodation in this beautiful part of the country, ~~ranging~~ **ranges** from modern hotels to rambling farmhouses, **and** ~~from~~ historic houses to country inns. This information sheet will provide prospective weekend visitors with a choice of places in which to stay in the Vale. All the accommodation has been inspected and classified under the National Tourist ~~Authority~~ **Assoc'n** **Silver** Triangle Scheme. Several of the hotels have won additional awards for their restaurants, wine lists or range of beers. All accommodation has en-suite bathrooms, colour TV, central heating and tea or coffee-making facilities in rooms.

> Leave a space here at least 3cm wide & 6cm high & no more than 3.25 × 6.5 cm. Don't rule

A visit to Darlock Vale could include activities such as golfing, fishing, cycling, and horse-riding. Details ~~of locations and organisers~~ are to be found in the Darlock Vale Activites leaflet ~~which can be obtained~~ from local offices of the National Tourist ~~Authority~~. **Association**

The Good Food in Darlock Vale leaflet gives the visitor details of the many excellent restaurants, inns and hotels providing appetising and nourishing meals.
*

Visitors taking weekend breaks during May and June will be given free Pass to the Past Vouchers allowing up to 50% discounts on admissions charges to museums, art galleries and historic houses in the area. Please ask for details when booking. *(embolden this para)*

Quality Cuisine
White Wood Farm Anna Morris at has won many prizes for her excellent English country fare. Spring Mount Hall's manager and chef, Archibald Mackie, has gained 4 Silver Triangles for his fresh & innovative creations. *(Please check name)*

Comfortable Surroundings
Look no further than the following for pleasant, warm and attractive décor & furnishings:

Glebe Villa
The Lilac Grove
The Corn Dolly Inn

Mt Spring Hall
Lwr Hallburn ~~Hall~~ Farm

Display in alphabetical order in one column

*Move to * please*

DARLOCK VALE – NTA WEEKEND BREAKS – SPRING AND SUMMER

<u>Hotels And Guest Houses</u>

Name of Establishment	Address and Tel No	Silver Triangle Award	Owner/ Proprietor/ Manager	Type	Price for Weekend Break
32 High Street*	32 High Street Darlock DV1 8JH 01565-883423	▼▼	Helen Miller	BB	£38 pp
Glebe Villa*	210 East Minton Road Claybury DV8 9FG 01565-874523	▼▼	David Parker	BB BBEM	£39 PP £75 pp
Lower Hallburn Farm*	North Road Hallburn DV8 6HY 01565-865906	▼▼▼	Ben Oates	BB BBEM	£37 pp £82 pp
Spring Mount Hall	Spring Mount Mittenford Darlock DV3 9AS 01565-896589	▼▼▼▼	Alistair Mackie	BB BBEM	£42 pp £90 pp
The Corn Dolly Inn*	The Green East Minton DV7 2CV 01565-878681	▼▼	William Hughes	BB	£40 pp
The Lilac Grove	Woodbridge Way Darlock DV2 5DE 01565-882231	▼▼▼	Jayne Green	BBEM	£80 pp
White Wood Farm	Darlock Road Telbridge DV10 7JU 01565-876548	▼▼	Anna Morris	BBEM	£70 pp

KEY:

BB – Bed and Breakfast
BBEM - Bed, Breakfast and Evening Meal

* Participating in 3 nights for price of 2 offer in September

UNIT 11 DOCUMENT DESIGN

At the end of Unit 11 you should have learnt how to:

◎ produce a document containing an element of design
◎ apply borders and shading to enhance the appearance of the document
◎ add full-page borders.

Document presentation

Document presentation combines the effective use of text in various fonts and sizes with various visual effects, including:

◎ text boxes
◎ drawings
◎ graphics
◎ diagrams
◎ columns
◎ ClipArt
◎ borders.

The electronic age has brought desk top publishing (DTP) into the office. This means that even basic documents can be enhanced relatively simply with a little know-how and flair. Word 2000 allows you to combine many methods of document design within the same program.

DTP is still recognised as a profession in its own right and there are many courses which specialise in this subject to advanced levels. The purpose of this section of the book, however, is to provide you with sufficient knowledge and information to meet the standards of the OCR/RSA Stage III Document Presentation Part 2 examination. Once you have learnt the basic techniques, you will be able to apply them more creatively in other situations.

In the examination make sure you follow all the instructions given – do not allow your creative urges to run away with you. You can use Word 2000's more advanced design features later to impress your boss or your friends.

Think carefully about the message you want to convey, your audience and your resources.

It is a good idea to draft out the layout of the page on a piece of rough paper first. Positioning the design elements beforehand will often provide you with a clearer outline of the end result you want to achieve. Include all headings/items. Arrange the layout in a logical manner using your own initiative, but according to any instructions given. You will get better with practice.

Check all instructions that specify certain sizes – eg font sizes, text boxes. Don't use too many different font types – the document will look cluttered and amateurish.

Make good use of the paper size – don't squash everything together! The end result should look clear and presentable. Clever use of the 'white space' on the page – eg margins, space between paragraphs – can contribute to the overall documentation presentation.

Document presentation and layout

Some of the requirements of the OCR/RSA Stage III Document Presentation Part 2 examination include the following:

◎ Recalling text that has been previously stored.
◎ Carrying out amendments to the recalled text.
◎ Changing the font, typeface/character, point size, line spacing and alignment of text – within headers and footers as well as within the main text.
◎ Paginating documents so that no less than two lines of a paragraph appear at the top and bottom of each page – ie avoiding widows and orphans.
◎ Numbering pages correctly.
◎ Using drawing facilities to create text boxes, shapes and diagrams with or without shaded backgrounds.
◎ Importing graphics/ClipArt images into the document.
◎ Creating and inserting borders/dividers into the document.
◎ Inserting special characters – eg mathematical symbols, accents, fractions, bullet points, subscript and superscript.
◎ Presenting information in columns – this may apply to a specified section of the page only.
◎ Carrying out ruling using the word processor and not by hand.
◎ Carrying out an aspect of modification as instructed (eg search and replace, case conversion, use of house style).
◎ Using appropriate top, bottom, left and right margins – these must not be less than 13 mm.
◎ Using consistent spacing between and within similar items within a document.

Add borders, lines and shading

You can add a wide range of lines, boxes or shaded backgrounds to enhance headings, paragraphs, portions of text, tables and pictures.

Mouse and menu method
Select: The item – eg paragraph text, heading – to which you want to add a border or shading Select: **Borders and Shading** from the **Format** menu

The **Borders** dialogue box appears on screen (Figure 11.1).

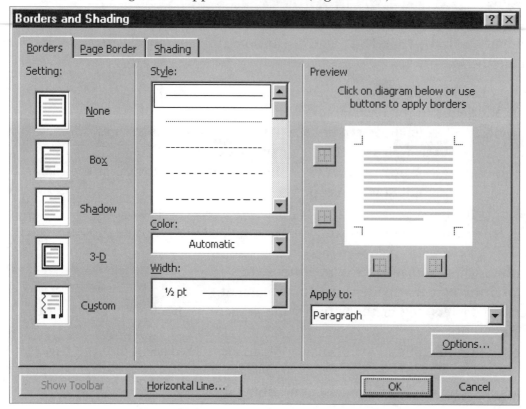

Figure 11.1   Borders dialogue box

To add a border or line(s)

Click: The **Borders** tab

Select: The required border display from the **Setting**, **Style**, **Color** and **Width** sections – you can view your choices in the **Preview** section

Select: How far you want the border to extend in the **Apply to** box (eg **Paragraph**, **Table**, **Cell**)

Click: **OK**

Note: The **Horizontal Line** button relates to borders and lines that can be applied to a Web page.

To adjust the distance between the border lines and the inside

Click: The **Options** button

Key in: The required internal margin specifications

To add shading

Click: The **Shading** tab

The **Shading** dialogue box appears on screen (Figure 11.2).

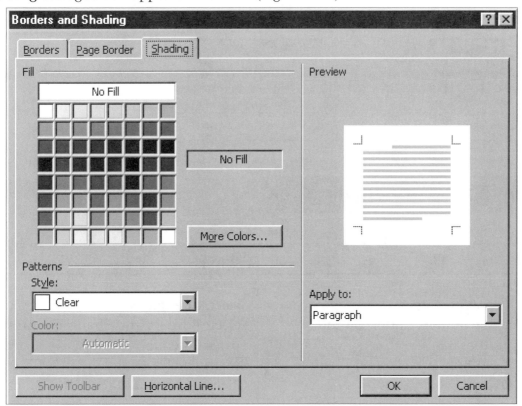

Figure 11.2   Shading dialogue box

Select: The required shading from the **Fill**, **Style** and **Color** sections – you can view your choices in the **Preview** section
Select: How far you want the border to extend in the **Apply to** box (eg **Paragraph**, **Table**, **Cell**)
Click: **OK**

Tool bar method

Select: The item – eg paragraph text, heading – to which you want to add a border or shading
Select: **Toolbars** from the **View** menu
Select: **Tables and Borders**

The **Tables and Borders** Tool Bar appears on screen (Figure 11.3).

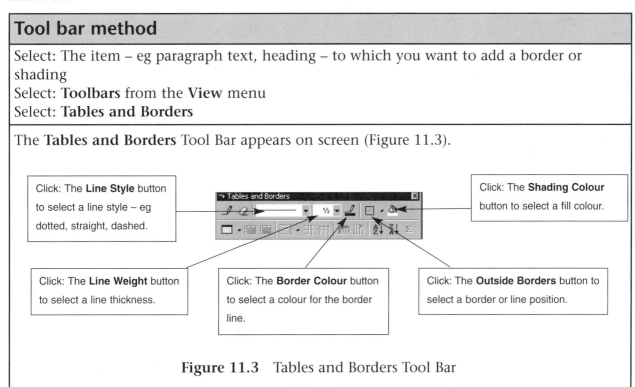

Figure 11.3   Tables and Borders Tool Bar

To adjust the width of the border or shading

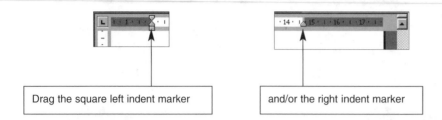

Drag the square left indent marker

and/or the right indent marker

Remove borders or shading

Borders	Shading
Select: The bordered item Click: The ▣ ▾ **Borders** button on the Formatting Tool Bar Click: The **No Border** button on the drop-down grid	Select: The shaded item Select: **Borders and Shading** from the **Format** menu Select: The **Shading** tab Click on: **No Fill** in the **Fill** section

Copying borders and shading format

Refer back to Unit 7 for use of the Format Painter tool to copy formats. You could also use the F4 repeat key to repeat the appropriate formatting command where appropriate.

Exercise 11A

11.1 Starting with a new document, key in the following text. After keying in all the text, add the formatting – bold, borders and shading – to the selected sections as indicated. (Remember, you can use Format Painter or F4 to copy/repeat formatting commands.)

◎ Use Times New Roman font size 12 for the document text.
◎ Use Arial font size 12 for the main heading and the subheadings.

Refer back to Unit 1 if you need to refresh your memory on bullets and their formatting. Save your document under filename **EX11A**. Using the Print Preview facility, check your work against the copy shown in this unit. If you find any errors, correct them and print one copy.

BORDERS TAB
Setting: 3-D
Colour: Auto
Width: 3 pt
SHADING TAB
Grey 12.5%

BORDERS TAB
Setting: Box
Colour: Auto
Width: 1 pt
SHADING TAB
Grey 10%
Apply bold to all
subheadings

THE SCOTTISH HIGHLANDS

LOCHS, GLENS and NATURE RESERVES

The glens and hills near Balquidder, where the notorious outlaw Rob Roy spent his last days, celebrate the beginning of the Highlands. Within the central Grampian Highlands lies the tree-fringed Loch Tummel, once so admired by Queen Victoria that it became known as the Queen's View. The Caledonian Canal, which connects Scotland's east and west coasts, passes through the infamous Loch Ness, alleged habitat of the legendary monster. Over in the forest-clad slopes of the Trossachs lie the vast 23-mile long bonnie banks of Loch Lomond that inspired many of the poems and novels of Sir Walter Scott.

SEA, SEALIFE, SEABIRDS and FARMLAND

Thousands of seabirds flock together on the steep red-sandstone cliffs that sweep down to sheltered sandy coves along the Moray Firth. The bustling fishing port of Lossiemouth, birthplace of James Ramsay MacDonald who became Prime Minister in 1924, hosts the Fisheries and Community Museum. Strathmore's fertile farmland by the sea hosts a mixture of cattle farms, steep braes and splendid beaches. The rocky headland across the West Voe of Sumburgh boasts a huge variety of wildlife and visitors looking out towards the Fair Isle can sometimes catch glimpses of dolphins and killer whales. The milder climate of the Ayrshire coast sees holiday resorts dotted amongst rocky coves and sandy beaches. In the farmland of the Shetlands Islands, there are more sheep and Shetland ponies than people and the islands are home to wildlife including:

- Gulls
- Skuas
- Puffins
- Seals

Indent
bulleted
section by
2.54 cm

St Andrews, named after Scotland's patron saint, is situated within one of Britain's finest stretches of coastline, bordered on three sides by the Firth of Forth, the Firth of Tay and the North Sea.

SHADING TAB
Grey - 10%

Full-page borders

You can apply a range of full-page decorative borders to enhance the appearance of your document.

Select: **Borders and Shading** from the **Format** menu
Select: The **Page Border** tab
Select: The required border display from the **Setting**, **Style**, **Color**, **Width** or **Art** sections – you can view your choices in the **Preview** section
Click: **OK**

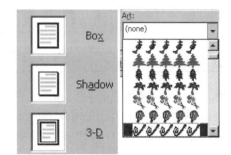

To specify a particular page or section of the document for the border to appear in

Click: The option you want in the **Apply to** drop-down menu box

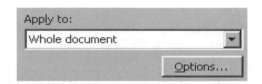

To specify the exact position of the border on the page
Click: **Options**

In the **Margins** section: Adjust the **Top**, **Bottom**, **Left** or **Right** margin settings

In the **Measure from** box: Choose where you want the border to be measured from – **Text** to measure from the page margins and **Edge of Paper** to measure from the edge of the page

In the **Options** section, choose: Whether to include the header and/or footer in the border – remove the tick to deselect ☐ or insert a tick to select ☑

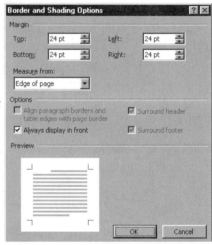

To position the border on a selected side(s) of a page

You can use the **Page Borders** facility to insert a ruled line at one side of the page only:

Click: **Custom** in the **Setting** section

Select: The display settings required as normal (select an option from the Art section if you want a graphical border)

Under **Preview**, click: The diagram or use the border buttons to specify where you want the border to appear

Click: **OK**

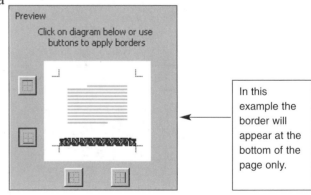

In this example the border will appear at the bottom of the page only.

11.2 Retrieve the file **EX11A** unless it is already on your screen. Save the file as **EX11B**. Amend the document following the instructions given below and resave the file. Check your work with the printout at the back of the book, correct any errors and print one copy of your work.

◎ Change the main heading only to Arial font size 18.

◎ Add the text below to the end of the document making it consistent with the original display.

◎ Using Times New Roman font size 9, insert a header **GLORIES OF SCOTLAND** at the top right of the document and a footer **TOURIST ATTRACTIONS** at the bottom centre of the document.

◎ Insert a page break in a sensible place and number the pages at bottom right of the page.

◎ Add a full-page border:

    – Settings: **Shadow**

    – Colour: **Grey-50%**

    – Width: **3 pt**

    – Click: The **Options** button

    – Select: **Text** from the **Measure from** box

    – Enter top, bottom, left and right margins of **12 pt**

    – Do not include the header and footer in the page border

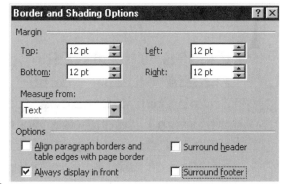

Note: The term **pt** is short for **point size** – point size is a measurement which may relate to the width of a line or border, the size of a font or the amount of margin space.

CASTLES, MANSIONS and DISTILLERIES
Castles of Scotland have a lasting fascination. Eilean Donan, set on a rocky islet in Loch Duich, is an admirable reconstruction of a MacKenzie fortress. Deeside and Donside have a wealth of historic castles including Balmoral, Highland home of the Royal Family. In the region of Perth and Dundee, Guinevere, King Arthur's Queen, was incarcerated at Barry Hill and ghosts are still said to haunt the corridors of Glamis Castle. Travel back 300 years in time tasting the aromas and sound effects of Edinburgh's Scottish Whisky Heritage Centre.

Alternatively, Scotland offers a multitude of whisky distilleries where visitors can sample the delights of time-honoured techniques and processes. A few to try would be:

a) The famous Glenfiddich distillery founded in 1887
b) Clynelish – one of Scotland's finest malt whisky distilleries
c) Glenturret distillery, established in 1775, displaying traditional methods

SKI SLOPES, CLIFFS AND MOUNTAINS

Britain's highest mountain, the giant Ben Nevis, rises 4406 feet, from a sea loch to a bleak plateau, in the Great Glen. The jagged mountains of the Isle of Skye offer a serious challenge for the most experienced climbers. The tiny village of Torredon is set against a backdrop of magnificent, sculptured sandstone peaks. Spectacular cliff-top walks around Banff and Buchan allow breathtaking views of Highland scenery and dramatic sunsets.

Winter sports abound on the northern snow-covered slopes of the sub-arctic plateaus of the Cairngorm Mountains where Aviemore, in particular, is renowned as a popular skiing resort.

CITIES, VILLAGES and ISLES

Dubbed 'The Athens of the North', Scotland's proud capital Edinburgh balances its high, dark buildings of the medieval Old Town with the classical architecture of the Georgian New Town. Edinburgh Castle, home of Scottish Kings and Queens down the centuries, dominates the city from its perch of volcanic rock. Scattered villages, surrounded by moors of red deer, still tell the tales of murder and treachery from days gone by.

Ruined strongholds, wooded valleys, and heather-clad hamlets surround the villages and towns of Ayr and Kilmarnock, once the inspiration of Scotland's national poet, Robert Burns. The Inner Hebrides Isles form landscapes of wild beauty steeped in history including the 1775 Jacobite rebellion led by Bonnie Prince Charlie. The rugged moorlands of prehistoric standing stones, graves and brochs of the Outer Hebrides stretch in a 130-mile chain against Atlantic storms. The Orkney Isles take the traveller back in time to Stone Age tombs and Iron Age underground earth houses.

Exercise 11C

11.3 Starting with a clear screen, key in the following document, following all the instructions. Save the document using the filename **EX11C** and print one copy.

◎ Use a document line length of 13 cm and a justified right-hand margin throughout.

◎ Use Perpetua font size 11 for the document text and Arial font size 12 with bold for the main and subheadings (you may use alternative fonts if those stated are not available).

◎ Add a border and shading to the main heading as shown.

◎ Add shading only to all the subheadings and also the clear line space below as shown in the first two examples shown in the exercise.

◎ Add a full page border – select an appropriate decorative border from the Art drop-down menu.

TREES AND SHRUBS

PLANTING

Generally, deciduous trees and shrubs are best planted between November and March whilst in a leafless state. Evergreens are usually planted in September and October, or preferably April when they start to make new growth. However, if plants are put out from pots, exceptions can be made since this does not disturb the roots, but no plants should ever be moved when the soil is icy or covered in snow. Plant in deeply dug and manured soil in a suitable situation for the species, ensuring that the planting hole is large enough to take the roots comfortably. Tread down periodically, leaving the soil slightly higher than the surrounding land to allow for normal levelling later. Young standard trees may need the support of a stake for several years until they become firmly established.

AFTER CARE

Soak the tree well if the ground seems dry at planting time. During the first summer, it is wise to spray the foliage of evergreens occasionally. Remove pernicious weeds, and apply a mulch (eg peat, bracken, leaves) to retain moisture and provide humus. Be careful not to dig too close to the shrubs to avoid damaging any feeding roots near to the surface. Very tender plants can benefit from a screen to protect them from the wind in their first year.

PROPAGATION
There are various methods of increasing stock such as seed, cuttings, layering, air layering, grafting, budding and division.   Cuttings tend to be the most widely used method of propagation. There are two different techniques — half-ripe cuttings that are taken during the summer and hard-wood cuttings that are taken during the autumn.

Growing from seed can be great fun and also very cheap. The best time to sow seeds is in early spring, about March.

Division simply involves lifting a tree or shrub and splitting it into several parts, making sure that each has some fibrous roots attached. The separated portions are then replanted. Division is best attempted in early spring before new growth begins.

GENERAL PRUNING
Pruning is vital for ensuring the maximum amount of good quality blooms, berries and fruits, and also to achieve balance, safety and shapeliness. As well as cutting back or removing sound branches, it is also essential to take out any dead or diseased wood. Methods of pruning vary, so it is wise to consult a good gardening book to become familiar with the habits of growth and flowering of particular species. Using incorrect techniques can lead to disease or infection setting in.

Use a 2-column layout for this section

USE IN THE GARDEN

A carefully positioned tree or shrub can be used to mask off any unsightly aspects which detract from the beauty of the garden. They are also useful for forming windbreaks from any areas subject to prevailing winds, or to provide privacy from passers-by. Trees can be features in their own right, particularly those with attractively shaped or coloured leaves, flowering or berry trees, and those with coloured bark. Trees can also provide varying height levels to create balance and avoid the garden from becoming too flat-looking.

Exercise 11D

11.4   Starting with a clear screen, key in the following document, following all the instructions given below. Save the document using the filename **EX11D** and print one copy.

◎   Use a document line length of 12.5 cm and centre the text as shown.

◎   Use Times New Roman font size 12 unless otherwise indicated.

◎   Add borders and/or shading where indicated.

◎   Add a full-page border – select an appropriate decorative border from the Art drop-down menu.

◎   Click: The **Options** button.

◎   Select: **Text** from the **Measure from** box.

◎   Enter top, bottom margins of **15 pt**, left and right margins of **30 pt**.

SEAFARERS SAILING CLUB
Special Events

Cassia font size 28 Bold or alternative font

Grey 10% Shading and 3/4 pt border

EARLY EVENING BOAT CRUISES

Aboard the Princess Guinevere Every Sat and Sunday evening: July and Aug
6.30-9.30 pm
Adults: £5.50, Children and OAP's: £3.00

Cruise along the Breedale River between Derrin Valley and Guildbury Bridge,
stopping for drinks at the Fox & Partridge

Shade all headings as in this example with grey 12·5 % and Embolden

SUNDAY LUNCH SPECIALS

Shade these paragraphs with grey 10%

Aboard the Michelangelo or the Rembrandt
Traditional 3-Course Sunday Lunch
Extensive choice of menu
Every Sunday: June-September
12.00 noon- 3.00/2.30 pm
Adults: £12.50
Children & OAPs: £8.00

Relax and enjoy the sights and sounds of the surrounding countryside whilst listening to the gentle
melodies of our own on-board music quartet

AFTERNOON TEA ON THE BONNY BREE

Use a 2-column layout for this section

Aboard the Bonny Bree Breeze
Afternoon tea, scones with strawberries and fresh cream
Every Sunday afternoon throughout the season
2.00-4.30 pm
Adults: £5.50, Children and OAP's: £3.00

Enjoy a short 45-minute stop-off at Breedale Crafts Centre

leave at least 1.27cm here

Seafarers Sailing Club, Briedale Riverbank, Derrin Valley, DA3 GYU
Tel no: 01459 348891

emphasise with italic and apply a 1 pt Box Border

UNIT 12 DRAWING TOOLS

By the end of Unit 12 you should have learnt how to:

◎ use Word 2000's drawing tools to produce shapes, diagrams and dividers
◎ insert a text box into a document
◎ apply shading to text boxes and drawing shapes
◎ insert text into a drawing shape.

In the next units you will learn how to place different types of graphics into your documents. The basic types of graphics are drawing objects, text boxes and pictures.

 ## Drawing objects

Drawing objects include the following:

◎ Ready-made AutoShapes – basic shapes such as circles or squares, flowchart elements, stars and banners, and callouts. You can resize, rotate, flip, colour and combine shapes with other shapes to make more complex shapes. You can also add text to these shapes.

◎ Lines and curves – you can combine different lines and curves, and also combine lines and curves with shapes:

   – use Curve for greater control and accuracy

   – use Scribble to look like it was drawn with a pen

   – use Freeform for a more refined shape without jagged edges

◎ WordArt drawing objects – you can create shadowed, skewed, rotated and stretched text, as well as text that has been fitted to predefined shapes. Because a special text effect is a drawing object, you can also use other buttons on the Drawing Tool Bar to change the effect — for example, to fill a text effect with a picture.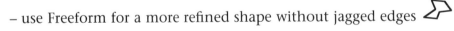

 ## Text boxes

Text boxes allow you to add callouts, labels and other text to your graphics, positioning these on the document page as you would a drawing object. You can use the Drawings options to enhance the text as you would for any other drawing object. Alternatively, you could use an AutoShape with text added to it as a text box.

> **Text boxes let you convert text into drawing objects.**

Pictures

Pictures are graphics that were created from another file and may include previously drawn images, scanned pictures and photographs, and ClipArt. Word 2000 comes with a ClipArt

 Gallery of pictures from scenic backgrounds to maps and from buildings to people. This makes it easier for you to insert pictures into your documents with professionally designed images instead of having always to create them yourself. You can also import pictures or photographs from other programs if you wish.

Whereas text always fits within preset page margins, drawing shapes, text boxes and graphics/pictures may not. You need to be aware of this both for layout and for design purposes – there may be times when you want to put a shape or picture into the margin to enhance the document display. Alternatively, shapes or pictures may overlap into the margin 'accidentally' and then you would need to move their position on the page according to the instructions provided later in the unit.

Drawing tools

In the OCR/RSA Stage III Document Presentation Part 2 examination you will need to be able to produce a diagram for use within a document. Word 2000 offers a range of drawing tools within the same software program, thus allowing you to combine text and drawings with relative ease. Word 2000's drawing tools can be used in a variety of ways. You will need to familiarise yourself with the different functions of the drawing tools in order to analyse the best use for each tool in relation to the type of diagram or shape required. The best way to learn is to practise.

Display (or hide) the Drawing Tool Bar

Click: the Drawing Tool Bar button on the Standard Tool Bar. The **Drawing** Tool Bar appears on screen

Draw a basic shape

Click: The required shape on the Drawing Tool Bar, eg the Line, Arrow, Rectangle or Oval

Position insertion point: Where you want to start drawing – the cursor changes to a $+$ cross hair pointer

Hold down: The left mouse button

Drag: The shape in the appropriate direction until it is the required size:

To draw a perfect circle, square or straight line

Hold down: The **Shift** key whilst drawing the shape – the oval shape for a circle, and the rectangle shape for a square: ◯ ▢ ━━

Format or change a shape

Before you can edit a shape, you need to select it.

Select a shape

Click the mouse pointer: On the graphic – the cursor changes to a four-headed arrow

The shape is selected when it appears with small 'handles' around it, eg:

Select several shapes

Click: The **Select Objects**  icon on the Drawing Tool Bar

Move the arrowhead to: The shapes

Hold down: The mouse button *and* drag the dotted outline around the
group of shapes to select so that each of the shapes will display 'handles' around it

OR

Hold down: The **Shift** key *and*

Select: Each shape in turn still holding the **Shift** key down

Release: The **Shift** key when all the objects are selected

Deselect a shape

Click the mouse pointer: In any area of white space

Resize a shape

You can resize a shape by making it larger or smaller: stretching or shrinking it vertically, horizontally or both:

Select: The shape to be edited

 Point to: The appropriate handle – a double headed arrow is displayed:

 Click: The ↔ arrow or the ↕ arrow to alter the shape horizontally or vertically
and

Drag the mouse: In the direction required either to increase or decrease the size.

Click: The ↘ arrow or the ↗ arrow to alter the shape horizontally or vertically
and

Drag the mouse: In the direction required either to increase or decrease the overall shape size

Note: To keep the same overall proportions, hold down the **Shift** key whilst resizing the shape.

Move a shape

Click: The shape to be moved/repositioned. The insertion point changes to a ✛ four-headed arrow

Drag: The drawing object to its new position

Shade, colour or pattern a shape

Click: The 🖌 **Fill Color**, 🖌 **Line Color**, 🔺 **Font Color**, ≡ **Line Style**, ▦ **Dash Style**, ⇄ **Arrow Style** buttons on the Drawing Tool Bar

Select: From the menu choices offered

Copy a shape

Select: The shape to be copied

Operate: The normal *copy* and *paste* commands *and*

Drag: The duplicate shape to the required position on the page

Cut/delete a shape

Select: The shape to be cut/deleted

Operate: The normal *cut/delete* commands

Group shapes together

Select: All the shapes to be grouped

Click: The Dr̲aw **Draw** button on the Drawing Tool Bar

Select: **Group** from the list of options offered

A selected group

Note: Any further changes will affect all the objects in the group, ie you may *colour*, *resize* or *move* them all together.

Ungroup previously grouped shapes

Select: The group

Click: The Dr̲aw **Draw** button on the Drawing Tool Bar

Select: **Ungroup** from the list of options offered

Send a shape in front or behind another shape

Select: The shape to be repositioned

Click: The Dr̲aw **Draw** button on the Drawing Tool Bar

Select: **Order**

Choose: The appropriate command from the list of options offered, eg **Send to Back**, **Bring to Front**

Send a shape in front or behind text

Send Behind Text

Select: The shape to be repositioned

Click: The Dr̲aw **Draw** button on the Drawing Tool Bar

Select: **Order**

Choose: The appropriate command from the list of options offered, eg **Send behind Text**, **Bring in Front of Text**

Flip, rotate or reshape the shape

Shape flipped vertically

Select: The shape to be repositioned

Click: The Dr̲aw **Draw** button on the Drawing Tool Bar

Select: **Rotate** or **Flip**

Choose: The appropriate command from the list of options offered

Align shapes or distribute evenly

Uneven alignment   Shapes aligned at top

A group of shapes which are not aligned with each other or distributed evenly

The same group of shapes after they have been **Aligned to the Top** and **Distributed Horizontally**

Select: The shapes to be aligned with each other or distributed evenly

Click: The `Draw` **Draw** button on the Drawing Tool Bar

Select: **Align** or **Distribute**

Ensure that: There is not a tick in the **Relative to Page** – if there is, click on the option to remove the tick

Choose: The appropriate command from the list of options offered depending on whether you want to align different shapes with each other or distribute them evenly on the page

Note: When you choose the **Distribute evenly** command (either horizontally or vertically), Word will distribute the shapes or graphics evenly between the first and last shape or graphic positioned on the page. You should therefore position the first and last shape or graphic where you want the shapes to finish (a bit like goal posts at the opposite end of a football pitch). Word will distribute the rest of the shapes between the first and last shapes.

Draw AutoShapes

You can draw and edit AutoShapes (ready-made shapes) in exactly the same way as a standard shape:

Select: **AutoShapes** from the Drawing Tool Bar `AutoShapes`

The drop-down list contains several different types of shapes, including lines, basic shapes, block arrows, flowchart elements, stars, banners and callouts. Many have a small yellow diamond-shaped adjustment handle that lets you change the most prominent feature of a shape, eg the size of the arrow point.

Choose: A shape from the submenu of options

Draw the shape as normal – using the cross-hair pointer to position the shape and the left mouse button to determine its size

Note: The option `More AutoShapes...` will be dealt with in Unit 13.

Add shadow or 3-D to a shape

Normal   Shadow   3-D

Select: The shape to be edited

Click: The ▣ **Shadow button** or the ▨ **3-D** button on the Drawing Tool Bar

Choose: From the menu of options offered

Add text to a shape

You can add text to shapes and AutoShapes:

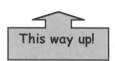

This way up!

Right-click: The shape

Click: **Add Text** on the shortcut menu

Key in: The text

Note: If you *move* the shape, the text will move with it.

If you *rotate* or *flip* the shape, the text does *not* rotate or flip with it. You can change the *colour* of the text using the 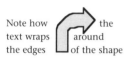 **Font Color** button.

You can rotate the text in a shape or text box 90 degrees to the left or right by selecting **Text Direction** from the **Format** menu.

Wrap text around a shape

You can wrap text around a shape of any size and shape. You can choose specific sides of the shape you want the text to wrap around and also the distance between the shape and the text that surrounds it:

Note how text wraps the edges the around of the shape

Key in: The text
Insert: The required AutoShape in the required position
Select: The shape
Select: **AutoShape** from the **Format** menu
Click: The **Layout** tab
Select: The text wrapping style you require from the options shown

Insert text above or below drawing shapes

Press: **Ctrl + Home** to move the insertion pointer above drawing shapes and to be able to key in or edit text above the drawing
Press: **Ctrl + End** to move the insertion pointer past drawing shapes and to be able to key in or edit text below the drawing

Snap to gridlines

This facility can be used if you want to align shapes, or draw shapes with set dimensions. Gridlines are not printed or displayed on the screen:

Click: The ⬚ **Draw** button on the Drawing Tool Bar
Select: ⊞ **Grid**
Click: The **Snap objects to grid** box to select the option – a tick will appear when the option is selected
Click: The **Snap objects to grid** box again to deselect the option – the tick will disappear when the option is not selected

These shapes were drawn with identical grid proportions by using the snap to grid feature

Note: The default spacing of gridlines is normally 0.32 cm – to alter the amount of space between both vertical and horizontal gridlines enter a new measurement in the Horizontal or Vertical spacing boxes.

To change the point at the left edge of the page where you want the gridlines to begin (normally defaulted to start at the 0 cm point on the horizontal and vertical rulers) enter a new measurement in the Horizontal or Vertical **Grid origin** box.

Determine the exact size or position of a shape

Right-click: The shape
Select: **Format AutoShape** from the quick menu
Click: The **Size** or **Layout** tab as appropriate and enter the required settings

Insert WordArt

Click: The **◢ Insert WordArt** button on the Drawing Tool Bar
Select: A **WordArt style** from the options displayed
Key in: Your text in the **Enter WordArt Text** box
Use: The text formatting tools to make any appropriate changes
Click: **OK**

When you click on the WordArt, the **WordArt Toolbar** is displayed on screen. You can now **Format WordArt** text just as you would any graphic, using the WordArt Tool Bar buttons and other drawing facilities to resize, reposition, align, rotate, flip, edit the text, colour or line etc.

Note: You can press the right mouse button to bring up the quick menu to format or edit shapes – this is sometimes quicker than using the Drawing Tool Bar. You can use the F4 key to repeat actions – this is useful, for example, when you want to repeat the copy command for multiple copies of the same shape.

Exercise 12A

12.1 Starting with a clear screen, display the **Drawing Tool Bar** on screen and practise using Word 2000's drawing facilities. Have fun!

- ◎ **Draw** some **Basic Shapes**, eg line, square, rectangle, circle, oval etc.
- ◎ **Draw** some **AutoShapes** eg Lines, Block Arrows, Callouts, Stars and Banners.
- ◎ **Resize** the shapes you have drawn – try enlarging and reducing them.
- ◎ Add different **Fill Colors**, **Line Color**, **Line Style**, **3-D** and **Shadow** to the shapes.
- ◎ **Move** the shapes around the screen, then **Copy** and **Delete** some of them.
- ◎ Position a shape in front of another shape – use the **Send to Front** and **Send to Back** facilities.
- ◎ Key in a few words, move a shape in front of the text, then use the **Send Behind Text** facility.
- ◎ **Rotate** and **Flip** some of your shapes – practise using the **Free Rotate** facility.
- ◎ Use the **Align** or **Distribute** command to align several shapes with each other.
- ◎ **Group** two or more shapes together, then **Ungroup** them.
- ◎ Practise drawing shapes using the **Grid** feature.
- ◎ **Add text** to a shape and change the **Font Color**.

12.2 Close the file without saving or printing your work at this stage.

Exercise 12B

12.3 Starting a new document, display the **Drawing Tool Bar** and turn on the **Snap objects to grid** facility with **Horizontal and Vertical spacing** set at **0.25 cm**. Follow the guidelines on the next page to reproduce the drawing of a mill factory. It doesn't matter if your finished drawing is not exactly the same – this exercise is just for practice and for fun!

Remember to use the **Send to Front/Back** facility to position the shapes, and to use the **Group** facility to keep objects together once you are satisfied with their position (remember, you can **Ungroup** and reposition individual shapes at any time if you need to).

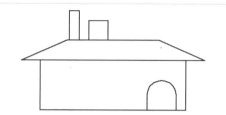

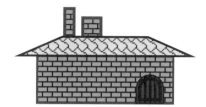

Step 1. Use the **Rectangle** shape for the main building and chimneys. Use the **Trapezoid** ▽ shape, from AutoShapes, Basic Shapes, for the roof using the Flip Vertical drawing facility to reposition it. Use the **Flowchart: Delay** ◻ shape using the Rotate Left drawing facility to reposition it as shown. You can adjust the sizes of the shapes as you go along. It doesn't matter if the shapes are not exactly the same size as shown.

Step 2. Click on each shape in turn and apply different colours and effects, patterns and line styles using the **Fill Color**, **Line Color** and **Line Style** buttons from the Drawing Tool Bar – you can choose different fill patterns if you want to. Remember that you may use Format Painter to copy formats from one shape to another, eg the walls and chimneys in the above drawing.

Step 3. In order to draw 'freehand', turn the Snap objects to grid facility off. Use the **Flowchart: Or** shape from AutoShapes, Flowchart, to draw a circular 'window' shape. (The example given used Fill Color, Fill Effects, Gradient, Two colors, Shading styles, From center.) Copy the circle twice.

Step 4. Position the circles as shown, using the Align Bottom and Distribute Horizontally facilities to line them up evenly. Use the Cloud Callout from AutoShapes, Callouts, to draw a puff of smoke as shown – use Fill Color effects to shade (you may need to use the small yellow adjustment handle to position it). Use the Sun shape, from AutoShapes Basic Shapes, to draw a sun shape at top right.

Step 5. Group all the shapes together. If necessary, make the drawing bigger (or smaller if your drawing is already quite large) – hold down the Shift key while you stretch the drawing to keep the same proportions. Using a suitable font and size, **Add Text** to the sun shape: **SUN MILL**. Use **WordArt** to create special effects for the text: **WELCOME TO A NEW SHOPPING EXPERIENCE** and position it to the right of the drawing as shown. Draw a **Rectangle** with no border lines above the WordArt and **Add Text** in bold, italic and centred: **Open 7 days a week 9.00am – 5.00pm**

12.4   Save and print a copy of your work using the filename **SUN MILL**.

 Exercise 12C

12.5   Starting with a clear screen, try to reproduce the diagrams shown below – they have all been completed simply by using Word 2000's drawing tools. You do not have to draw them in the exact sizes or fill shown – the purpose of this exercise is for you to practise using combining different shapes to create a drawing. Remember to use the Align command to line up the shapes and the Order command to position the shapes in front or behind each other. Save and print a copy of your work using the filename **DRAWINGS**.

Insert a text box

You have already used text boxes as a method of allocating space within documents in Unit 7. Text boxes are primarily used as 'drawing objects' and act as containers for text that can be positioned anywhere on a page. Text boxes allow you to use new graphical effects to manipulate text in a more exciting way. A text box is useful for creating a *watermark* where text appears on top or behind existing text. For example, companies sometimes print 'Confidential' in light print across the pages of a document.

> This is an example of text entered into a text box. You can edit the size of the box to allow enough room for the text, and apply decorative finishes using the Drawing Tool Bar.

Use the Drawing Tool Bar to apply 3-D effects, shadows, border styles and colours, fills and backgrounds to the text box. You can group text boxes together, change the alignment or distribution of them as a group, rotate and flip text boxes, and change the orientation of the text with the **Text Direction** command.

Click: The 📧 **Text Box** icon on the Drawing Tool Bar (a cursor in the shape of a **+** appears on screen,
Hold down: The left mouse button
Drag: The box until it is an appropriate size for the text

Note: Text boxes do not automatically increase in size if you key in more text than the original box size will allow for – you must select the text box and make it larger to make room for the extra text.

Position the insertion pointer: Inside the text box
Key in: The text

Note: Text in a text box is formatted with the normal style – you can change the style of part or all of the text in a text box in the same way you would reformat text in the main document.

To adjust the space between the text box border and the text inside
Click: The text box border to select it
Select: **Text Box** from the **Format** menu (*or* right click and
select: **Format Text Box** from the quick menu)
Select: The **Text Box** tab
Key in: A value in the **Internal Margin** boxes
Click: **OK**

 Standard internal margins

Internal margins adjusted

To change the orientation of the text in a text box
Click: The text box to select it
Select: **Text Direction** from the **Format** menu
Click: The direction required in the **Orientation** box – use the Preview box to view the layout
Click: **OK**

To format a text box
Click: The text box to select it
Select: **Text Box** from the **Format** menu
Select: The appropriate tab shown on the **Format Text Box** dialogue box: **Color and Lines, Size, Layout, Text Box** to alter the display or format of the text box

12.6 Starting with a clear screen, reproduce the following diagram. Use Arial font size 8, and embolden and centre the text in all boxes. You may find it easier if you use the Grid facility:

◎ Use grey-filled text boxes for the rectangle shapes for **LOCHS**, **SEA**, **CITIES**, **SKI**, **RIVERS** and **CASTLES**. (You can complete the first text box and then copy it five times for the others. However, after using the *copy* command you *must* position the insertion pointer outside the text box before using the *paste* command otherwise you will get a box within a box.)

◎ Use text boxes with No Line and No Fill for the text entries **where history**... and **landscape of** ... Do not embolden the text in these boxes.

◎ Use a text box with a White Font Colour for the text **SCOTLAND**... and a Black Fill Colour for the background to produce the ‘reverse video’ effect.

◎ **Draw** the lines, using 2¹/₄ pt Line Style, connecting the boxes as shown – use the **Send to Back** facility to hide the ends of each line behind the boxes.

◎ **Group** all the shapes together.

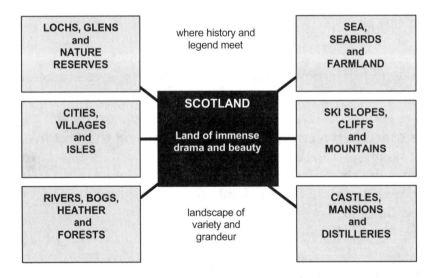

12.7 Save your work using filename **SCOTLAND**. Close the file without printing at this stage.

12.8 Open the file **EX11B** you saved earlier in Unit 11. Resave the file using the filename **EX12D**. Position the cursor at the very end of the document, ie after the section headed **CITIES, VILLAGES and ISLES** on page 2.

12.9 Select **File** from the **Insert** menu. Select the file **SCOTLAND** and insert it into the document. (If you have difficulty fitting the diagram on to the page, reduce the size of the document text.)

12.10 Position the diagram in a sensible place on page 2 of the document. Resave the file to include your new work. Do not print at this stage.

Create dividers (rules) using drawing tools

Dividers or rules are used to organise the miscellaneous elements in a document and to separate one item from another. There are several different methods of inserting dividers into a document using Word 2000.

A simple divider can be created using a grey-shaded rectangle with or without border lines. You can copy and paste this throughout the document.

Another simple divider can be inserted using the Line tool from the Drawing Tool Bar. Format it with the Line Style, Arrow Style and Line Color tools.

Examples

You could create a more decorative divider by combining several different drawing shapes together. Group the shapes and paste the graphic divider as appropriate throughout the document.

Examples

Exercise 12D (continued)

12.11 With Exercise 12D on screen, refer to the instructions 'Create dividers (rules) using drawing tools' above. Create a divider approximately 5 cm wide using the Drawing Tool Bar. Insert the divider between the end of the text on page 2 and the diagram.

12.12 Resave the file using the filename **EX12D**. Use the Print Preview facility to check your layout against the printout check at the back of this book. If your layout is correct, print page 2 only by selecting **Print** from the **File** menu, then clicking **Pages** and enter **2** as the page range.

12.13 Exit the program if you have finished working or continue straight on to the next unit.

UNIT 13 CLIPART IMAGES AND GRAPHICAL DIVIDERS

> **By the end of Unit 13 you should have learnt how to:**
>
> ◎ import and position a ClipArt image from the ClipArt Catalogue
> ◎ use symbols for graphics
> ◎ import and position picture files from the Microsoft Picture File.

In the Stage III Document Presentation Part 2 examination, there will be an instruction to add an appropriate ClipArt image to the document. This unit will introduce you to the different methods of importing and formatting ClipArt. However, you will also need to familiarise yourself with the range of ClipArt stored on your computer as this will vary between systems. When completing the exercises for this unit, if you do not have the ClipArt file suggested, try to find a similar picture file from the choices available on your system.

 ## Insert ClipArt from the ClipArt Catalogue

You can insert a ClipArt image or a picture into your document from the ClipArt Catalogue. After inserting it, you can convert the ClipArt image to drawing objects and then use options on the Drawing Tool Bar to edit different parts, eg change the fill or line colours.

View the ClipArt Catalogue
Position the insertion pointer: At the place where you want to insert the ClipArt image
Select: **Picture** from the **Insert** menu
Select: **ClipArt**

OR

Click: The 🖳 **Insert ClipArt** button on the Drawing Tool Bar
Click: The **Pictures** tab

The Microsoft ClipArt Catalogue appears on screen (Figure 18.1).

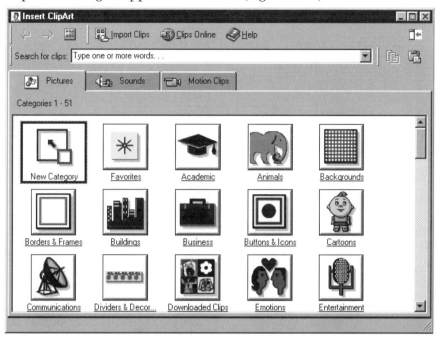

Figure 13.1 Microsoft ClipArt Catalogue

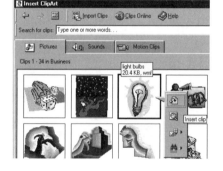

Insert a ClipArt image

Click: A **Category** from the ClipArt Catalogue options

Click: The **Clip** you want *or*

Click: ⇥⊞⊞ Keep Looking to view some more clips

Click: The **Insert clip** button on the drop-down menu to the right of the clip to insert the image into your document (Figure 13.2)

Figure 13.2 Insert ClipArt dialogue box

OR

Click: **Preview clip** to view the image before insertion

Click: **Add to Favorites** if you want to make up your own personal catalogue of favourite clips

Click: **Find similar clips** to view other clips which are either similar in 'Artistic Style' or 'Color and Shape'

Click: The **Back** arrow to go back a step *or*

Click: The **All Categories** to view all the different categories again

Click: The **Change to Small Window** button to reduce the size of the dialogue box – you can leave this on screen whilst you are working if you wish

Click: The **Change to Full Window** button again to toggle back to full view

Display the Picture Tool Bar

It is often easier to edit/format pictures by using the Picture Tool Bar which appears on screen when you select the graphic image. If the tool bar does not appear on screen:

Right-click: The image and select **Show Picture Toolbar** from the quick menu *or*
Select: **Toolbars** from the **View** menu
Click: **Picture**

You can use these tools to crop the image, add a border to it or adjust its brightness and contrast (Figure 13.3).

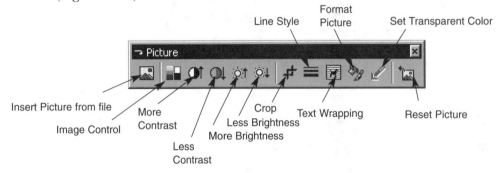

Figure 13.3 Picture Tool Bar

Format a ClipArt image

You can format a ClipArt image using some of the drawing tools just as you would a drawing shape.

Examples

Apply Shadow   Send to Back   Apply a Fill Color to the background

---

Resize a ClipArt image

Select: The image (it is selected when small rectangular handles appear around it)

Click: A handle arrow (eg ↔ ↕ ↗ ↘)

Drag: The mouse in the direction required to increase or decrease the size

To keep the same overall proportions:

Hold down: The **Shift** key whilst resizing the image:

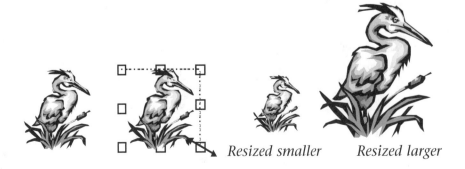

Resized smaller   *Resized larger*

To determine the exact size of a ClipArt image

Select: The graphic image

Select: **Picture** (or **AutoShape**) from the **Format** menu

OR

Click: The **Format Picture** button on the **Picture Tool Bar**

The **Format Picture** dialogue box appears on screen (Figure 13.4).

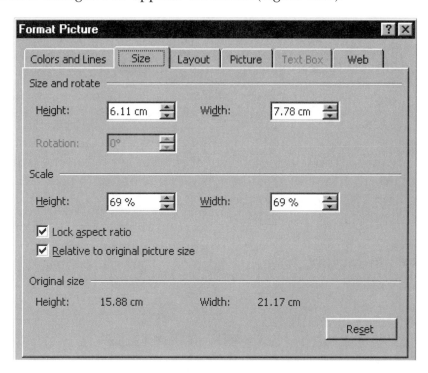

Figure 13.4 Format Picture dialogue box

Click: The **Size** tab

The size of the image is shown as exact **Height** and **Width** measurements under **Size and rotate** *or* as a percentage of the original size under **Scale**. If the **Lock aspect ratio** check box is selected, the height and width settings change automatically in relation to one another.

Move/copy/paste/cut a ClipArt image

Click: The image
Drag: The image to its new position to *move* it *or*
Use: The normal *copy*, *paste* and *cut* commands as required

Wrap text around the ClipArt picture

You can wrap text around a drawing object of any size and shape. You can specify particular sides of the graphic you want the text to wrap to and also the distance between the graphic and the text that surrounds it:

Select: The image
Select: **Picture** (or **AutoShape**) from the **Format** menu
Click: The **Layout** tab
Select: From the options in the **Wrapping style** section
Click: The **Advanced** button if you need to set vertical and horizontal alignment as well as additional wrapping options

OR

Click: The **Text Wrapping** tool on the **Picture Tool Bar**
Select: The text wrapping option you require from the options shown

Position an image in relation to text or to the page

Select: The graphic object or picture you want to position
Select: **Picture** (or **AutoShape**, **Text Box**, **Object**) from the **Format** menu
Click: The **Layout** tab
Click: **Advanced**
Select: The required options for your horizontal and vertical anchors in the **From** boxes
Enter: The distances from the anchors in the **Horizontal** and **Vertical** boxes

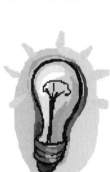

You can attach an object to a paragraph so that if you move the paragraph the object moves with it:

Ensure that: There is a tick mark in the **Move object with text** check box under **Format**, **Picture**, **Layout**, **Advanced** (the selected object becomes anchored to the paragraph and always moves up or down with it – if you do not want the object to be attached to the paragraph, deselect the option to remove the tick)

You can ensure the selected object is always anchored in the same position on the page if you move it by making sure there is a tick mark in the **Lock anchor** check box.

Exercise 13A

13.1   Open **EX3D** and save as **EX13A**.

13.2   Following the instructions 'Insert a ClipArt image' above, insert one of the ClipArt images from the **Business** ClipArt Category into your document. The position is not important at this stage.

13.3   Following the instructions 'Resize a ClipArt image' above, decrease the size of the graphic, keeping the same overall proportions, until it is about 4 cm high. Use the ruler at the left of the screen to help you to estimate this measurement.

13.4   Wrap the text around the image:

Click: The image to select it (unless it is already selected)
Select: **Picture** from the **Format** menu
Click: The **Layout** tab
Select: **Tight** from the **Wrapping style** section
Click: **OK**

13.5   Move the image to the right-hand side of the second paragraph of the memo (look at the printout check at the back of the book if you need to check the position). The text should flow up to the left edge of the image.

13.6 Make a copy of the image and decrease the copy by about 50%, keeping the same overall proportions. With the **Picture Tool Bar** on screen, click the **Image Control** tool and select **Watermark**. With the image selected, choose **In Front of text** for the **Wrapping style**. (You may find it easier to select the **Wrapping** button from the Picture Tool Box which should now be displayed on screen.)

13.7 Make four more copies of the watermark graphic and position these across the page between the left and right margins.

13.8 With the **Drawing Tool Bar** on screen, select all five watermark images using the **Select Objects** button. Use the **Align or Distribute** command from the **Draw** menu, select **Align Top** and then **Distribute Horizontally**.

13.9 **Group** all five graphic images together. Move the grouped picture to the centre of the last paragraph that begins **Please could you send** ...   With the image group selected, choose **Behind text** for the **Wrapping style**.

13.10 Resave the document. Check your work on screen (using the Print Preview facility) with the printout at the back of the book. If your layout is correct, print a copy of your document.

Exercise 13B

13.11 Open the document **EX11C** and save as **EX13B**. Apart from the main heading, reduce all the document text to font size 10. Insert a ClipArt picture from the **Plants** category into your document. If necessary, resize the image and position the picture in the middle of the white space at the bottom of the page. (Click on the picture, then select **Format, Object, Layout, In front of text, OK**, so that you can move the picture to different positions on the page.)

13.12 Make a copy of the ClipArt picture. Decrease the size of the copy only by about 50%. Make a copy of the smaller sized ClipArt picture so that you have one large and two small copies of the same image. Arrange the trio as below (it doesn't matter if you don't match the exact sizes):

13.13 Use the **Shadow** tool on the Drawing Tool Bar to apply a shadow setting to each graphic.

13.14 Resave and print one copy.

Position the insertion pointer: Where you want to insert the picture
Select: **Picture** from the **Insert** menu
Select: **From File**
Check: That the Microsoft ClipArt Directory (or other directory in which the picture is stored) is displayed in the **Look in** box, eg **MSOffice**, **ClipArt** – this should be under Program Files on C: drive or, alternatively, you could use a special ClipArt CD-ROM in D: drive

The **Insert Picture** dialogue box appears on screen (Figure 13.5).

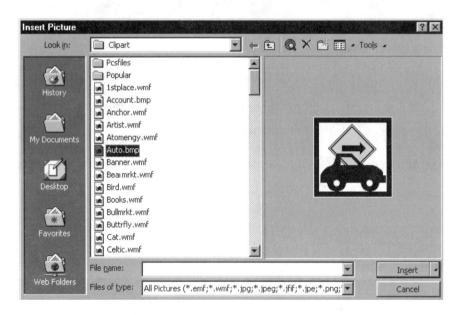

Figure 13.5 Insert Picture dialogue box

Click: The **Preview** button on the **Insert Picture** dialogue box so that you can view the choices
Click: The filename for the picture you want to insert
Click: **Insert**

Format the picture using the same methods as described earlier under 'Insert ClipArt from the ClipArt Catalogue', eg adjust the size or position, text wrapping etc.

Note: You will need to check what ClipArt pictures are available on your particular computer – these may vary from the examples shown. Choose appropriate alternatives if necessary.

Insert a picture into a text box

You can predetermine the amount of space and the position which the picture takes up on the page by inserting it into a text box:

Draw: A text box where you want the picture to appear on the page
Click the insertion pointer: Inside the text box
Insert: The picture as described above – the picture will fill the text box boundaries

Note: You can still increase or decrease the size of the picture afterwards – the text box boundaries will also be increased or decreased accordingly.

You can format the text box and the picture using the usual methods.

Use symbols as graphics
To insert a symbol into the document
Select: **Symbol** from the **Insert** menu

Select: The **Symbols** tab

Select: A **Font** from the drop-down menu to display its character set in the grid below, eg **Wingdings**

Click: The symbol you want to insert into your document, eg ☠ or other symbol of your choice

Click: **Insert**

Click: **Close**

To increase or decrease the size of the symbol ☠ ☠ ☠
Select: The symbol as you would normal text

Select: A point size from the **Font Size** menu on the Formatting Tool Bar *or*

Press: **Ctrl +]** until you have the required size

To display in reverse video ☠
Select: **White Font Color** and **Black Highlight** from the Formatting Tool Bar

To move a symbol graphic around the page
You can insert the symbol into a text box:

Click: The text box button on the Drawing Tool Bar

Position: The insertion pointer inside the text box

Select: The symbol to be inserted following the previous instructions 'To insert a symbol into the document'

You can then increase, decrease or format both the text box and the symbol using the usual methods. You can remove the text box to show no lines if you only want to be able to see the symbol.

Exercise 13C

13.15 Open **EX11D** and save as **EX13C**. Carry out the following changes:

- ◎ Delete the two words **Tel No**: at the bottom of the page.
- ◎ Position the insertion point immediately before the **01459 348891** (telephone number).
- ◎ Select **Symbol** from the **Insert** menu, then select the **Wingdings** font.
- ◎ Click on the **telephone** symbol (on the top row). Click: **Insert**, **Close**.
- ◎ Increase the telephone symbol size to **16 pt**.

13.16 Draw two identical text boxes in the white space at either side of the **SUNDAY LUNCH SPECIALS** section – make these approximately 2.5 cm high by 3.5 cm wide.

With both text boxes selected:

- ◎ Select: **Text Box** from the **Format** menu
- ◎ Click: The **Size** tab
- ◎ Enter: The **Height** and **Width** settings

13.17 Insert a ClipArt image:

Note: Choose appropriate alternative graphics if the ones that are suggested at steps 13.17 and 13.18 are not available on your computer.

◎ Position the insertion pointer: Inside the text box at the left-hand side of the page.

◎ Select: **Picture** from the **Insert** menu.

◎ Select: **From File**.

◎ Check that the **MSOffice**, **ClipArt** folder is displayed in the **Look in** box.

◎ Click: The **Preview** button on the Insert Picture dialogue box so you can view the choices.

◎ Insert the picture: **Dinner1.wmf** into the text box.

◎ Repeat the above, but inserting the picture **Jazz.wmf** into the text box at the right-hand side of the page.

◎ Remove the border lines from both text boxes.

13.18 Insert the picture **Sail.wmf** into the white space at the bottom of the page below the **Afternoon Tea** section. Do not use a text box this time – you will need to select **In front of text** for the **Wrapping Style** section. Resize the picture if necessary and position centrally in the space available.

13.19 Resave your file. You do not need to print at this stage.

Insert picture file borders

In Unit 11 you learnt how to apply a border around the page using the **Page Border** facility. As an alternative, Word 2000 also offers you some decorative picture border files.

To insert the picture file border
Refer back to the instructions: 'Insert pictures from other files'. Follow exactly the same procedures to insert decorative borders that have been prestored as picture files. (You will be able to see which files can be used as decorative borders from the Preview box.)

After inserting the picture border into your document
Select: **Behind Text** for the **Wrapping style**
Select: **Whole Page** from the **Zoom** button on the Standard Tool Bar so that you can see the full page
Click: The picture border and stretch it vertically and/or horizontally to the required position across the page:

Document page

ClipArt border inserted into document

ClipArt border stretched across the page

Note: If you want to set precise measurements for the border, you can select **Picture** from the **Format** menu to bring up the **Format Picture** dialogue box, then select the **Size** tab to enter specific Height and Width measurements.

Insert picture file dividers

To insert the picture file divider

Refer back to the instructions 'Insert pictures from other files'. Follow exactly the same procedures to insert decorative dividers that have been prestored as picture files. (You will be able to see which files can be used as decorative dividers from the Preview box.)

Examples

Divider3.wmf   Flourish.wmf   Nouveau2.wmf   Arrows6.wmf

Note: You will need to check what picture file dividers are available on your particular computer – these may vary from the examples shown here.

Format and edit picture file borders and dividers

Format the border or divider using the same methods as described earlier in the unit under 'Inserting ClipArt from the ClipArt Catalogue', eg adjust the size or position, text wrapping etc.

Exercise 13C (continued)

13.20 With the document **EX13C** on screen, remove the page border:

- ◎ Select: **Borders and Shading** from the **Format** menu.
- ◎ Select: The **Page Border** tab.
- ◎ Click: **None** in the Setting section.
- ◎ Click: **OK**.

13.21 Referring to the instructions 'Insert picture file dividers':

- ◎ Insert a ClipArt divider from the ClipArt picture file, eg **Divider3.wmf**.
- ◎ Position the divider between the **Early evening boat cruises** and **Sunday lunch specials** section.
- ◎ Copy: The divider.
- ◎ Position the second divider between the **Sunday lunch specials** section and the **Afternoon tea on the Bonny Bree** section.
- ◎ Adjust the line spacing to fit all the text on the page (if necessary).

Note: If for any reason you cannot access the Microsoft ClipArt file, create a divider using the drawing tools as described in Unit 12 and insert as instructed above.

13.22 Refer to the section 'Insert picture file borders':

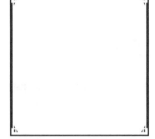

◎ Insert a ClipArt border from the ClipArt picture file, eg **Hangle.wmf**.

◎ In **Whole Page** view, stretch the border across the page to the top, bottom, left and right margins and so that it clears the text.

◎ Select: **Picture** from the **Format** menu to bring up the **Format Picture** dialogue box.

◎ Click: The **Layout** tab.

◎ Select: **In front of text** for the **Wrapping style**.

◎ Select: **Centre** from the Horizontal alignment section.

◎ Click: The **Size** tab.

◎ Enter: **Height: 25 cm Width: 17 cm** in the **Size and rotate** section.

◎ Ensure there are no ticks in the **Lock aspect ratio** and **Relative to original picture size** boxes.

◎ Click: **OK**.

Note: If for any reason you cannot access any suitable borders using the Microsoft ClipArt file, create a border using the Insert Page Border facility described in Unit 11.

13.23 Resave the document using the same filename **EX13C**. Check your document layout with the printout at the back of the book. If your layout is correct, print a copy of your work.

Exercise 13D

13.24 Starting with a clear screen, key in the following text. Follow all the manuscript instructions given and refer back to the information given in this unit where necessary. Save and print a copy of your work using the filename **EX13D**.

13.25 Exit the program if you have finished working or continue straight on to the next unit.

Parties for Special Occasions ←

CREATING THE RIGHT ATMOSPHERE ←

There is no magic formula for creating the right atmosphere to suit the occasion.

However, with careful preparation and attention to details such as the nature of the invitation, displaying appropriate decorations, and serving special foods associated with the occasion, the atmosphere can be influenced.

SAINT VALENTINE'S DAY

Traditionally, this is the day when love blossoms, particularly among young people.

Hearts, cupids and posies cut from pink card or paper, and small heart-shaped cakes and sandwiches, will help to set a romantic party mood.

HALLOWEEN

For the night traditionally associated with witches and mischief, decorations can be made to represent black cats, spiders, owls, witches and lanterns. Lanterns can be made from hollowed out turnips or pumpkins, or even jam jars covered with black paper silhouettes.

Traditional foods are roasted chestnuts, various different nuts and fruit, especially apples. Ducking apples is the traditional game for parties on this day.

EASTER

Easter eggs, lambs, chickens and the famous Easter rabbit are all symbolic of this springtime celebration. Names of guests can be written or painted on to hard-boiled eggs. Small prizes such as little chocolate eggs, or small bags of sugar eggs, can be attractive for both children and adults. An attractive table centre-piece would be a small farmyard filled with small plastic animals. Amusing little egg figures can also be made from eggs and eggshells using pipe cleaners for arms and legs, wool or cotton for hair and pieces of felt for clothing.

UNIT 14 REFORMAT A DOCUMENT TO A THREE-COLUMN LAYOUT

By the end of Unit 14 you should have learnt how to:

◎ display documents in a specified house style indicated on a separate reference sheet
◎ produce specialist business documents, such as an agenda and minutes
◎ reformat a document to a three-column layout
◎ apply triple line spacing.

Special business documents and house styles

As part of the Stage III examination – and often in the workplace – you will be required to produce specialist business documents which follow the layout of the organisation's house style. Examples of these may include technical documents, notices of meetings and agendas, minutes of a meeting etc. You may have been used to displaying your work to a particular layout, eg leaving a clear line space after headings. However, when following a specified house style you should follow the instructions or visual display given.

Although you will still be expected to follow written instructions, you will also have to interpret house style requirements from a separate resource or reference sheet. Examine the display shown on the resource/reference sheet very carefully. Note how the layout displays headings, margin alignment, space allocation, enumeration or bulleted points, column layout, text alignment etc and apply the house style format to the specified document.

Notice of a meeting and agenda

Notification of a meeting and the list of items to be discussed are often combined in one document. This is sent out to everyone who is entitled to attend a meeting approximately two weeks in advance of the date. The secretary of the organisation or committee is usually responsible for the preparation of the agenda in consultation with the chairperson, although nowadays many managers send out their own agendas for less formal in-house meetings.

Minutes of a meeting

The minutes of a meeting are issued to all members who were present at the meeting as an agreed record of the key topics of discussion. Minutes are often displayed in a three-column layout. The first column indicates the items discussed in numbered order. The second column provides a brief description of the key issues arising from each item and any action to be taken. The third column is used to record the name of the person who will take further action, usually by his or her initials.

Triple line spacing

Select: The text you want to edit
Select: **Paragraph** from the **Format** menu
Select: **Multiple** from the **Line spacing** drop-down menu
Enter: **3** in the **At** box
Click: **OK**

Red Blue Green Brown Pink White Yellow	Red Blue Green Brown	Red Blue Green
Single	*Double*	*Triple*

Line spacing

Exercise 14A

14.1   Starting a new document, key in the following notice and agenda. Save the document using the filename **EX14A** and print one copy.

> PANACHE TRADING LTD
> A meeting of the Executive Management Team of P— T—
> L— will be held on Fri 22 Aug in the Renaissance
> Conference Room, 67 Firth Rd, Huddersfield, at 3:30pm.
>
> AGENDA ← (Arial font size 12 and bold)
>
> 1) Apologies for absence
> 3 2) Matters arising from the minutes
> 2 3) Minutes of the last meeting
> 4) Financial analysis of assets and stock
> 5) Review of marketing strategy
> 6) Review of health and safety policy
> 7) Any other bus
> 8) Date and time of next meeting
>
> B RIDGEWAY
> Honorary Sec
>
> (This section in triple line spacing)
>
> (use Times New Roman font size 12 apart from where indicated)

Exercise 14B

14.2   Starting a new document, key in the following minutes:

◎   Use Times New Roman font size 12.

◎   Insert a two-column table after the **PRESENT** section with sufficient rows to take the numbered items.

- Make the first column approximately 1.5 cm wide leaving the second column to stretch to the right margin. Set a left-aligned tab in the second column for the indented items. (Remember to use **Ctrl + T** to wrap the text around the tab setting, and to press **Ctrl + Tab** to move to the next tab stop when in a table.)
- Enter the text as shown in the example below.
- Use the **No Borders** facility so that the table lines are not printed out.
- Save using the filename **EX14B** and print a copy of the document.

(Refer back to Unit 8 if you need to refresh your memory on using tables.)

Example of the layout to be followed for Exercise 14B

1	APOLOGIES FOR ABSENCE – Hélène de Courcy, John Fern.
2	MINUTES of previous meeting were approved and signed.
3	MATTERS ARISING 3.1 The Auditor's Report was satisfactory. 3.2 The review of management salaries was postponed until the Personnel Director returned from sick leave.

MINUTES OF THE EXECUTIVE MANAGEMENT TEAM MEETING OF PANACHE TRADING LTD

(Insert date from EX14A)   AT 3.30 PM IN THE RENAISSANCE ROOM

(CONFERENCE)

(PRESENT) Kellern Jordan (Chair)
    Redknapp Kim
(embolden) Richardson Gina
    Normanton Alvin
    Arif Surayah

Deneuve Estelle
Feathers Victor

1   APOLOGIES FOR ABSENCE – Hélène de Courcy, John Fern.

2   MINUTES of previous meeting were approved and signed.

3   MATTERS ARISING
    3.1   The Auditor's Report was satisfactory.
    3.2   The review of management salaries was postponed until the Personnel Director returned from sick leave.

4   FINANCIAL ANALYSIS OF ASSETS AND STOCK
    The financial report showed healthy ratios of assets and stock held by the company. It was agreed to conduct a more detailed analysis of frequency of stock turnover and to explore the benefits of 'just-in-time' control stock methods. (Action SA)

REVIEW OF MARKETING STRATEGY ~~months~~
The corporate Marketing Plan for the next 3 ~~years~~ was presented to the ✓
Executive Team by Kim Redknapp, Marketing Manager. Agreed that
Jordan Kellern would present this to the next Board meeting for approval.
(Action JK)

REVIEW OF HEALTH AND SAFETY POLICY [6.1   Following the
recent appointment of Roger Whitely as the new Health and Safety
Officer, it was agreed that the current policy should be reviewed
immediately. (Action RW)

6.2 Several written complaints had been received by
staff about a number of the procedures being impractical,
and these would be considered within the review.
It was agreed that the Quality Manager, Gina
Richardson, would circulate a questionnaire to all
staff to analyse any other areas of staff concern and
feed this back to RW. (Action GR)

ANY OTHER BUSINESS
Following the ~~huge~~ interest shown at the (insert name of Fair from Ex.3D)
Fair, Alvin Normanton outlined ~~forthcoming~~ plans for a 10% expansion of
the Sales Team. The Marketing Manager, K——— R———, was
thanked for representing the company's interests at the Fair and
coordinating departmental activities.

DATE OF NEXT MEETING
To be notified.

Make sure the document fits on one page

Reformat a document to a three-column layout

The most appropriate method of reformatting a document to a three-column layout is to use the **Tables** facility. You can use the rows and columns to line up all the items as appropriate, then remove the table border lines. Refer back to Unit 8 if you need to refresh your memory on using this feature. After completing the task it is important to double-check that all items and sub-items of the three-column layout are in the right sequence and position, and numbered correctly if appropriate.

Note: If you convert text into columns using Word 2000's **Columns** facility, the text flows freely from the first column to the last. This makes the **Column** facility unsuitable when you want to position specific portions of text in specific columns.

Insert a column
Draw Table method
Display: The **Tables and Borders Tool Bar** unless it is already on your screen (select: **Toolbars, Tables and Borders** from the **View** menu)
Select: The **Draw Table** button (the insertion pointer changes to a pencil)
Using the pencil, draw: The new column line on the table where you want it to appear

Adjust: The column dividers to the appropriate position on the horizontal ruler to alter the column width and text display (if necessary)

Double-check that: All items and sub-items of the three-column layout are in the right sequence and position, and numbered correctly if appropriate

Table menu method

Check that: The horizontal ruler is displayed on screen and that you are in **Print Layout View**

Click the insertion pointer: In the column next to where you want to insert a column

Select: **Insert** from the **Table** menu

Select: **Columns to the left** or **Columns to the right** depending on where you want to insert the new blank column(s)

P11	Blue damask curtains. £45.00
P12	Green cotton curtains. £16.00
P13	Red velour curtains. £75.00

P11	Blue damask curtains. £45.00	
P12	Green gingham curtains. £16.00	
P13	Red velour curtains. £75.00	

Adjusting the column width

Sometimes the existing columns do not automatically reduce in width to allow room for the new column(s) to fit on the page, and the column at the right-hand side of the table appears to disappear off the page. If this happens, select **Normal** view from the **View** menu before proceeding with the next step so that you can see the full table outline:

Drag: The column dividers for each column to the appropriate position on the horizontal ruler to alter the column width and text display (if necessary)

Double-check that: All items and sub-items of the three-column layout are in the right sequence and position, and numbered correctly if appropriate

Insert a row

You may need to insert an extra row(s) when reformatting the two-column layout to a three-column layout, eg if there are any additional row headings:

Follow either of the methods given above for 'Insert a column', but replacing 'column' with 'row' in the instructions (full instructions on editing tables are provided in *Extending Word 2000*).

Exercise 14C

14.3 Read through the instructions 'Reformat a document to a three-column layout' above. Recall the document stored as **EX14B**. Save the document using the filename **EX14C**. Amend it where indicated in the next exercise and display it according to the house style shown on the reference sheet at the end of this unit, adding an **ACTION** column as shown. Print one copy.

Check the layout on the reference sheet at the end of this unit very carefully. Note the enumeration style, alignment of text and the general layout of each section of the display.

MINUTES OF THE EXECUTIVE MANAGEMENT TEAM MEETING OF PANACHE TRADING LTD FRIDAY 22 AUGUST AT 3.30 PM IN THE RENAISSANCE CONFERENCE ROOM

PRESENT   Kellern Jordan (Chair)
Redknapp Kim *(Marketing Manager)*
Richardson Gina *(Quality Manager)*
Normanton Alvin *(Sales Manager)*
Arif Surayah *(Finance Manager)*
Deneuve Estelle *(Personnel Manager)*
Feathers Victor *(Technology Manager)*
Ridgeway Barry *(Honorary Sec)*

[handwritten annotation: align at the left margin under PRESENT]

[handwritten annotation: Sort into alphabetical order of surname]

1   APOLOGIES FOR ABSENCE – Hélène de Courcy, John Fern.

2   MINUTES of previous meeting were approved and signed.

3   MATTERS ARISING
   3.1   The Auditor's Report was satisfactory.
   3.2   The review of management salaries was postponed until the Personnel Director returned from sick leave.

4   FINANCIAL ANALYSIS OF ASSETS AND STOCK
   4.1   The financial report showed healthy ratios of assets and stock *[handwritten: although some stock items were slow moving]*. It was agreed to conduct a more detailed analysis of frequency of stock turnover and to explore the benefits of 'just-in-time' stock control methods. (Action SA)

5   REVIEW OF MARKETING STRATEGY
   5.1   The corporate Marketing Plan for the next 5 years was presented to the Executive Team by Kim Redknapp, Marketing Manager. Agreed that Jordan Kellern would ~~present this to~~ *[handwritten: table the Plan at]* the next Board meeting for approval. (Action JK)

6   REVIEW OF HEALTH AND SAFETY ~~POLICY~~ *PROCEDURES*
   6.1   Following the recent appointment of Roger Whitely as the new Health and Safety Officer, it was agreed that the current policy should be reviewed ~~immediately~~ *[handwritten: before the end of next month]* (Action RW)
   6.2   Several written complaints had been received by staff about a number of the procedures being impractical, and these would be ~~considered~~/within *[handwritten: addressed]* the review. It was agreed that the Quality Manager, Gina Richardson, would circulate a questionnaire to all staff to analyse any other areas of staff concern and feed this back to RW. (Action GR)

7   ANY OTHER BUSINESS
   7.1   Following the interest shown at the Local Industry Innovation Fair, Alvin Normanton outlined plans for a 10% expansion of the Sales Team. The Marketing Manager, Kim Redknapp, was thanked for representing the company's interests at the Fair and coordinating departmental activities.

8   DATE OF NEXT MEETING
   ~~To be notified.~~ *[handwritten: Arranged for Mon 15 Sep at 1430 hours in the R___ C___ R___]*

A short-term Marketing Plan, focusing on immed issues and actions ~~rates presented~~ for the next yr, was also presented. Questions were raised about the implications of new technologies on the marketing strategy and Victor Feathers was asked to report/make a detailed at the next meeting. (Action VF)

Make this the second item under REVIEW of MARKETING STRATEGY

It was noted that there had been a 7½% increase in the number of accidents on co premises over the last year.

This is the first item under REVIEW OF HEALTH AND SAFETY PROCEDURES

K_R_ was asked to circulate feedback on the outcomes of the co's participation in the fair to all Heads of Department. (Action KR)

Make this the second item under ANY OTHER BUSINESS

- number second and subsequent pages only at bottom right of page, ie do not number the first page
- change 'Redknapp' to 'Rednape' throughout
- change 'agreed' to upper case 'AGREED' throughout
- split the table in a sensible place for page 2 (Select: Split Table from the Table menu)

Exercise 14D

14.4 Recall the document **EX14B** again. Save as **EX14D**. Amend it where indicated in the next exercise and display it according to the reference sheet at the end of this unit, adding an **ACTION** column as shown. Print one copy.

◎ Number all pages at the bottom centre of the page.

◎ Change **Redknapp** to **Rendap** throughout.

◎ Change **sales team** to **Sales Force** throughout.

◎ Format the text in column 2 only to a justified right margin.

(this heading centred and bold)

MINUTES OF THE EXECUTIVE MANAGEMENT TEAM MEETING OF PANACHE TRADING LTD FRIDAY 22 AUGUST AT 3.30 PM IN THE RENAISSANCE CONFERENCE ROOM

PRESENT

Kellern Jordan ~~(Chair)~~ (Chairperson)
Redknapp Kim (Marketing Manager)
Richardson Gina (Quality Manager)
Normanton Alvin (Sales Manager)
Arif Surayah (Finance Manager)
Deneuve Estelle (Personnel Manager)
Feathers Victor (Technology Manager)
Ridgeway Barry (Honorary Sec)

sort into alphabetical order by job title

1 APOLOGIES FOR ABSENCE – Hélène de Courcy, John Fern.

2 MINUTES of previous meeting were approved and signed.

3 MATTERS ARISING
   3.1 The Auditor's Report was satisfactory *but there were several weak areas to be reviewed*
   3.3 The review of management salaries was postponed until the Personnel Director returned from sick leave. *long-term*

4 FINANCIAL ~~ANALYSIS OF ASSETS AND STOCK~~ REPORT
   The financial report showed healthy *trading* ratios of assets and stock. It was agreed to conduct a more detailed analysis of frequency of stock turnover and to explore the benefits of 'just-in-time' stock control methods. (Action SA)

5 REVIEW OF MARKETING STRATEGY
   5.1 The corporate Marketing Plan for the next 3 years was ~~presented~~ *outlined* to the Executive Team by Kim Redknapp, Marketing Manager. Agreed that Jordan Kellern would present this to the next Board meeting for approval. (Action JK)

6 REVIEW OF HEALTH AND SAFETY POLICY
   6.1 Following the recent appointment of Roger Whitely as the new Health and Safety Officer, it was agreed that the current policy should be reviewed *(and updated)* immediately. (Action RW)
   6.2 Several ~~written~~ complaints had been received *from* ~~by~~ staff about a number of the procedures being impractical, and these would be ~~considered within~~ *included* in the review. It was agreed that the Quality Manager, Gina Richardson, would circulate a questionnaire to all staff to analyse any other areas of staff concern and feed this back to RW. (Action GR)

use consistent enumeration and apply to each item

7 ANY OTHER BUSINESS
   Following the interest shown at the Local Industry Innovation Fair, Alvin Normanton outlined plans for a ~~10%~~ *12½%* expansion of the Sales Team. The Marketing Manager, Kim Redknapp, was thanked for representing the company's interests at the Fair and coordinating departmental activities.

8 DATE OF NEXT MEETING
   ~~To be notified.~~ *Arranged for Wed 17 Sep at 1530 hours in the Georgian Conference Room. The meeting ended at 4.30 pm.*

More info was requested on the Profit and Loss Account. (Action SA)

make this the second item under FINANCIAL REPORT

Correspondence on agenda items was now being marked "% Barry Ridgeway, Honorary Sec, to aid coordination.

make this the first item under MATTERS ARISING

TIP: to insert the % symbol, select Symbol from the Insert menu and locate from the normal font or use subscript + superscript

There were issues in the Marketing Plan that may affect the operation of the sales team. Agreed that Alvin Normanton should assess the impact of improved marketing on sales and report back at the next meeting. (Action AN)

make this the second item under REVIEW OF MARKETING STRATEGY

It was agreed that the new Staff Appraisal Scheme was working well. Estelle Deneuve to advise on any Departments where the new scheme had not been implemented. (Action ED)

make this the first item under ANY OTHER BUSINESS

14.5 Exit the program if you have finished working or continue straight on to the next unit.

Reference sheet for Exercises 14C and 14D

Note: The information below is not to be keyed in. It indicates the house style required for the documents. Use capitalisation and three-column layout as in this specimen layout for minutes.

> **Note**
> Please ensure that initials are moved to the ACTION column as shown below, and align the initials directly opposite the relevant part of the text in the second column.

PRESENT

Janice Walker	(Chair)	
Vanya Turton	(Secretary)	
Mark Severn	(Treasurer)	
Drew Barker	(Finance Director)	
Henry Walsh	(Marketing Manager)	

		ACTION
1	MINUTES of the previous meeting were agreed and signed.	
2	MATTERS ARISING	
	2.1 The staff appraisal scheme was still under review.	
	2.2 Orders for the new computer equipment were ready to be placed.	DB
3	MARKETING STRATEGY	
	3.1 Agreed to develop a new company marketing brochure.	HW

UNIT 15 CONSOLIDATION 3

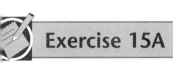

Exercise 15A

15.1 Key in the following document using a consistent typeface and layout. Use a justified right margin and a typing line length of 13 cm. Use Times New Roman font size 12 for the main body text and follow the amendments shown. Save and print a copy of your document using the filename **EX15A**.

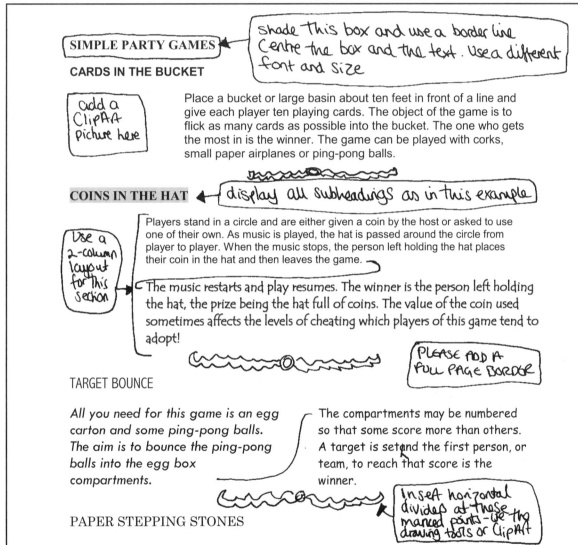

15.2 Key in the following document. Check your work with the copy below. Save and print a copy of your document using the filename **EX15B**.

TRAINING COURSES IN INFORMATION TECHNOLOGY

A number of short training courses in information technology will be available during the summer term. We will be able to offer a limited number of places for participants to receive help with:

Free course fees
Free examination fees
Assistance with the cost of resources/materials
Assistance with the cost of travel
Assistance with the cost of childcare

> Insert the text in this section in a 2-column table.

For a personal interview, contact our training team on 01422 379789: Janet Shearing, Suhail Akudi, Cleo Derrington

AWP18	Word processing - intermediate and advanced. Tuesday or Wednesday afternoon: 2.00-3.30 pm. Tuesday or Wednesday night: 6.30-8.30 pm. Tutor: Janet Shearing
AIB2	Introduction to the Internet – beginners. Tuesday or Thursday morning: 9.30-11.00 am. Tuesday or Thursday night: 7.00-8.30 pm. Tutor: Cleo Derrington
ADP7	Desk top publishing – all levels. Wednesday or Thursday afternoon: 2.30-4.00 pm. Monday or Wednesday night: 6.00-8.30 pm. Tutor: Suhail Akudi
SDA3	Spreadsheets and databases – all levels. Monday or Wednesday morning: 9.30-11.00 am. Monday or Thursday night: 7.00-8.30 pm. Tutor: Suhail Akudi
AWP12	Word processing - absolute beginners. Tuesday or Wednesday morning: 10.00-11.30 am. Monday or Thursday night: 6.30-8.30 pm. Tutor: Janet Shearing

---

Exercise 15C

15.3 Retrieve the document **EX15B** unless it is already on your screen. Save it as **EX15C** and carry out the following amendments:

◎ Change the main heading to Arial font size 14 and bold.

◎ Display the document according to the reference sheet at the end of this unit, reformatting it to a three-column layout as shown, and following all other reformatting indicated.

- Sort the courses in ascending order by code.
- Change **night** to **evening** throughout the document.
- Resave your work. Check your document layout with the printout check at the back of the book. If it is correct print one copy.

Exercise 15D

15.4 Key in the following document using a consistent typeface and heading layout:

- Insert a header **INSERTING SYMBOLS** and a footer **DOCUMENT PRESENTATION TECHNIQUES** on each page using a point 8 font size.
- Number the pages at the foot of the page in the centre, starting with page 8.
- Adjust the line length to 12 cm and use a ragged right-hand margin.

15.5 Save and print a copy of your document using the filename **EX15D**.

INSERTING SYMBOLS INTO A DOCUMENT   (centre and bold)

(after words)

In the days when the typewriter was the only available equipment to prepare typed documents, spaces had to be left in the text so that any special symbols in the draft manuscript could be inserted afterwards by hand (using a pen). With the introduction of the computer, however, it became possible to insert symbols by keying in a single character or string of characters in the ANSI character set. For example, in the font Times New Roman the result of the field { SYMBOL 211 \f "Symbol" \s 12 } is the 12 point character: © (the copyright symbol).

You can insert many common symbols by keying in the appropriate ANSI character code on the numeric keypad, such as typing ALT + 0189 to insert ½.

INSERTING SYMBOLS WITH WORD 2000   (inset this section only by 1.5 cm at left and right margins)

One of the many advantages of Word 2000 software is that it offers a much much easier way of inserting symbols or special characters into a document. You can simply select **Symbol** from the **Insert** menu and then click on the preferred **Font**. When you click on a symbol, Word 2000 even allows you a close-up view before you insert it into your document. In the **Subset** list, there is also a list of extended language characters, such as Latin, Greek, Cyrillic (Russian), or Hebrew.

(please insert here the diagram shown on the Reference Sheet at the end of this unit.)

SYMBOL TYPES

The variety of symbols that can be inserted depends on which fonts are available on your particular computer. The default symbol font in Word 2000 is **(normal text)**. This includes:

or number forms

Fractions such as ⅔, ½, ¾, ⅝. (Word 2000 will automatically insert fractions such as ½ as when you key in 1/2.)

International characters such as Ã, Œ, ë, Б. These are particularly useful when keying in foreign names such as *Françoise Viète*.

Viète

International monetary symbols such as £, F, Pts, ₫. %o

General punctuation such as ‡, †, along with others not available on the standard keypad.

use bullet points for these four points

SPECIAL CHARACTERS

By switching to the **Special Characters** tab of the **Insert, Symbol** dialogue box, you can improve the appearance of text and insert special characters into your document. A few examples of these include ™ (Trademark), ... (Ellipsis), ¶ (Paragraph), § (Section). ® *(Registered),*

many

Although you may never need to use ~~the majority~~ of these symbols it is useful to know what is available for those that do appear from time to time.

print the last section only in triple line spacing

indent this paragraph by 2.5 cm at left and right margins

retain the bold emphasis on any words which are displayed in bold in the text

15.6 Exit the program if you have finished working or continue straight on to the next unit.

Reference sheet for Exercise 15C

This information page is not to be copied. It indicates the house style required for the documents.

- Free course fees

- Free examination fees

- Assistance with the cost of resources/materials

For a personal interview, contact our training team on 01422 379789:
Janet Shearing
Suhail Akudi
Cleo Derrington

CODE	COURSE DETAILS	TUTOR
ADP7	Desk top publishing – all levels. Wednesday or Thursday afternoon: 2.30-4.00 pm. Monday or Wednesday evening: 6.00-8.30 pm.	Suhail Akudi
AIB2	Introduction to the Internet – beginners. Tuesday or Thursday morning: 9.30-11.00 am. Tuesday or Thursday evening: 7.00-8.30 pm.	Cleo Derrington

Reference sheet for Exercise 15D

This diagram does not have to be reproduced in the exact size and can be adjusted to fit the space available in your document. You may choose your own pattern or shading to fill the shapes, and either circles, squares, rectangles or ovals can be used.

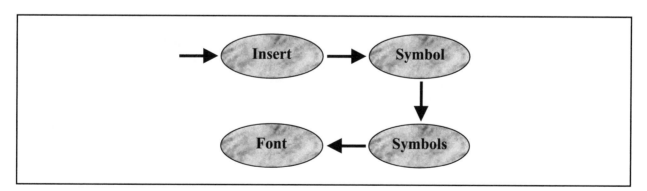

UNIT 16 EXAMINATION PRACTICE 3

> By the end of Unit 16 you should have completed a mock examination for the OCR/RSA Stage III Document Presentation Part 2 Award.

OCR/RSA Stage III Document Presentation Part 2

This examination assesses your ability to apply advanced processing and production skills to meet presentation requirements. You will be assessed on your ability to produce from handwritten and typewritten drafts a variety of complex and/or specialist business documents, using recalled text and supplementary information, and to display them in an appropriate manner. Documents to be produced will include an element of design, column styles and fonts, boxes, text boxes, diagrams and ClipArt. The award demonstrates competence to the level demanded by NVQ Level 3.

In addition to being assessed against standard word processing criteria (eg omissions and additions, typing/spelling/punctuation errors, abbreviations, transposition and misplacement etc) you will also be assessed on your presentation techniques. You should refer back to the section in Unit 11 headed 'Document presentation and layout' to refresh your memory on some of the criteria you will be assessed against. However, it is recommended that you also check the OCR/RSA's published performance and assessment criteria for the examination for full details of the scheme.

The examination lasts for $1^3/_4$ hours and you must complete four documents using a word processor. Printing is done outside this time. The invigilator will give you instructions concerning the recalling of stored files.

Examination hints

When sitting your examination:

◎ You may use a manual prepared by the centre or the software manufacturer.
◎ Put your name, centre number and document number on each document.
◎ Check your work very carefully before printing – proofread, spellcheck.
◎ Assemble your printouts in the correct order at the end of the examination.

You are now ready to try a mock examination for Stage III Document Presentation Part 2. Take care and good luck!

The list of assessment criteria for this examination is long and detailed. To be sure you have reached the required standard to be entered for an examination, you need to work through several past papers and have these 'marked' by a tutor or assessor who is qualified and experienced in this field.

Key in using a consistent typeface and layout. Display as indicated on the reference sheet. Save as **Unit16Doc1** and print a copy of your document on one side of a piece of A4 paper.

STIR FRY SUCCESS

WHY STIR FRY?

Use a justified right hand margin and apply bold to all headings

Stir frying has gained in popularity as a healthy ~~method~~ *way* of cooking food, providing modest amounts of oil are used. Because it does not involve large quantities of liquid, it retains vitamins and minerals which are often lost when boiling or steaming.

add a ClipArt picture here

Apart from preserving nutrients, stir frying also tends to bring out the full flavour of complementary foods.

Firm fish fillets or chunks of fish are ideal for stir fry dishes. All poultry stir fries well, but must be cut into small pieces. Tough cuts of meat or poor quality mince should be avoided

Use a 2-column layout for this section

Fast and Easy
A boon for today's busy lifestyles, stir frying is fast and easy and does not require any special skills or techniques.

It may be necessary to spend some time preparing some of the ingredients, but frozen and tinned ingredients may also be stir fried if time is ~~of the essence.~~ *precious*

EQUIPMENT

~~STIR FRY WOK~~ *Pan* The traditional domed metal wok is the classic pan for stir frying. There is a wide choice of *Pan* available, including non-stick, which offer various advantages, but deep sides and a well domed base are essential.

UTENSILS

~~OTHER EQUIPMENT~~ A long handled stirring implement or spatula and a large scoop or draining spoon are useful. Remember that metal utensils should not be used on non-stick surfaces.

BASIC POINTS   Cut up the food fairly finely, and in similar sized pieces, so that it cooks quickly. (Food can be marinated in advance for extra flavour if preferred.) Trim any fat from meat and cut it across the grain as this gives the most tender results. Heat enough oil or other fat and evenly coat the pan before adding the ingredients. Add the ingredients in batches.

Stir and turn the food, keeping it moving from the outside to the middle and vice versa. Cooked pieces can be pushed to one side of the pan. A small amount of liquid can be added to the pan to make a sauce just before the food is cooked. Once the stir fry is ready, it should be served promptly.

but minced steak, lamb or pork are suitable. Most vegetables, cooked or canned beans and pulses, cooked rice or pasta, can all be added to the stir fry.

Recall the document stored as **Unit16Doc1** and amend as shown. Save as **Unit16Doc2** and print a copy on one side of a piece of A4 paper.

[Handwritten annotation: Centre and use a larger font size]

STIR FRY SUCCESS

[Handwritten annotation: Insert a text box in the centre 1.5cm high and 10cm wide with the words: Stir frying is an ancient cooking technique which is ideal for contemporary living. Centre the box, text and use a different font and size]

WHY STIR FRY?

Stir frying has gained in popularity as a healthy way of cooking food, providing modest amounts of oil are used. Because it does not involve large quantities of liquid, it retains vitamins and minerals which are often lost when boiling or steaming. Apart from preserving nutrients, stir frying also *and* tends to bring out the full flavour of complementary foods.

Firm fish fillets *or* chunks of fish are ideal for stir fry dishes. All poultry stir fries well, but must be cut into small pieces. Tough cuts of meat and poor quality mince should be avoided but minced steak, lamb or pork are suitable. Most vegetables, cooked or canned beans and pulses, cooked rice or pasta, can all be added to the stir fry.

[Handwritten annotation: Please add a full page border of your own choice]

QUICK

~~FAST~~ AND EASY

~~A boon for today's busy lifestyles,~~ Stir frying is fast and easy and does not require any special skills or techniques. It may be necessary to spend some time preparing some of the ingredients, but frozen and tinned ingredients may also be stir fried if time is precious.

[Handwritten annotation: method of lightly cooking food]

EQUIPMENT

WOK   The traditional domed metal wok is the classic *cooking* pan for stir frying. There is a wide choice of pans available, including non-stick, which offer various advantages, but deep sides and a well domed base are essential.

UTENSILS   A long handled stirring implement or spatula and a large scoop or draining spoon are useful. Remember that metal utensils should not be used on non-stick surfaces.

[Handwritten annotation: • shade this box • Centre both the box and the text • Use a different font and size for the text]

BASIC POINTS

[Handwritten annotation: into / slices or cubes]

Cut up the food fairly finely ~~and in~~ similar sized ~~pieces~~, so that it cooks quickly. (Food can be marinated in advance for extra flavour if preferred.) Trim any fat from meat and cut it across the grain as this gives the most tender results. Heat enough oil or other fat and evenly coat the pan before adding the ingredients. Add the ingredients in batches. Stir and turn the food, keeping it moving from the outside to the middle and vice versa. Cooked pieces can be pushed to one side of the pan. A small amount of liquid can be added to the pan to make a sauce just before the food is cooked. Once the stir fry is ready, it should be served promptly.

[Handwritten annotation: Add the slowest-cooking ingredients to the wok first. Fry the food until it becomes tender but still remains crisp.]

Document 3

Recall the document stored as **EX15D**. Save as **Unit16Doc3**. Amend as shown, using a consistent typeface and heading layout. Change the header to **SYMBOLS AND SPECIAL CHARACTERS** and the footer to **INSERT SYMBOL FACILITY** on each page and change them both to a point 10 font size. Number the pages at the foot of the page, in the centre, starting with page 12. Adjust the line length to 14 cm and use a justified right margin. Resave the document and print one copy.

INSERTING SYMBOLS INTO A DOCUMENT

Inset this section by 1.5cm from left margin

In the days when the typewriter was the only equipment available to prepare typed documents, spaces had to be left in the text so that any special symbols in the draft manuscript could be inserted afterward by hand (using a pen). With the introduction of the computer, however, it became possible to insert symbols by keying in a single character or string of characters in the ANSI character set. For example, in the font Times New Roman the result of the field { SYMBOL 211 \f "Symbol" \s 12 } is the 12 point character: © (the copyright symbol). You can insert many common symbols by keying in the appropriate ANSI character code on the numeric keypad, such as typing ALT+0189 to insert $^1/_2$.

INSERTING SYMBOLS WITH WORD 2000

One of the advantages of Word 2000 software is that it offers a much easier way of inserting symbols or special characters into a document. You can simply select **Symbol** from the **Insert** menu and then click on the preferred **Font**. When you click on a symbol, Word 2000 even allows you a close-up view before you insert it into your document. In the **Subset** list, there is also a list of extended language characters, such as Latin, Greek, Cyrillic (Russian), or Hebrew.

remove indent at left and right margins

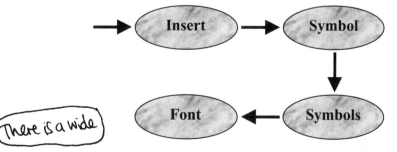

SYMBOL TYPES

There is a wide

The variety of symbols that can be inserted *depending* depends on which fonts are available on your particular computer. The default symbol font *installed* in Word 2000 is **(normal text)**. This includes:

- Fractions or number forms such as ⅔, ½, ¾, ⅝. (Word 2000 will automatically insert fractions such as ½ as you key in.)

- International characters such as Ã, Œ, ë, Б. These are ~~particularly~~ especially useful when keying in foreign names such as Françoise Viète.

- International monetary symbols such as £, ₣, ₧, ₫.

- General punctuation such as ‡, ‰, †, ~~along with~~ and others that are not available on the standard keypad.

SPECIAL CHARACTERS

By switching to the **Special Characters** tab of the **Insert, Symbol**

dialogue box, you can improve the ~~appearance~~ ~~look~~ of text and insert

special characters into your document. A few examples of these

include ™ (Trademark), … (Ellipsis), ® (Registered), ¶ (Paragraph), §

(Section).

display as a bulleted list

keep the indent at left and right margins

Although you may never need to use

many of these symbols it is useful to

know what is available for those that do

appear from time to time.

use single line spacing throughout the document

use a different type of bullet point for bulleted items, than the original, but be consistent with the bullet point style used for both lists in the document

Additional ~~Default~~ Font Symbols

In addition there are bullets, arrows, ~~and also~~ scientific and mathematical symbols. You may find more symbol fonts, such as Botanical or Wingdings, which include a range of decorative symbols. Fonts such as Math A or Math C include a wider range of mathematical fonts, which would be useful if you were preparing documents for a statistician, or a teacher of mathematics.

insert this section immediately ~~before~~ The SPECIAL CHARACTERS section

statistician

THE EURO CURRENCY SYMBOL

Word 2000 allows you to display the euro currency symbol €. The fonts needed to display the e — c — ~~symbol~~ *symbol* / should have been ~~is~~ installed when the Word 2000 software was installed. However, if the euro symbol prints out as a box you will need to check that yr printer has the euro symbol in its resident fonts. If not, you will need to check with your printer salesperson how to update yr printer fonts to include the e — c — symbol.

insert this section immediately before the last paragraph of the document

Please insert here the diagram shown on the Reference Sheet ~~as the last item in the document~~

please change 'many' to 'some' Throughout the document

Key in the following document. Use a two-column table layout for the lower section which begins **TEXTILE CRAFTS** … Save the document as **Unit16Doc4P1**. Print one copy and check it against the copy below.

CORONA CRAFTSHOP RESIDENTIALS

Learn a new craft and make new friends at one of our weekend craftshop residentials. Unlike the 'workshop' approach, our craftshops place the emphasis on: fun, friendship, relaxation, enjoyment of learning new skills.

As part of our package, we offer high quality accommodation with TV and tea/coffee making facilities in all rooms. Accommodation is on a full board basis.

Prices to be added to the craftshop fee are:

Single room with shared bathroom/toilet facilities: £45pp/pn
Single room with en suite facilities: £55pp/pn
Double room with shared bathroom/toilet facilities: £35pp/pn
Double room with en suite facilities: £45pp/pn

All our craftshop residentials are staffed by professional instructors who have a wealth of experience and expertise in their chosen specialism.

TEXTILE CRAFTS	Silk screen-printing, tie dying, cross-stitch, collage, embroidery (hand and machine), patchwork, lace making, quilting. Cost - £85.00
PAINT EFFECTS	Stippling, sponging, stencilling, clouding, rag-rolling, marbling, wood graining, liming, crackle-glaze, dragging, verdigris, bronzing and gold leaf. Cost - £110.00
STONE & WOOD CRAFTS	Pottery, ceramics, stone carving, coal carving, plaster casting, mosaics, marquetry, woodturning, pyrography (poker work), garden ornaments. Cost - £95.00
PAPER CRAFTS	Calligraphy, papier-mâché, origami, quilling, Chinese lantern making, paper flower making, fancy dress masks, bookbinding. Cost - £75.00
COUNTRY CRAFTS	Basket and corn dolly making, dough modelling, pressed flower pictures, 3-D decoupage, china painting, candle making, glass painting. Cost - £105.00

Document 4 Part 2

Retrieve the document **Unit16Doc4P1** unless it is already on your screen. Save the document as **Unit16Doc4P2**. Apply bold, centring and Arial font size 14 to the main heading. Display the document according to the reference sheet at the end of this unit, reformatting it to a three-column layout as shown, and following any other reformatting indicated.

Apart from the table section, print the document in double line spacing. Sort the items of the table in ascending order of **ACTIVITY** in the first column. Number all pages. Resave the file and print one copy.

Situated in the heart of The Yorkshire Dales, Corona Cottage offers visitors a unique experience. Not only can you 'get away from it all' to sample the delights of the surrounding countryside, you can expereince the satisfaction of learning a new skill and discovering hidden talents you never knew you had.

make this the second sentence of the first paragraph

Please bring overalls or other suitable clothing.

make this the second paragraph in the PAINT EFFECTS section

Kite making will be offered as an alternative option to bookbinding.

make this the second paragraph in the PAPER CRAFTS section

Part of the craftshop day will take place at a nearby pottery in the local village (transport will be provided.

make this the first sentence in the STONE & WOOD CRAFTS section

Silk painting techni techniques may also be available on the day for no extra charge.

make this the second paragraph in the TEXTILE CRAFTS section

Reference sheet for Document 1

This information is not to be copied. It indicates the house style required for the documents.

Key in the equipment at the left-hand margin and indent the text as indicated.

WOK	The traditional domed metal wok is the classic pan for stir frying. There is a wide choice of pans available, including non-stick, which offer various advantages, but deep sides and a well domed base are essential.
UTENSILS	A long handled stirring implement or spatula and a large scoop or draining spoon are useful. Remember that metal utensils should not be used on non-stick surfaces.

Reference sheet for Document 3

This diagram does not have to be reproduced in the exact size and can be adjusted to fit the space available in your document. You may choose your own pattern or shading style to fill the shapes. Insert the diagram at the very end of the document, after all the text.

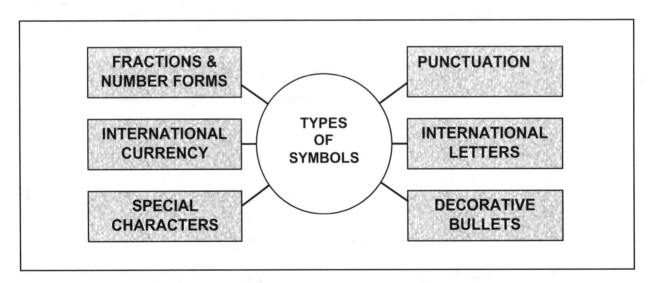

Reference sheet for Document 4 Part 2

This information is not to be copied. It indicates the house style required for the documents.

Unlike the 'workshop' approach, our craft shops place the emphasis on:

- *FUN*

- *FRIENDSHIP*

- *RELAXATION*

- *ENJOYMENT OF LEARNING NEW SKILLS*

> ➤ Use capitalisation, bold, italic, and 3-column layout where indicated here.
> ➤ Please use bullet points indicated and inset by 2.54 cm at the left margin. Display the list of bulleted items as shown.
> ➤ Align the text in the 3-column display as shown below.

Prices to be added to the craftshop fee are:

- Single room with shared bathroom/toilet facilities: £45pp/pn

- Single room with en suite facilities: £55pp/pn

ACTIVITY		COST
COUNTRY CRAFTS	Basket and corn dolly making, dough modelling, pressed flower pictures, 3-D decoupage, china painting, candle making, glass painting.	£105.00
PAINT EFFECTS	Stippling, sponging, stencilling, clouding, rag-rolling, marbling, wood graining, liming, crackle-glaze, dragging, verdigris, bronzing and gold leaf.	£110.00

Progress Review Checklist

Unit	Topic	Date completed	Comments
1	Document formatting revision (EX1A)		
	Page numbering from a given page		
	Changing appearance of headers and footers		
	Footnotes		
2	AutoCorrect		
	Apostrophes		
	Spelling in context		
	Abbreviations		
	Fractions		
	Accents		
	Symbols		
	International characters		
3	Memorandum and business letter layout		
	Printing on preprinted forms and using templates		
	Multiple enclosures		
	Page numbering and continuation sheet(s)		
	Postdating documents		
	Confirming facts		
	Routing of copies		
4	Consolidation 1		
5	Examination Practice 1 Stage III Text Processing Part 1		
6	Pagination		
	House style		
	Locating and selecting information		
7	Formatting fonts		
	Margin alignment and line spacing		
	Consistency of presentation		
	Using styles		
	Allocating vertical space		
	Allocating horizontal space		
	Allocating space using text box		
	Newspaper columns – whole document		
	Newspaper columns – section of document		
	Copying text from one document to another		
8	Creating tables		
	Using different types of tab settings		

Unit	Topic	Date completed	Comments
	Applying ruling (borders) to a table		
	Setting tabs inside a table		
	Changing paper size to landscape orientation		
	Complex table layouts		
9	Consolidation 2		
10	Examination Practice 2 Stage III Word Processing Part 2		
11	Document presentation and layout		
	Adding and removing borders, lines and shading		
	Full-page borders		
12	Displaying the Drawing Tool Bar		
	Drawing shapes		
	Selecting, formatting and manipulating drawing shapes		
	Inserting text into a drawing shape		
	Inserting WordArt		
	Inserting a text box		
	Formatting a text box		
	Applying shading to drawing shapes and text boxes		
	Creating dividers using the drawing tools		
13	Inserting ClipArt images from the Microsoft ClipArt Catalogue		
	Adjusting, moving, copying, formatting a ClipArt picture		
	Wrapping text around a ClipArt picture		
	Positioning a graphic object in relation to text or to the page		
	Inserting pictures from other files		
	Inserting a picture into a text box		
	Using symbols as graphics		
	Inserting picture file borders and dividers		
14	Special business documents and house styles		
	Examples of specialist business documents – agenda and minutes		
	Triple line spacing		
	Reformat a two-column document to a three-column layout		
15	Consolidation 3		
16	Examination Practice 3 Stage III Document Presentation Part 2		

Glossary

Action	Keyboard	Mouse	Menu
Accents (combination keys)	Select: **International characters** from the **Help** index to see the combinations Hold down/Press keys: As shown *See also*: Symbols		
Alignment of text	Select: **View, Tool bars, Drawing**; Click: Text Box on the Drawing Tool Bar; Click: anywhere		
Allocate a rectangular space using text box	Select: **View, Tool bars, Drawing**; Click: 🔲 Text Box on the Drawing Tool Bar; Click: anywhere in document Select: **Text box** from **Format** menu; Click: **Size**; Key in: The required dimensions in **Size and rotate** section Click: **Line**; Select: **No line** Click: **Layout**; Select: **Square**; Click: **OK** Drag: **Text box** to required position		
Allocate clear lines	Press: ↵ once for each line required, plus one		
Allocate horizontal space from left or right margin		Select: The text to be positioned at side of space or position cursor just before first character Drag: The **Left Indent** or **Right Indent** marker to the required position on ruler	
Allocate vertical space			**Format, Paragraphs, Indents and Spacing** Key in: The measurement required in the **Before** spin box
Allocate vertical space across full typing line			**Format, Paragraphs, Spacing, Before** Key in: The required measurement
AutoCorrect			**Tools, AutoCorrect**
AutoFormat	Press: **Alt + Ctrl + K**		**Format, AutoFormat**
Blocked capitals	Press: **Caps Lock** key		
Bold text	Press: **Ctrl + B**	Click: **B** on the Formatting Tool Bar	**Format, Font**
Borders		Click: 🔲 on the Formatting Tool Bar	**Format, Borders and Shading, Borders**
Borders and lines		Select: The area to which you want to add a border Click: 🔲 **Borders** on **Formatting Tool Bar**	Select: The area to which you want to add a border **Format, Borders and Shading, Borders** Select: From the **Setting, Style, Color** and **Width** sections Select: The area of text to apply the border to in the **Apply To** box *or* Select: **View, Tool Bars, Tables and Borders** to use the tool bar method
– full-page borders			**Format, Borders and Shading, Page Border** Select: From the Setting, Style, Color, Width and Art sections Select: The area of page to apply the border to in the Apply To box

Action	Keyboard	Mouse	Menu
– to remove		Click: **No Border** option on the Borders button	Repeat the above menu commands but select the **None** option
Bulleted lists		Click: ▤ on the Formatting Tool Bar	**Format, Bullets and Numbering** Select: **Bulleted** Click: The required style
Capitalise letters	Press: **Ctrl + Shift + A**		**Format, Change Case, Uppercase**
Case of letters (to change)	Press: **Shift + F3**		**Format, Change Case**
Centre text	Press: **Ctrl + E**	Click: ≡ on the Formatting Tool Bar	**Format, Paragraph, Indents and Spacing, Alignment, Centred**
Change case	Select: The text to be changed Press: **Shift + F3** until required format is displayed		**Format, Change case**; Select: The required case; Click: **OK**
ClipArt (from the Microsoft ClipArt Catalogue) – from other files			**Insert, Picture, ClipArt** Select: The required image from the categories shown Click: **Insert clip** **Insert, Picture, From File** Select: The correct drive or folder that contains the file you want in the **Look in** section Select: The required image from the selected file Click: **Insert**
Close a file (clear screen)	Press: **Ctrl + W**		**File, Close**
Copy a block of text Highlight text to be copied	Press: **Ctrl + C**	Click: ▣ on the Standard Tool Bar *or* Press: Right mouse button and Select: **Copy**	**Edit, Copy**
Position cursor where text is to be copied to	Press: **Ctrl + V**	Click: ▣ on the Standard Tool Bar *or* Press: Right mouse button and select: **Paste**	**Edit, Paste**
Copying text from one document to another	Select: **Window**; Select: The source document Select: The text to be copied; Copy: The text in normal way Select: **Window**; Select: The destination document Position the cursor: In the required position Paste: The text in normal way		
Cursor movement Move cursor to required position Move to top of document Move to end of document Move left word by word Move right word by word Move to end of line Move to start of line Move to top/bottom of paragraph Move up/down one screen	Use arrow keys: → ↑ ← ↓ Press: **Ctrl + Home** Press: **Ctrl + End** Press: **Ctrl + ←** Press: **Ctrl + →** Press: **End** Press: **Home** Press: **Ctrl + ↑** *or* **Ctrl + ↓** Press: **PgUp** *or* **PgDn**	Click: Left mouse button in required position	
Cut text	*See*: Delete/cut a block of text		
Date insertion	Press: **Alt + Shift + D**		**Insert, Date and Time**

Action	Keyboard	Mouse	Menu
Delete/cut a block of text	Select: Text to be deleted Press: ← (**Del**) or Select: Text to be deleted Press: **Ctrl + X**	Select: Text to be deleted/cut Click: ✂ on the Formatting Tool Bar	Select: Text to be deleted/cut Select: **Edit, Cut** or Press: Right mouse button; select: **Cut**
Delete/cut a character	Move cursor to correct character; Press: **Del** or Move cursor to right of incorrect character; Press:← (**Del**)		
Delete/cut a word	Move cursor to end of word Press: ← (**Del**) or Select: Word to be deleted Press: **Ctrl + X**	Select: Word to be deleted/cut Click: ✂ on the Formatting Tool Bar	Select: Word to be deleted/cut Select: **Edit, Cut** or Press: Right mouse button; select: **Cut**
Dividers and rules – using the drawing tools – using ClipArt	Refer to the section on *drawing tools* – use the same principles and facilities to create simple dividers or borders. Refer to the section on *ClipArt* - use the same principles and facilities to insert prestored graphic dividers or borders.		
Drawing Tool Bar (to display)		Click: ▦ **Drawing** on the **Standard Tool Bar**	**View, Toolbars, Drawing**
Enumeration	Key in: The enumeration e.g. **A)** Press: **Tab** key Key in: The rest of the text Repeat for each enumerated paragraph	Click: ▤ on the Formatting Tool Bar	**Format, Bullets and** **Numbering** Select: **Numbered** Click: The required style
Exit the program	Press: **Alt + F4**	Click: Control button at right of Title Bar	**File, Exit**
Find text	Press: **Ctrl + F**		**Edit, Find**
Font colour: to change		Click: ✎▾ on **Formatting** **Tool Bar**	**Format, Font** Select: A **Color** from the colour drop-down menu
Font size Next larger point size Next smaller point size	Press: **Ctrl + Shift + P** Choose desired size Press: **Ctrl +]** Press: **Ctrl + [**	Click: 10 ▾ on the Formatting Tool Bar Choose desired size	**Format, Font** Choose desired size
Font typeface style	Press: **Ctrl + Shift + F** Choose desired font	Click: [font] on the Formatting Tool Bar Choose desired font	**Format, Font** Choose desired font
Footnote separator: to remove			**View, Normal** **View Footnotes** Select: **All footnotes** Select: **Footnote separator** Highlight and delete: **Line**
Footnotes (to insert)	**Alt + Ctrl + F**		**Insert, Footnote** Select: **Options** Click: **OK** Enter: The footnote text
Format Painter (to copy formats)	Position cursor in text with the required format Press: **Ctrl + Shift + C** Select: Text to be formatted Press: **Ctrl + Shift + V**	Position the cursor: In the text with the required format Click: ▨ **Format Painter** on **Formatting Tool Bar** To copy one word: Click: The word To copy a block of text: Select: The text Click: The left mouse button	

Action	Keyboard	Mouse	Menu
Formatting, to review	Press: **Shift + F1** Click: Text to be reviewed Press: **Shift + F1** to reverse		Select: The text to be reviewed Check: The displayed formats on Formatting Tool Bar
Fractions: using superscript and subscript	Press: **Ctrl + Shift + +** (plus sign) Key in: The numerator Press: **Ctrl + Spacebar** Key in: Solidus (/) Press: **Ctrl + =** Key in: Denominator Press: **Ctrl + Spacebar**		**Format, Font, Effects, Superscript, OK** Key in: The numerator **Format, Font, Effects, Superscript, OK** Key in: Solidus (/) **Format, Font, Effects, Subscript, OK** Key in: The denominator **Format, Font, Effects, Subscript, OK**
Go to (a specified page)	Press: **Ctrl + G** *or* **F5**		**Edit, Go To ...**
Grammar tool	Press: **F7**	Click: on the Standard Tool Bar	**Tools, Spelling and Grammar**
Headers and Footers To delete:	 Select: The actual text or page number Press: ← (**Del**)		Select: **View, Header and Footer** Key in: The header text and/or footer text
Headers and footers: changing text formatting			**View, Header and Footer** **Format, Font** Select: The required format Click: **OK** Click: **Close**
Help function and Office Assistant	Press: **F1** (for Contents) Press: **Shift + F1** (for **What's This?** – context-sensitive help)	Click: on the Formatting Tool Bar for the **Office Assistant**	**Help**
Highlight/shade text		Click: on the Formatting Tool Bar	**Format, Borders and Shading, Shading**
Indent function Indent at left to next tab stop Indent at left to previous tab stop Indent as a hanging paragraph Unindent and return to standard margin	 Press: **Ctrl + M** Press: **Ctrl + Shift + M** Press: **Ctrl + T** Press: **Ctrl + Q**	Click: on the Formatting Tool Bar Click: on the Formatting Tool Bar *Using ruler* first-line indent left indent first-line and left indent right indent	**Format, Paragraph, Indents and Spacing**
Insert special character/symbols			To insert a symbol: Position cursor: Where you want the character/symbol to appear Select: **Insert, Symbol**
Insert text	Simply key in the missing character(s) at the appropriate place – the existing text will 'move over' to make room for the new text. If **OVR** is displayed (overtyping), Press: **Ins(ert)** key to remove		

Action	Keyboard	Mouse	Menu
Italics	Press: **Ctrl + I**	Click: *I* on the Formatting Tool Bar	**Format, Font**
Justified right margin	Press: **Ctrl + J**	Click: ▤ on the Formatting Tool Bar	**Format, Paragraph, Indents and Spacing, Alignment, Justified**
Landscape orientation			**File, Page Setup, Paper Size** Click: **Landscape**
Line break (to insert)	Press: **Shift + ↵**		
Line length – to change	Select text. Display horizontal ruler. Move margin markers to required position on ruler		
Line spacing – to set – triple line spacing	Press: **Ctrl + 1** (single) Press: **Ctrl + 2** (double) Press: **Ctrl + 0** (to add or delete a line space)		**Format, Paragraph, Indents and Spacing, Line Spacing** Select: Either single or double from the Line Spacing drop-down menu box Select: **Multiple** from the **Line Spacing** drop-down menu box Enter: **3** in the **At** box
Mail merge – add record		**Switch to Data Form** Click: **Add New** Key in: The record Click: **Add New** *or* **Switch to View Source** Click: **Add New** Record Key in: The record	
Mail merge – amend fields		**Switch to View Source** Click: ▦ on the Database Tool Bar	
Mail merge – create data source	Select: **Tools, Mail Merge, Get Data** in Section 2, **Create Data Source**		
Mail merge – create main document	Select: **Tools, Mail Merge, Create** in Section 1, **Form Letters, Active Window**		
Mail merge – delete record		Select: **Switch to Data Form** Select: **Find Record** Click: **Delete** *or* Select: **Switch to View Source** Select: The required record Select: **Delete**	
Mail merge – enter records		**Switch to Data Form** Key in: The record Select: **Add New**	
Mail merge – find record		**Switch to Data Form** Click: **Find** Click: ▦ Key in: The data Select: **In Field** Click: **Find First** *or* **Switch to Data Form** Click: **View Source** Click: ▦	
Mail merge – insert merge codes		**Switch to Main Doc** Click: **Insert Merge Field** Select: The required filename	
Mail merge – open data source		Select: **Tools, Mail Merge** Click: **Get Data** in Section 2 Select: **Open Data Source**	
Mail merge – print merged file		Click: ▦	

Action	Keyboard	Mouse	Menu
Mail merge – select records		Select: **Query Options** in the **Mail Merge Helper** dialogue box Select: The required field Key in: The required options	
Mail merge – sort data source		**Switch to View Source** Place the cursor: In the appropriate column Click: [A↓] or [Z↓]	
Mail merge – switch between Data Source and Main Document		Click: [icon] Select: **Edit** in Section 1 or 2 *or* Click: [icon] or [icon] on the Database Tool Bar	**Window, Main Doc** **Window, Datafile**
Mail merge – view merged file		**Switch to Main Doc** Click: [icon]	
Margins (to change)	Use the mouse pointer to drag the left and/or right margin boundaries to the appropriate place on the horizontal ruler. Press: The **Alt** key at the same time [icon] to view the measurements on screen		**File, Page Setup, Margins**
Move around document	*See*: Cursor movement		
Move a block of text Select: Text to be moved Position cursor where text is to be moved to	Press: **F2** *or* **Ctrl + X** Press: **Ctrl + V** *or* ↵	Click: [icon] on the Standard Tool Bar Click: [icon] on the Standard Tool Bar *drag and drop moving:* Select: Text to be moved Click: Left mouse button in middle of text and keep held down Drag: Selection to required location Release: Mouse button	**Edit, Cut** **Edit, Paste** *or* Press: Right mouse button Select: **Cut** Press: Right mouse button Select: **Paste**
Newspaper columns – changing column width		Position cursor in section to be changed: Drag: **Column markers** to required position on ruler	
Newspaper columns – for section of document			Select: The text to be formatted into columns: Operate commands as for **Newspaper columns (for whole document)**
Newspaper columns – for whole document		Click: [icon] **Columns** on **Standard Tool Bar** Drag: Across grid to select number of columns	**View, Page Layout, Edit, Select All** **Format, Columns** Select: The columns required in the **Presets** section Click: **OK**
Newspaper columns – insert column break			Position the cursor: Where the new column is to start: **Insert, Break, Column break**
Newspaper columns – inserting vertical lines between			Position the cursor: In the section to be changed: **Format, Columns, Line between**
Newspaper columns – to remove column formatting		Position the cursor: In the section to be changed: Click: [icon] **Columns** on **Standard Tool Bar** Drag: Across grid to select one column	**View, Page Layout, Edit, Select All** **Format, Columns** Select: One column in the **Presets** section Click: **OK**

Action	Keyboard	Mouse	Menu
Open an existing file	Press: **Ctrl + O**	Click: 📂 on the Standard Tool Bar	**File, Open**
Open a new file	Press: **Ctrl + N**	Click: 🗋 on the Standard Tool Bar	**File, New**
Page break (to insert)	Press: **Ctrl + ↵**		**Insert, Break, Page break**
Page numbering	Press: **Alt + Shift + P**		**Insert, Page Numbers**
Page numbering from given page			**Insert, Page numbers** Select: **Position and alignment** Select: **Format** Select: **Start at** Key in: The page number for the first page
Page Setup			**File, Page Setup** Choose from **Margins, Paper Size, Paper Source** and **Layout**
Paragraphs – splitting/joining	*Make a new paragraph (ie split a paragraph into two):* Move cursor to first letter of new paragraph: Press: ↵ twice *Join two consecutive paragraphs into one:* Move cursor to first letter of new paragraph: Press: ← (**Del**) twice (backspace delete key) Press: **Space Bar** (to insert a space after full stop)		
Print out hard copy	Press: **Ctrl + P**	Click: 🖨 on the Standard Tool Bar	**File, Print**
Print Preview	Press: **Ctrl + F2**	Click: 🔍 on the Standard Tool Bar	**File, Print Preview** Select: **Zoom** *or* **Full Page**
Ragged right margin	Press: **Ctrl + L**	Click: ☰ on the Formatting Tool Bar	**Format, Paragraph, Indents and Spacing, Alignment, Left**
Remove text emphasis First, select the emphasised text to be changed back to normal text	Press: **Ctrl + Space Bar** *or* Press: **Ctrl + Shift + Z**	Click: Appropriate emphasis button on the Formatting Tool Bar (to deselect)	**Format, Paragraph, Indents and Spacing**
Repeat typing or actions (redo)	Press: **F4** to repeat previous action *or* Press: **Ctrl + Y**	Click: ↻ on the Formatting Tool Bar To redo (repeat) sets of actions, drag down the **Redo** drop-down list; select: The group of actions you wish to repeat	**Edit, Repeat Typing**
Replace text	Press: **Ctrl + H**		**Edit, Replace**
Replace text – typeover Word will fit the replacement	1 Select: The incorrect text and then type in the correct entry 2 Move cursor: To incorrect entry Press: The **Ins** key (typeover on) and overtype with correct entry Press: The **Ins** key again (typeover off) to stop overtyping of text		
Restore deleted text	Press: **Ctrl + Z**	Click: ↶ on the Formatting Tool Bar	**Edit, Undo Typing**
Ruler – to display			**View, Ruler**
Save work to disk Save a file for the first time	Press: **F12**		**File, Save As, Enter Filename** Select: Correct Directory/Drive Click: **OK**
Save an active file which has been saved previously Save all open files	Press: **Ctrl + S** *or* Press: **Shift + F12**	Click: 💾 on the Standard Tool Bar	**File, Save** **File, Save All**

Action	Keyboard	Mouse	Menu
Scroll bars (to view)			**Tools, Options, View** Select: Horizontal Scroll Bar and Vertical Scroll Bar options
Search for text	*See* Find text		
Select text One character (or more) One word To end of line Start of line A full line A paragraph Whole document Any block of text	Press: **Shift** + → *or* ← Press: **Shift + Ctrl** + → *or* ← Press: **Shift + End** Press: **Shift + Home** Press: **Shift + End** *or* **Home** — Press: **Ctrl + A** —	Click and drag pointer across text Double-click on word Click and drag pointer right or down Click and drag pointer left or up Click in selection border Double-click in selection border Triple-click in selection border Position pointer at start of text and hold down **Shift**. Then, position pointer at end of text and click	
Remove selection		Click in any white space	
Shading First, select the area to add shading to		Click: 🅰 ▾ **Highlight** on **Formatting Tool Bar** *and/or* Click: ✐ **Font Color** on **Formatting Tool Bar**	**Format, Borders and Shading, Shading** Select: From the **Fill**, **Style** and **Color** sections Select: The area of text to apply the shading to in the **Apply To** box *or* Select: **View, Tool Bars, Tables and Borders** to use the tool bar method
– to remove			Repeat the above menu commands but select the **None** option
Small capitals	Select: The text to be changed **Ctrl + Shift + K**		**Format, Font** Select: **Small caps** in the **Effects** section
Sort (rearrange) items			Select: The items or text to be sorted Select: **Table, Sort …**
Spaced capitals	Press: **Caps Lock** key. Leave one space after each letter. Leave three spaces after each word		
Spellcheck	Press: **F7**	Click: 🔤✓ on the Standard Tool Bar	**Tools, Spelling and Grammar**
Standard Paragraph Files To create/store standard paragraphs:	Key in: The portion of text to be saved as a standard paragraph file Save it in a separate file using normal **Save** procedures		
To insert standard paragraphs into your document:	Position the cursor: Where you want the standard paragaph to be inserted Select: **File** from the **Insert** menu Select/key in: The appropriate filename		
Status Bar			**Tools, Options, View** Select: Status Bar option
Styles (using)	Select: The text to be formatted Normal style: Press: **Ctrl + Shift + N** Heading 1 style: Press: **Alt + Ctrl + 1** Heading 2 style: Press: **Alt + Ctrl + 2**	Select: The text to be formatted: Select: The required style from **Style** drop-down menu on the **Formatting Tool Bar**	
Subscript	**Ctrl + =** (equal sign) **Ctrl + Space Bar** to revert to normal text		**Format, Font** Select: **Subscript** in **Effects** section Select: **Subscript** again to revert to normal text

Action	Keyboard	Mouse	Menu
Superscript	**Ctrl + Shift + +** (plus sign) **Ctrl + Space Bar** to revert to normal text		**Format, Font** Select: **Superscript** in **Effects** section Select: **Superscript** again to revert to normal text
Switch on and load Word		Double-click: **Microsoft Word Icon**	Select: **MS Word from Start**
Symbols	*See*: Insert special characters/symbols		
Symbols/Accents/Fractions			**Insert, Symbol** Select: The required font Click: On the required symbol Select: **Insert, Close**
Symbols as graphics			Position cursor: Where you want the graphic symbol to appear: **Insert, Symbol** Select: The appropriate **Font** Click: The required graphic symbol Click: **Insert, OK**
Tabs – to add/set	Click: On the **Tab Alignment button** at far left of horizontal ruler until the type of tab alignment you want is displayed: Left-aligned tab � Decimal tab ⊡ Right-aligned tab ▪ Centred tab ⊥ Click: The mouse pointer on the horizontal ruler at the place where you want to set the tab stop		**Format, Tabs** Enter: The appropriate position and alignment for each tab required
– to delete/clear	Click: On the tab marker Drag: It off the horizontal ruler		**Format, Tabs** Select: The appropriate tab stop Select: **Clear**
– to move	Click: On the tab marker Drag: It to the left or right on the horizontal ruler		**Format, Tabs** Select: The appropriate tab stop and follow the instructions *to delete/clear*. Then, set the tab stop in its new position following the instructions above *to add/set*
Tables Insert table		Click: ⊞ on the Standard Tool Bar	**Table, Insert Table**
Tables and borders		Click: ▱ on the Standard Tool Bar	**Table, Draw Table**
Tables – to apply ruling/borders		Click: ▱▾ **Borders** on **Formatting Tool Bar**	Select: The table cell(s) to apply ruling to: **Format, Borders and Shading, Borders**
Tables – to add/set/delete tabs inside a table	Select: The column in which you want to edit the tab settings: Make any tab stop changes in the normal way – see *tabs*.		
– to move between tabs in a table	Press: **Ctrl + Tab** Click: At the required position		

Action	Keyboard	Mouse	Menu
Text box (to add)		Click: 🔻 **Drawing icon** on the **Standard Tool Bar**	**Insert**, **Text Box** Drag the cross-hair cursor across the screen until the text box is the required size
– to format		Click: 📧 **Text Box** icon on the Drawing Tool Bar Click: The text box Press: The right mouse key Select: **Format Text Box** Select: From the options on the **Format Text Box** dialogue box	Click: The text box **Format**, **Text Box** Select: From the options on the **Format Text Box** dialogue box *or* **View**, **Toolbars**, **Picture** to format the text box using the Picture Tool Bar
Underline text Single underline Double underline	Press: **Ctrl + U** Press: **Ctrl + Shift + W** Press: **Ctrl + Shift + D**	Click: **U** on the Formatting Tool Bar	**Format**, **Font**, **Underline**
Undo mistakes, typing or actions	Press: **Ctrl + Z**	Click: ↶ on the Standard Tool Bar. To undo sets of actions, drag down the **Undo** drop-down list; select: The group of actions you wish to undo	**Edit**, **Undo Typing**
Units of measurement			**Tools**, **Options**, **General**, **Measurement Units** Select: Desired unit from drop-down menu
View magnified pages		Click: 100% on the Standard Tool Bar Click: **Magnifies** on Print Preview	**View**, **Zoom**
View – normal view	Press: **Ctrl + F2**	Click: The 📄 **Normal View** button at left of document window	**View**, **Normal**
View – outline view		Click: The ⊞ **Outline View** button at left of document window	**View**, **Outline**
View – page layout view		Click: The ▤ **Print Layout View** button at left of document window	**View**, **Page Layout**
View – Print Preview	Press: **Ctrl + F2**	Click: 🔍 on the Standard Tool Bar	**File**, **Print Preview** Select: **Zoom** *or* **Full Page**
Widow/orphan control			**Format**, **Paragraph**, **Line and Page Breaks**
WordArt		Click: ✎ **Insert WordArt** on the **Drawing Tool Bar**	**View**, **Toolbars**, **WordArt** Select: From the options shown

**Unit 1
Exercise 1A continued**

CREATIVE PASTIMES

The name *arte povera* (the poor man's art) was given to the use of cut-outs to decorate Venetian furniture with chinoiserie figures in the style of Oriental lacquer ware. This work is now far from the reach of the poor – it fetches very high prices at auction.

European gentlewomen of the 18th century incorporated decoupage into their (sometimes very impressive) repertoire of artistic pursuits. Together with music, painting and needlework, decoupage gave them an opportunity to create some excellent works. They did not simply amuse themselves; their work still provides us with many excellent pieces.

In the mid 19th century with the mass production of Victorian scrap sheets (collections of colourful images), decoupage became widespread and no longer confined to the gentry. The whole family would be involved in a project such as the production of a scrap screen for the nursery. Work carried out in this way is often rather haphazard as if the main aim of the venture had been to cover every spare inch of the available space rather than to plan and prepare a work of artistic merit. However, the value of the work to those involved was probably of a personal domestic, rather than aesthetic, nature.

The skill declined in popularity at the beginning of the 20th century but is now enjoying a revival. This renewed interest has been helped by the advent of the photocopier and the invention of special varnishes.

No special equipment or tools are needed for decoupage projects. This fact makes it ideal as a new hobby which will not prove to be too expensive as many pastimes do. The average household already contains most of the materials and tools you will need to begin.

DECOUPAGE TODAY

Nowadays, the basic motifs or designs are of two types. Some people use special black-and-white printed designs and apply colour using pencils, inks or paints. Others prefer to use printed designs from wrapping paper, wallpaper, cards and magazines. The latter method follows the Victorian tradition of scrap sheets, whilst the former mimics the Venetian *arte povera* and allows more scope for individual creativity.

2

**Unit 1
Exercise 1A**

CREATIVE PASTIMES

<u>THE ART OF DECOUPAGE</u>

If you are looking for an interesting artistic hobby which is not too difficult to learn and won't break the bank, perhaps decoupage is for you. Many of us admire the design work and paintings produced by others but feel we ourselves cannot make anything of worth. Decoupage demands only patience!

PROJECTS

You can use your new skills to decorate picture frames, boxes, vases and bowls. If you are really ambitious, you could make an attractive room screen or decorate the top of a coffee table. After practising on small objects to begin with, you will soon come up with other, larger projects.

No special equipment or tools are needed for decoupage projects. This fact makes it ideal as a new hobby which will not prove to be too expensive as many pastimes do. The average household already contains most of the materials and tools you will need to begin.

A beginner's kit should comprise:

1 Small scissors or scalpel
2 Large scissors
3 A natural sponge
4 Soft rags
5 Brushes
6 Finger bowl and water
7 Wallpaper paste
8 Coloured pencils and paints

You will probably find most of these items in a cupboard or in your decorating kit.

DECOUPAGE THROUGH THE AGES

Decoupage (from the French découper – to cut out) became very popular during the 15th century when German furniture was being decorated with elaborate borders simulating 'tarsia' work. The work was so skilfully executed that it was difficult, from a distance, to distinguish it from the complicated wood inlay work which it reproduced.

1

CREATIVE PASTIMES

THE ART OF DECOUPAGE

If you are looking for an interesting artistic hobby which is not too difficult

to learn and won't break the bank, perhaps decoupage is for you. Many of

us admire the design work and paintings produced by others but feel we

ourselves cannot make anything of worth. Decoupage demands only

patience!

PROJECTS

You can use your new skills to decorate picture frames, boxes, vases and bowls. If you are really ambitious, you could make an attractive room screen or decorate the top of a coffee table. After practising on small objects to begin with, you will soon come up with other, larger projects.

No special equipment or tools are needed for decoupage projects. This fact makes it ideal as a new hobby which will not prove to be too expensive as many pastimes do. The average household already contains most of the materials and tools you will need to begin.

A beginner's kit should comprise:

1 Small scissors* or scalpel
2 Large scissors
3 A natural sponge
4 Soft rags
5 Brushes
6 Finger bowl and water
7 Wallpaper paste
8 Coloured pencils and paints

You will probably find most of these items in a cupboard or in your decorating kit.

It may be necessary to prepare the surface you are going to decorate and so you may find that sandpaper, primer, scrapers and paint stripper will be required. It is always worth spending time to prepare the wood or metal correctly to ensure a good final finish.

---

* *Sharp-pointed, curved manicure scissors are ideal. They should be good quality and very sharp.*

Your name

4

CREATIVE PASTIMES

DECOUPAGE THROUGH THE AGES

Decoupage (from the French découper – to cut out) became very popular during the 15th century when German furniture was being decorated with elaborate borders simulating 'tarsia' work. The work was so skilfully executed that it was difficult, from a distance, to distinguish it from the complicated wood inlay work which it reproduced.

The name *arte povera* (the poor man's art) was given to the use of cut-outs to decorate Venetian furniture with chinoiserie figures in the style of Oriental lacquer ware. This work is now far from the reach of the poor – it fetches very high prices at auction.

European gentlewomen of the 18th century incorporated decoupage into their (sometimes very impressive) repertoire of artistic pursuits. Together with music, painting and needlework, decoupage gave them an opportunity to create some excellent works. They did not simply amuse themselves; their work still provides us with many excellent pieces.

In the mid 19th century with the mass production of Victorian scrap sheets (collections of colourful images), decoupage became widespread and no longer confined to the gentry. The whole family would be involved in a project such as the production of a scrap screen for the nursery. Work carried out in this way is often rather haphazard as if the main aim of the venture had been to cover every spare inch of the available space rather than to plan and prepare a work of artistic merit. However, the value of the work to those involved was probably of a personal domestic, rather than aesthetic, nature.

The skill declined in popularity at the beginning of the 20th century but is now enjoying a revival. This renewed interest has been helped by the advent of the photocopier and the invention of special varnishes.

No special equipment or tools are needed for decoupage projects. This fact makes it ideal as a new hobby which will not prove to be too expensive as many pastimes do. The average household already contains most of the materials and tools you will need to begin.

DECOUPAGE TODAY

Nowadays, the basic motifs or designs are of two types. Some people use special black-and-white printed designs and apply colour using pencils, inks or paints. Others prefer to use printed designs from wrapping paper, wallpaper, cards and magazines. The latter method follows the Victorian tradition of scrap sheets, whilst the former mimics the Venetian *arte povera* and allows more scope for individual creativity. Whatever the level of your artistic ability, you should be able to produce an item to be proud of.

Your name

5

CREATIVE PASTIMES

THE ART OF DECOUPAGE

If you are looking for an interesting artistic hobby which is not too difficult to learn and won't break the bank, perhaps decoupage is for you. Many of us admire the design work and paintings produced by others but feel we ourselves cannot make anything of worth. Decoupage demands only patience!

PROJECTS

You can use your new skills to decorate picture frames, boxes, vases and bowls. If you are really ambitious, you could make an attractive room screen or decorate the top of a coffee table. After practising on small objects to begin with, you will soon come up with other, larger projects.

No special equipment or tools are needed for decoupage projects. This fact makes it ideal as a new hobby which will not prove to be too expensive as many pastimes do. The average household already contains most of the materials and tools you will need to begin.

A beginner's kit should comprise:

- Small scissors or scalpel
- Large scissors
- A natural sponge
- Soft rags
- Brushes
- Finger bowl and water
- Wallpaper paste
- Coloured pencils and paints

You will probably find most of these items in a cupboard or in your decorating kit.

It may be necessary to prepare the surface you are going to decorate and so you may find that sandpaper, primer, scrapers and paint stripper will be required. It is always worth spending time to prepare the wood or metal correctly to ensure a good final finish.

DECOUPAGE THROUGH THE AGES

Decoupage (from the French découper – to cut out) became very popular during the 15th century when German furniture was being decorated with elaborate borders simulating 'tarsia' work. The work was so skilfully executed that it was

Your name   1

CREATIVE PASTIMES

difficult, from a distance, to distinguish it from the complicated wood inlay work[1] which it reproduced.

The name arte povera (the poor man's art) was given to the use of cut-outs to decorate Venetian furniture with chinoiserie[2] figures in the style of Oriental lacquer[3] ware. This work is now far from the reach of the poor – it fetches very high prices at auction.

European gentlewomen of the 18th century incorporated decoupage into their (sometimes very impressive) repertoire of artistic pursuits. Together with music, painting and needlework, decoupage gave them an opportunity to create some excellent works. They did not simply amuse themselves; their work still provides us with many excellent pieces.

In the mid 19th century with the mass production of Victorian scrap sheets (collections of colourful images), decoupage became widespread and no longer confined to the gentry. The whole family would be involved in a project such as the production of a scrap screen for the nursery. Work carried out in this way is often rather haphazard as if the main aim of the venture had been to cover every spare inch of the available space rather than to plan and prepare a work of artistic merit. However, the value of the work to those involved was probably of a personal domestic, rather than aesthetic, nature.

The skill declined in popularity at the beginning of the 20th century but is now enjoying a revival. This renewed interest has been helped by the advent of the photocopier and the invention of special varnishes.

No special equipment or tools are needed for decoupage projects. This fact makes it ideal as a new hobby which will not prove to be too expensive as many pastimes do. The average household already contains most of the materials and tools you will need to begin.

DECOUPAGE TODAY

Nowadays, the basic motifs or designs are of two types. Some people use special black-and-white printed designs and apply colour using pencils, inks or paints. Others prefer to use printed designs from wrapping paper, wallpaper, cards and magazines. The latter method follows the Victorian tradition of scrap sheets, whilst the former mimics the Venetian arte povera and allows more scope for individual creativity. Whatever the level of your artistic ability, you should be able to produce an item to be proud of.

1 Use of different woods to form a design
2 Influenced by Chinese art
3 Type of varnish giving a very smooth, glassy coating

Your name   2

The local residents didn't know that they'd have to visit the local Council office to see the plans. They weren't pleased to find that the builders hadn't taken the trouble to consider local feelings. They're to make a protest through their local Councillor as they don't think that the proposed development is appropriate. They'll take their findings along to the meeting.

The theatre's auditorium was full for the play's last performance. The critics' review had been excellent, praising the designer's flair and the cast's enthusiasm. The audience waited in anticipation as the lights dimmed and the orchestra's instruments began to produce the music which had become familiar to so many people.

This plant grows on chalk downland and its shape is described as squat and spiny. However, it's also found in pine woods, where it's been known to grow to tree size. It's native to north-western Europe, Asia and North America, where its value is mainly for ornamental purposes. A similar tree grows in the Mediterranean where its uses are culinary and it's valued for its aperitif and digestive properties. Its foliage has a pleasant aromatic scent and it's distilled to produce an essential oil, when its properties are employed for its alternative product – perfume.

The Technological Age

THE VICTORIANS

British society and economy had been transformed during the Industrial Revolution and the effects of the changes were felt throughout the Empire and the rest of the world.

The Victorians developed science, invention and engineering skills to an unprecedented level in a relatively short space of time, using technology to improve the quality of life.

The Victorian age was a time when self-confidence was displayed by the nation. Scientists and engineers, such as Isambard Kingdom Brunel and Robert Stephenson, were the heroes of the age and their achievements have delivered long-lasting benefits on a large scale. They created wealth through their expertise and the values of enlightenment and democracy accompanied their enterprises. Public enterprise resulted in many magnificent public buildings and several ambitious civil engineering projects were undertaken.

Public Enterprise

On a grand scale, the Thames Embankment and the Vyrnwy Valley reservoir[1] remind us of the public works which were carried out during the Victorian era. On a smaller scale, towns and cities benefited from gas street lighting and a burst of house-building activity. In Newcastle upon Tyne, described as 'the best designed Victorian town in England', 13,000 homes were built in the first 70 years of the 19th century, leaving a permanent testimony of the age, at least in its grand buildings.

Public Health

Diseases such as cholera, tuberculosis and anthrax claimed very many lives, and often at an early age. During the latter half of the 19th century, new work was carried out in the science of bacteriology.[2]

---

[1] Supplying the City of Liverpool
[2] Robert Koch working in Berlin

Your name

1

Unit 2
Exercise 2D

The Technological Age

THE VICTORIANS

British society and economy had been transformed during the Industrial Revolution and the effects of the changes were felt throughout the Empire and the rest of the world.

The Victorians developed science, invention and engineering skills to an unprecedented level in a relatively short space of time, using technology to improve the quality of life.

The Victorian age was a time when self-confidence was displayed by the nation. Scientists and engineers, such as Isambard Kingdom Brunel and Robert Stephenson, were the heroes of the age and their achievements have delivered long-lasting benefits on a large scale. They created wealth through their expertise and the values of enlightenment and democracy accompanied their enterprises. Public enterprise resulted in many magnificent public buildings and several ambitious civil engineering projects were undertaken.

Public Enterprise

On a grand scale, the Thames Embankment and the Vyrnwy Valley reservoir[1] remind us of the public works which were carried out during the Victorian era. On a smaller scale, towns and cities benefited from gas street lighting and a burst of house-building activity. In Newcastle upon Tyne, described as 'the best designed Victorian town in England', 13,000 homes were built in the first 70 years of the 19th century, leaving a permanent testimony of the age, at least in its grand buildings.

Public Health

Diseases such as cholera, tuberculosis and anthrax claimed very many lives, and often at an early age. During the latter half of the 19th century, new work was carried out in the science of bacteriology.[2]

Surgery became less hazardous as antisepsis was promoted and vaccination against diseases such as anthrax was introduced. The nursing profession traces its roots to the Victorian era with its most famous practitioner, Florence Nightingale, working to relieve suffering in the Crimea.

Professor Wilhelm Conrad Röntgen of Würzburg discovered, almost by accident, the effect of light on a piece of barium platinocyanide paper. After further investigation and research this discovery became what we now call X-rays.

---

[1] Supplying the City of Liverpool
[2] Robert Koch working in Berlin

Your name

1

Unit 2
Exercise 2B continued

The Technological Age

Surgery became less hazardous as antisepsis was promoted and vaccination against diseases such as anthrax was introduced. The nursing profession traces its roots to the Victorian era with its most famous practitioner, Florence Nightingale, working to relieve suffering in the Crimea.

Transport

Railways dominated the scene, combining all the achievements of the Victorians in one service. Isambard Kingdom Brunel again demonstrated his tenacity and genius through his involvement in ship-building, railways and civil engineering projects.

Locomotives made in the 'manufactories' of Britain were delivered to South Africa, Australia, India, Japan and South America, as well as to most of Europe. A definite impact was made on the infrastructures of many foreign countries. The Metropolitan Underground Railway was opened in London in 1863.

Communications

A 'girdle' was placed around the world when telegraphy and telephony were invented. Improved communication systems supported the rapid developments in technology.

The Victorians developed science, invention and engineering skills to an unprecedented level in a relatively short space of time, using technology to improve the quality of life.

Your name

2

The Technological Age

Making Way For Progress

Although the aims of the Victorian entrepreneurs were usually altruistic, the railway companies caused the demolition of workers' housing as they forged their way into London. The princely sum of 1s 6d (7½p) compensation was paid towards the cost of their moving to other accommodation.

Parliament insisted that a special train be put on for the workers to travel to their places of work from their new lodgings in the suburbs and this was called the Workmen's Penny Train, the fare being 1d per journey.

Personal Transport

The boneshaker, or vélocipède as it was known in France, was developed by Michaux in Paris and improved on an earlier model – the Laufmaschine - made by Drais in 1817. The bicycle was to prove a most useful and enjoyable method of transport for many years until the motor car monopolised the roads.

The Victorians developed science, invention and engineering skills to an unprecedented level in a relatively short space of time, using technology to improve the quality of life.

Your name

3

The Technological Age

The Illustrated London News in April 1986 reported that the Duke and Duchess of York (later to become King George V and Queen Mary) had had their hands 'photographed' using X-rays and gave the additional comment that 'the Röntgen ray is no respecter of persons, and gives a touch of homeliness to the most illustrious anatomy'.

Transport

Railways dominated the scene, combining all the achievements of the Victorians in one service. Isambard Kingdom Brunel again demonstrated his tenacity and genius through his involvement in ship-building, railways and civil engineering projects.

Locomotives made in the 'manufactories' of Britain were delivered to South Africa, Australia, India, Japan and South America, as well as to most of Europe. A definite impact was made on the infrastructures of many foreign countries. The Metropolitan Underground Railway was opened in London in 1863.

Communications

A 'girdle' was placed around the world when telegraphy and telephony were invented. Improved communication systems supported the rapid developments in technology.

Applications For Warfare

The new technology made it possible for manufacturers to develop new devices and improve old ones in preparation for warfare. The late 19th century was a critical time for the development of naval warfare in the armouring of ships.

Sir John Brown of Sheffield was a pioneer manufacturer of steel using the method introduced by Henry Bessemer. He was concerned, like many others at the time, that the French were producing an armoured battleship. In his manufacturing base, Atlas Works, he made rolled armourplate to a thickness of 4½ inches, which he felt would be stronger than the hammered plate of the French ship.

Competition between the British, Italians and French in the development of naval guns culminated in the Italian ship 'Duilio' carrying 100-ton 17.7 inch muzzle loaders, making them 50 per cent more powerful than the British guns. The 100-ton guns were in fact produced by William Armstrong[3] of Elswick.

---

[3] A solicitor turned engineer in later life

Your name

2

PANACHE TRADING LTD

MEMORANDUM

PERSONAL

From: Kim Redknapp, Marketing Manager
To: Heads of Departments
Ref: KR/009/34
Date: today's

LOCAL INDUSTRY INNOVATION FAIR

May I draw your attention to the attached letter which sets out some proposals for a Local Industry Innovation Fair.

I would appreciate it if you could forward your ideas and suggestions as to how we could benefit from participating in such an event. I believe that the event would provide us with an ideal opportunity to promote our business services to both current and prospective clients. We would also be able to network with other companies in the area who may be able to open up new opportunities for us through sub-contracting arrangements.

If there is anyone who would be interested in working with me on this initiative, I would be grateful if you could let me know on your reply. As you are aware, two of my key staff are on long-term sickness, so even a few hours from you or your staff would be very much appreciated. It will be necessary to have names of people who would be willing to 'staff' the event on a rota basis, although I am currently awaiting confirmation of dates when this will take place.

Please could you send your comments to Sue Bridges, Marketing Officer, by Friday (date of Friday of next week) so that she can co-ordinate them in readiness for my first planning meeting.

Enc

Copy: Sue Bridges
      File

Copy: **Sue Bridges** ✓
      File

Copy: **Sue Bridges**
      File ✓

PANACHE TRADING LTD

67 Firth Road
HUDDERSFIELD
HD12 7GT

Tel no: 01484 489472   Fax no: 01484 489315
Internet: www.panache.co.uk   e-mail: sales@panache.co.uk

Today's date

URGENT

Mr Austin Phelps
Business Ideas Ltd
43 Lembark Road
HUDDERSFIELD
HD4 9ST

Dear Mr Phelps

LOCAL INDUSTRY INNOVATION FAIR

Thank you for your recent letter inviting us to participate in a Local Industry Innovation Fair, and requesting ideas and suggestions which may contribute to its success. First of all, may I congratulate you on piloting this exciting new initiative, which will be a great opportunity for local companies. I think many companies will greet your proposal with enthusiasm.

I have circulated your letter to all our Heads of Department to see if other colleagues in our organisation have any helpful ideas for the event. In the meantime, may I recommend that we convene a meeting between the various Marketing Managers of interested companies in order to brainstorm ideas and develop a draft plan and time schedule. Please let me know if you intend to coordinate such a meeting. Otherwise, perhaps I could make an appointment to meet with you separately to discuss a way forward.

I am enclosing our company catalogue and business information leaflets which will give you some background details about the organisation's activities and interests. I thought it might be useful for you to have prior sight of them to aid any pre-event publicity measures.

Yours sincerely

Kim Redknapp
Marketing Manager

Encs

PANACHE TRADING LTD

67 Firth Road
HUDDERSFIELD
HD12 7GT

Tel no: 01484 489472   Fax no: 01484 489315
Internet: www.panache.co.uk   e-mail: sales@panache.co.uk

Ref DM/SS/87

Today's date

Mrs Fiona Wetherby
45 Liverton Walk
HUDDERSFIELD
HD5 7HR

Dear Mrs Wetherby

ORDER CODE REFERENCE: TR77W

Thank you for your recent order which we received last week.

Our normal delivery time for orders is within 7 days. Unfortunately, the goods you specified are currently out of stock and there may be a slight delay of approximately 14 days before we are able to undertake delivery. We have placed a special order with our manufacturer and, in order to speed up the process, the goods will be sent to you direct from their own premises.

This means that this letter will act as your temporary invoice for the following goods ordered on your account:

Quantity	Item description	Price	Invoice no
1	Deluxe filing cabinet	£219.99	7/3769

Delivery will be made using the supplier's own carrier service and should be within 21 days. The carrier will contact you by telephone to arrange a suitable delivery time. Your telephone number is shown on our records as 01484 437251. If this has changed, or is incorrect, please contact our Answer Line on Freephone 0800 119 237 as soon as possible.

If you are unhappy with these arrangements, or dissatisfied with the goods after delivery, you may use the same Answer Line Freephone number and ask to speak to one of our Customer Service Agents. We will do our best to resolve any problems which may arise.

If you wish to cancel the order, again please use the Answer Line Freephone and ask to speak to one of our Sales Advisers.

The Answer Line is staffed during normal office hours of 9.00am to 5.30pm, Monday to Friday, but you may leave a message outside office hours on the voice mail and someone will return your call.

We aim to make your purchases with Panache Trading as trouble free as possible. If you have any further queries about our services, please don't hesitate to contact me.

Yours sincerely

Dyllis Morgan
Sales Supervisor

2

PANACHE TRADING LTD

MEMORANDUM

From: Dyllis Morgan, Sales Supervisor
To: Estelle Deneuve, Customer Services Manager
Ref: DM/376/21
Date: today's

I have received notification from one of our suppliers that they are unable to meet any orders from us until (*date of last Friday of next month*).

I am concerned that correspondence has already gone out to several of our customers advising them that there would only be a 3-week delay on their orders. I would appreciate it, therefore, if you could contact these clients immediately to explain the further delay and offer our apologies for any inconvenience caused. **We are able to offer them a 5% discount against the original purchase price as a financial incentive not to cancel their orders.** It would be helpful if you could confirm to our Finance Department which clients decide to take up this offer, along with your letter reference. Our supplier has assured me that outstanding orders will definitely be dealt with as a priority so I do not anticipate any further difficulties at this time. However, I have made an appointment to meet with them in a fortnight to double check their production schedule.

A list of clients is attached. If necessary, you may contact my secretary for any other information you need on each customer account. Most of those listed are long-standing customers and it is vital that we maintain good relations with them. Should you receive any complaints, please notify Jim McDonnagh's secretary so that Jim can deal with them at a more senior level.

Enc

Copy: Jim McDonnagh
      File

Copy: Jim McDonnagh ✓
      File

Copy: Jim McDonnagh ✓
      File ✓

Occupational Aspects

STRESS AND ILLNESS

It is an alarming fact that the majority of our waking hours (60% - 70% according to statistics) is spent working. If work involves being in contact with people we do not particularly like, in a job which we do not enjoy, where little appreciation of employees' achievements is shown, and where the financial remuneration is felt to be insufficient, then we become 'stressed' and a reaction of some type is triggered.

If, in addition to these negative factors at work, we are struggling to pay bills or having problems with our accommodation or in social or family relationships, it is not surprising that a few individuals display severe symptoms of distress.

Predisposing factors

You may have seen a list of life events or a life stress scale.[1] Each life event, ranging from death of a spouse at the top of the scale (100), and minor law breaking at the bottom of the scale (11), has a score out of 100. This list of life events does not only include so-called 'negative' events, such as being fired or divorced, but also includes events which are commonly perceived to be 'positive'. Examples are marriage or holidays.

It is said that an individual's risk of suffering a stress-related illness is related to their score on the life events scale during the previous year. Approximately 50% of people who exceed 200 on the scale develop health problems. Almost 80% of people who exceed 300 on the scale succumb to ill health.

---
[1] Sometimes called the Holmes Rahe scale after its authors

1

Modern Times

STRESS AND ILLNESS

Predisposing factors

You may have seen a list of life events or a life stress scale.[1] Each life event, ranging from death of a spouse at the top of the scale (100), and minor law breaking at the bottom of the scale (11), has a score out of 100. This list of life events does not only include so-called 'negative' events, such as being fired or divorced, but also includes events which are commonly perceived to be 'positive'. Examples are marriage or holidays.

It is said that an individual's risk of suffering a stress-related illness is related to their score on the life events scale during the previous year. Approximately 50% of people who exceed 200 on the scale develop health problems. Almost 80% of people who exceed 300 on the scale succumb to ill health.

It is an alarming fact that the majority of our waking hours (60% - 70% according to statistics) is spent working. If work involves being in contact with people we do not particularly like, in a job which we do not enjoy, where little appreciation of employees' achievements is shown, and where the financial remuneration is felt to be insufficient, then we become 'stressed' and a reaction of some type is triggered.

If, in addition to these negative factors at work, we are struggling to pay bills or having problems with our accommodation or in social or family relationships, it is not surprising that a few individuals display severe symptoms of distress.

The pecking order

Some authorities believe that the factor of 'being in control' is vital. Although senior business executives work hard, they do tend to be more in control of their work and the work itself is often varied. The ability to exercise control over tasks to be performed and use of time during their working day protects them, to some extent, from the effects of stress.

[1] Sometimes called the Holmes Rahe scale after its authors

Occupational Aspects

6

Occupational Aspects

The pecking order

Some authorities believe that the factor of 'being in control' is vital. Although senior business executives work hard, they do tend to be more in control of their work and the work itself is often varied. The ability to exercise control over tasks to be performed and use of time during their working day protects them, to some extent, from the effects of stress.

Unfortunately, this same ability to control their own environment may also give them the opportunity to exercise control over their 'inferiors' and, when this is perceived to be counter-productive by the 'controllee', it adds even more to the stress level of the latter. The manager of a department therefore should acknowledge and appreciate his or her responsibility for the health of colleagues in his or her charge.

The costs of stress

Individuals suffering the effects of stress can easily identify the costs in personal terms. Their health, relationships and ability to enjoy life are adversely affected. However, there is also enormous cost to commerce, industry and the professions.

The costs are shown as:

- increases in premature retirements
- increases in premature deaths
- higher health care costs
- higher absence rates

Persons under stress are more accident-prone – another factor affecting health, and generating 'costs' to the health service, the employer and the person concerned and their family.

2

Unit 4
Exercise 4B continued

Unfortunately, this same ability to control their own environment may also give them the opportunity to exercise control over their 'inferiors' and, when this is perceived to be counter-productive by the 'controllee', it adds even more to the stress level of the latter. The manager of a department therefore should acknowledge and appreciate his or her responsibility for the health of colleagues in his or her charge.

The costs of stress

Individuals suffering the effects of stress can easily identify the costs in personal terms. Their health, relationships and ability to enjoy life are adversely affected. However, there is also enormous cost to commerce, industry and the professions.

The costs are shown as:

1. increases in premature retirements
2. increases in premature deaths
3. higher health care costs
4. higher absence rates[2]

Invisible costs, although difficult to measure, have profound effects on performance and productivity within the workplace. It is only when the invisible costs become apparent that the full picture can be observed.

The invisible costs can include:

1. reduced mental performance
2. lack of concentration
3. impaired judgment
4. ineffective leadership
5. reduced creativity
6. fewer innovations
7. lack of decision-making skills

Persons under stress are more accident-prone[3] – another factor affecting health, and generating costs to the health service, the employer and the person concerned and their family. The tendency to have accidents can be related to forgetfulness, anxiety and impaired coordination.

[2] The highest absence rate is found in the transportation and communications industry (8.9%)
[3] 1.6 million accidents happen at work each year

Occupational Aspects

7

Unit 4
Exercise 4B continued

Highest risk groups

The most stressful occupations are considered to be nursing, social work, police and teaching.

In November 1994 a senior social worker won a High Court case for compensation against his employer. The judge said that he should have been given more support.

Occupational Aspects

8

PANACHE TRADING LTD

MEMORANDUM

From: Thomas A Darnborough, Events Sales Administrator
To: Timothy Wardell, Human Resource Department
Ref: TAD/Staff/S2000
Date: Date of typing

STAFF OUTINGS TO PANACHE EVENTS

Thank you for passing on Roger Lyness' name to me. I have written to him offering him a place on the sales unit waiting list for the Peak Woodworking Show.

As we discussed earlier today, I am writing to give you a list of the events due to take place in the forthcoming months which are reasonably local and may be of interest to members of staff.

Peak Woodworking Show	Darlock Vale	14/15 September
Northern Arts & Crafts Festival	Ilkley	20/21/22 August
Beautiful Gardens	Derby	6 July
21st Century Living	Harrogate	13/14 August
21st Century Living	Coventry	27/28 August
Media Mela	Manchester	21/22 September

We can offer half-price ticket entrance to all of the events which we organise. We are unable to offer any further discounts as catering, transport etc are sub-contracted.

I have arranged to have full details of each event sent to you in the next few days so that you can circulate them to staff. Your plan to encourage participation will, in my opinion, be well accepted and should increase awareness and interest amongst all departments and branches of the organisation. Please keep me informed and let me know if I can be of further assistance.

PANACHE TRADING LTD

67 Fifth Road
HUDDERSFIELD
HD12 7GT

Tel no: 01484 489472   Fax no: 01484 489315
Internet: www.panache.co.uk   e-mail: sales@panache.co.uk

Our ref: TAD/Lyn/S2000

Date of typing

Mr R Lyness
10 Sun Street
Penworth Hill
HUDDERSFIELD
HD9 8DW

Dear Mr Lyness

PEAK WOODWORKING SHOW

My colleague, Timothy Wardell, has passed your name to me informing me that you are interested in taking part in the Peak Woodworking Show to be held later this year.

The Show consists of demonstrations, sales points and exhibitions. It is to be held at the Central Exhibition Centre in Darlock Vale. One of the exhibitions will be staged by the Guild of Derbyshire Woodworkers and the other will be a display of work done by the students at Ashsage College.

I understand that you would like to take a sales unit to display your meditation stools.

Unfortunately, I cannot confirm a unit booking for you at the moment as all units have been allocated. Bookings are often made 12 months in advance. However, I will place your name on the waiting list and should a unit become available through cancellation, I will contact you. Occasionally, cancellations are made due to illness.

Please complete the enclosed application form and attach a cheque for £50. Your cheque will not be processed until your booking is confirmed. If you have any further queries, you can contact me by telephone or fax at the numbers given above or by e-mail.

I also enclose 2 complimentary tickets to the Show, worth £5 each, and hope that you will be able to utilise these or pass them to a friend or colleague who would enjoy the Show.

Yours sincerely

THOMAS A DARNBOROUGH
Events Sales Administrator

Encs

The following should be avoided:

1 'knots' – except in softwoods if less than ¾ in diameter
2 'shakes' where the timber has splits caused during the drying out process
3 'splits' across the timber caused during felling or compression
4 'warping' where the board is no longer flat and straight but curved in section
5 'waney' edges where the bark and sapwood have been left on
6 'heartwood' in softwood boards

Unfortunately, not all defects are immediately apparent; they emerge during manufacture.

CONVERTING LOGS TO TIMBER

The main aim is to obtain as much useful timber as possible. However, hardwood planks should show a specified grain pattern. Hardwood which is to be used for finished work where the grain is not important, eg on legs and rails, may simply be cut into boards of ½ in, ¾ in, or ⅞ in. Where the appearance of the grain is important, cuts are made carefully, perhaps using tangential or radial cuts to produce the optimum effect.

GRADES OF TIMBER

Grading is carried out according to the visual quality of one face of the board. 'Firsts and Seconds' are boards with one defect-free face. 'No 1 Common and Selects' may have some discolouration or blemishes on the reverse but a good quality face. 'Merchantable' grades are lower in quality.

However, interesting textures and patterns can be found in lower grades and, for certain projects, may be ideal.

SAWN TIMBER TERMINOLOGY

Pieces of timber are described according to their size, as follows:

Batten – softwood often 50 mm x 19 mm
Baulk – a squared log of at least 115 mm square
Board* - hardwood up to 32 mm thick
Plank – at least 280 mm wide and 50-150 mm thick
Slab** - regarded as waste and made from outside of logs
Strip – less than 102 mm x 50 mm

---

* sold S/E (square-edged) or W/E (waney-edged)
** useful for covering stacked timber

2

Unit 5
Document 3

SELECTING TIMBER

If you wish to avoid problems throughout the manufacturing process and with the finished product, you need to take great care in the selection of your raw materials. There are very many factors to be taken into account when choosing your timber or board.

HARDWOODS

There are two main classes of timber: hardwoods and softwoods. Hardwoods are not necessarily 'hard' in nature. They are derived from deciduous, broadleaved trees which grow in temperate climates and shed their leaves in winter. They have open cells which carry moisture through the tree by conduction.

SOFTWOODS

Softwoods are derived from cone-bearing (coniferous) trees with needle-like leaves.

The cells are not open and the sap (moisture) passes through the thin, semi-permeable cell walls.

HEARTWOOD

On the end grain of a section of round wood, there is an area of 'pith' which is the original sapling around which all later growth has occurred. As a matter of interest, if the 'heart' is off-centre, this is an indication that stress has been applied, perhaps through resisting gravity or prevailing gale-force winds and storms.

Timber is an expensive material and you need to be on the look-out for defects when you are purchasing it. Defects in the wood will have to be cut out, causing wastage.

1

GIVING A PRESENTATION

PREPARATIONS

Giving a presentation, seminar or lecture causes anxiety to almost everyone. It is sometimes assumed that people who do this regularly do not worry about it but this is not the case.

Being apprehensive before speaking in public is natural. However, there are several methods of preventing this anxiety from getting the better of you – and they are all related to preparation. A well-prepared presentation can be enjoyed by the audience and the presenter, as well as achieving its aims in terms of motivating, giving information etc.

Good basic groundwork is the key to success and should be done well in advance.

The following areas need to be researched:

> The occasion or event
> The audience/listeners
> The location

Clear information about the occasion can be obtained from managers, coordinators and colleagues. However, it may be necessary to ask pertinent, even persistent, questions to get definite facts in this respect. The list below may help:

> Department/organisation
> Formality/dress requirements
> Organisational objectives
> Programme/order of proceedings
> Questions and/or discussion opportunities
> Speakers/presenters involved
> Time allowance and start time

1

GIVING A PRESENTATION

Obviously, the audience must be the focus of the presentation and so it is vital to discover as much as possible about the size of the audience, their level of expertise, opinions, scope of influence and, last but not least, any tensions present in the group. The list below may help:

> Expectations of delegates
> Key figures likely to be present
> Number of delegates/visitors
> Possible hostility or opposition to the topic
> Pre-conceptions on the topic(s)
> Pre-existing conflicts between sections within the group
> Prior knowledge and/or skills

Being apprehensive before speaking in public is natural. However, there are several methods of preventing this anxiety from getting the better of you – and they are all related to preparation. A well-prepared presentation can be enjoyed by the audience and the presenter, as well as achieving its aims in terms of motivating, giving information etc.

2

Unit 6
Exercise 6B

PREPARATIONS

Giving a talk, seminar or lecture causes anxiety to almost everyone. It is sometimes assumed that people who do this regularly do not worry about it but this is not the case.

Being apprehensive before speaking in public is natural. However, there are several methods of preventing this anxiety from getting the better of you – and they are all related to preparation. A well-prepared talk can be enjoyed by the audience and the presenter, as well as achieving its aims in terms of motivating, giving information etc.

Good basic groundwork is the key to success and should be done well in advance.

The following areas need to be researched:

The occasion or event
The audience/listeners
The location

Clear information about the occasion can be obtained from managers, coordinators and colleagues. However, it may be necessary to ask pertinent, even persistent, questions to get definite facts in this respect. The list below may help:

Department/organisation
Formality/dress requirements
Organisational objectives
Programme/order of proceedings
Questions and/or discussion opportunities
Speakers/presenters involved
Time allowance and start time

GIVING A TALK

1

Unit 6
Exercise 6B continued

Obviously, the audience must be the focus of the talk and so it is vital to discover as much as possible about the size of the audience, their level of expertise, opinions, scope of influence and, last but not least, any tensions present in the group. The list below may help:

Expectations of delegates
Key figures likely to be present
Number of delegates/visitors
Possible hostility or opposition to the topic
Pre-conceptions on the topic(s)
Pre-existing conflicts between sections within the group
Prior knowledge and/or skills

The setting where a talk is given can have a profound effect on its outcome. A cramped, stuffy room can leave the audience feeling very uncomfortable whilst a room which is far too large can be impersonal and cold. At either extreme, the speaker can have difficulty in being successful. Visit the location beforehand and, if possible, have a rehearsal. Use the following checklist to help you:

Acoustics
Equipment, eg flipcharts, whiteboards, markers
Formality of setting
Layout of room including seating
Microphone/PA System
Projectors – type and method of use
Travel time and mode of transport

Being apprehensive before speaking in public is natural. However, there are several methods of preventing this anxiety from getting the better of you – and they are all related to preparation. A well-prepared talk can be enjoyed by the audience and the presenter, as well as achieving its aims in terms of motivating, giving information etc.

The above text was extracted from a staff development session delivered by Louisa Weston. She will repeat this session on the following dates and at the branches shown:

Branch	Date
Manchester	7 September
York	8 October
York	10 October
Huddersfield	12 October
Manchester	8 November
Huddersfield	10 November

GIVING A TALK

2

PANACHE TRADING LTD

67 Firth Road
HUDDERSFIELD
HD12 7GT

Tel no: 01484 489472
Fax no: 01484 489315
Internet: www.panache.co.uk
e-mail: sales@panache.co.uk

Our ref AM-L/your initials/T&D Ext 346

Date of typing

Mr J P Astley
Sovereign Business Solutions
26 Waverley Road
BRADFORD
BD5 2SM

Dear Mr Astley

Training and Development on Payroll Package

I am writing to give you further information on the above subject as requested.

Details of staff development sessions within the **Panache** Group are circulated monthly to all heads of units and departments. Information is also displayed on all notice boards throughout the organisation and in the weekly Staff Newsletter.

Proposals for new initiatives are made on Form TDPR1/1 which is available on the **Panache** intranet. I believe that you have already developed a proposal with one of our Training Officers. I enclose the draft proposal form for your attention.

Branches in Huddersfield, York and Manchester have custom-built training accommodation with computer terminals, and you are welcome to visit any or all of these sites prior to delivering the training sessions. A new facility in Derby will be ready for use in 3 months' time.

As you will see from the enclosed schedule, in order to support the introduction of the new system which is to be installed initially at the Huddersfield site, training will be held on 13/14 October and 11/12 November. This particular development is mandatory for all personnel and payroll staff. Unit managers from other branches will be expected to attend.

Please contact me within the next week so that we can finalise plans.

Yours faithfully
PANACHE TRADING LTD

Amanda Murray-Leith
TRAINING & DEVELOPMENT OFFICER

Enclosures: Schedule
                Draft proposal form

To apply for a place, please complete Application Form TDAP1/2 and return it to your

Head of Unit for authorisation.

Panache Training and Development Unit aims to ensure that all employees are given

free access to high quality training and personal development opportunities.

Trainees are requested to complete Evaluation Form TDEV1/5 after training so that

comments can inform the process of continuous improvement.

GIVING A TALK

3

The pecking order

Some authorities believe that the factor of 'being in control' is vital. Although senior business executives work hard, they do tend to be more in control of their work and the work itself is often varied. The ability to exercise control over tasks to be performed and use of time during their working day protects them, to some extent, from the effects of stress.

Unfortunately, this same ability to control their own environment may also give them the opportunity to exercise control over their 'inferiors' and, when this is perceived to be counter-productive by the 'controllee', it adds even more to the stress level of the latter. The manager of a department therefore should acknowledge and appreciate his or her responsibility for the health of colleagues in his or her charge.

The costs of stress

Individuals suffering the effects of stress can easily identify the costs in personal terms. Their health, relationships and ability to enjoy life are adversely affected. However, there is also enormous cost to commerce, industry and the professions.

The costs are shown as:

1   increases in premature retirements

2   increases in premature deaths

3   higher health care costs

4   higher absence rates[2]

Invisible costs, although difficult to measure, have profound effects on performance and productivity within the workplace. It is only when the invisible costs become apparent that the full picture can be observed.

---

[2] The highest absence rate is found in the transportation and communications industry (8.97%)

Occupational Aspects

STRESS AND ILLNESS

Predisposing factors

You may have seen a list of life events or a life stress scale.[1] Each life event, ranging from death of a spouse at the top of the scale (100), and minor law breaking at the bottom of the scale (11), has a score out of 100. This list of life events does not only include so-called 'negative' events, such as being fired or divorced, but also includes events which are commonly perceived to be 'positive'. Examples are marriage or holidays.

It is said that an individual's risk of suffering a stress-related illness is related to their score on the life events scale during the previous year. Approximately 50% of people who exceed 200 on the scale develop health problems. Almost 80% of people who exceed 300 on the scale succumb to ill health.

It is an alarming fact that the majority of our waking hours (60% - 70% according to statistics) is spent working. If work involves being in contact with people we do not particularly like, in a job which we do not enjoy, where little appreciation of employees' achievements is shown, and where the financial remuneration is felt to be insufficient, then we become 'stressed' and a reaction of some type is triggered.

If, in addition to these negative factors at work, we are struggling to pay bills or having problems with our accommodation or in social or family relationships, it is not surprising that a few individuals display severe symptoms of distress.

---

[1] Sometimes called the Holmes Rahe scale after its authors

Occupational Aspects

Unit 7
Exercise 7D

PANACHE DESIGN AND PRINT
Creative, reliable and speedy printing services
67 Firth Road
HUDDERSFIELD
HD12 7GT

<u>Design</u>
Leaflets
Brochures
Posters
Mailers
Presentation folders
Greetings cards

<u>Service</u>
Standard – maximum 3 weeks
Quick – maximum 10 days
Superstar – maximum 1 week

Please telephone 01484 486753 for our full-colour brochure giving prices, product descriptions and examples, colour chart and typeface selector.

Your document may not look exactly the same as this example as you may have used different fonts and sizes. However, the text should be the same as this.

Unit 7
Exercise 7B continued

Work in the 21st century

The invisible costs can include:

1   reduced mental performance
2   lack of concentration
3   impaired judgment
4   ineffective leadership
5   reduced creativity
6   fewer innovations
7   lack of decision-making skills

Persons under stress are more accident-prone[3] – another factor affecting health, and generating costs to the health service, the employer and the person concerned and their family. The tendency to have accidents can be related to forgetfulness, anxiety and impaired coordination.

Highest risk groups

The most stressful occupations are considered to be nursing, social work, police and teaching. In November 1994 a senior social worker won a High Court case for compensation against his employer. The judge said that he should have been given more support.

[3] 1.6 million accidents happen at work each year
Occupational Aspects

8

DARLOCK VALE SINGERS

Winter Programme

Traditional Carols and Christmas songs
The Market Cross, Dorlock
Saturdays in December from 2.00 pm to 4.00 pm

Spring Programme

North Country Folk Music
Lymeley Morris Dancers
The Market Cross, Dorlock
Sundays in May from 2.00 pm to 4.00 pm

Summer Programme

The Music of Shakespeare
Readings by the Morden Poetry Society
The Rose Garden, Vale Park
Sundays in August from 3.00 pm to 4.00 pm

Autumn Programme

English and European Sacred Music
The Cloisters, Morden Abbey
The Abbey will be floodlit
Saturdays in October from 6.00 pm to 7.00 pm

Public Collection

All proceeds to the Lymeley Hall Hospice. Please telephone the Secretary of the Darlock Vale Singers on 01234-2687419 for further details.

Membership

Participating members of the Singers come from all walks of life and most live within a 15-mile radius of Dorlock Vale. Meetings and rehearsals take place in 'The Red Rose' at Dorlock on Thursday evenings throughout the year except during local school holidays.

New members are always welcome. If you are interested, please contact the Secretary or just come along to the Function Room at The Red Rose between 7.30 pm and 9.30 pm most Thursdays. *You will be made very welcome.*

PANACHE PERSONAL INVESTMENTS

Most of us would like to become wealthy overnight, or at least increase our buying power considerably. Our chances of winning the lottery or 'coming up on the pools' are very, very slim, but we carry on trying because we think 'someone has to win'.

At first sight, investing in stocks and shares may seem less exciting than taking a chance but it can be extremely interesting and profitable. Property, works of art, gold and precious jewels have all been considered to be good stores of wealth in the past but, as our society's values have changed, these may have become less predictable investments.

Investing in the stock market is not as complex as it seems. Like all other institutions, it has its own jargon but the principles are reasonably simple.

Panache Investments, a branch of the Panache Trading Ltd Group of companies, has designed a series of one-day seminars, conveniently timed on Saturdays, for would-be investors. The Seminar programme aims to take the mystery out of the investment industry and make it accessible and, more importantly, profitable, for people who have always been interested but never felt able to take the plunge.

Just as no one house, job or car is right for everyone, so no one investment plan is appropriate for all potential investors. Our values differ and we have differing needs according to our age, occupation, life-style etc. The degree to which we are prepared to risk our hard-earned cash is an important factor. The Panache Investment Seminars could help you to decide on a strategy which is right for your circumstances and with which you feel comfortable.

Unlike most other Seminars, the Panache programme is not linked to a financial institution and therefore does not promote particular products nor receive commission. The short-lived 'high' experienced with taking a gamble and anticipating the result, is not for everyone. If you would prefer researched facts and supported decision-making, the Panache Seminars may be just what you have been waiting for. **Don't wait any longer – start making your fortune now!**

LAMONT LITERARY SOCIETY - SPECIAL SUMMER PROMOTIONS

CATEGORY	BOOK TITLE	AUTHOR	STANDARD PUBLISHER PRICE (£)	LAMONT SPECIAL OFFER PRICE (£)
Gardening	Water Garden Wonders	Evelyn Horrocks	21.99	15.99
DIY	Make it in a Day	Boris Zavedo	29.99	12.99
Gardening	Heavenly Herbs	Daniel de Courcy	16.99	9.99
Cookery	Quick Cuisine	Janette Scott	18.99	12.99
DIY	Rooms for a Change	Mark Durril	15.99	10.99
Cookery	Lavish Lunches	Peter Trent-Brown	9.99	7.99
Crafts	Modern Metalcraft	Austin Granger	8.99	6.99
Travel	Lakeland Excursions	Penny Walters	14.99	12.99
Crafts	Patchwork for Pleasure	Rhia Burns	18.99	14.99

SUMMER MEMBERSHIP OFFERS

WHAT WE OFFER

MEMBERSHIP LEVEL	MINIMUM BOOKS PER YEAR	MEMBERSHIP DISCOUNT
GOLD	12	25%
SILVER	6	20%
BRONZE	9	15%
PLATINUM	3	10%

Depending on which membership level you select, you can qualify for a further discount on the normal publisher price as shown in the MEMBERSHIP DISCOUNT column. Simply decide on the minimum number of books you wish to be delivered direct to your door each year and take advantage of our great money saving offer.

All membership levels will automatically receive a FREE 3-monthly colour review.

HARK THE HERALDS!

Warm the bleak midwinter with warm mince pies and mulled wine.

Take a break from the bustle of shopping and join in the singing around the Christmas Tree.

DARLOCK VALE SINGERS

Winter Programme
Traditional Carols and Christmas songs
The Market Cross, Dorlock
Saturdays in December from 2.00 pm to 4.00 pm

Plays and recitals on each day performed by local schools and youth groups.

You will be made very welcome.

All proceeds to the Lymeley Hall Hospice.

FORTHCOMING APPEARANCES OF THE DARLOCK VALE SINGERS:

Spring Programme
North Country Folk Music
Sundays in May from 2.00 pm to 4.00 pm

Summer Programme
The Music of Shakespeare
Sundays in August from 3.00 to 4.00 pm

Autumn Programme
English and European Sacred Music
Saturdays in October from 6.00 pm to 7.00 pm

Please telephone the Secretary of the Darlock Vale Singers on 01234-2687419 for further details.

Your document may not look exactly the same as this example as you may have used different fonts and sizes. However, the text which you copied from other documents should be the same as this.

BRINK ROYD PARK – SUMMER FETE

COMPETITION SCHEDULE

DATE AND TIME		COMPETITION TITLE	ENTRY FEE
Saturday 22 June	11.30 am	Flower arrangement	£2.00
Saturday 22 June	2.30 pm	Art – Landscapes (Water colours/Oils/Acrylics)	£2.50
Saturday 22 June	3.30 pm	Art – Portraits (Water colours/Oils/Acrylics)	£2.50
Saturday 22 June	3.30 pm	Art – Still Life (Water colours/Oils/Acrylics)	£2.50
Saturday 22 June	4.30 pm	Vegetables and Fruit	£2.00
Sunday 23 June	10.00 am	Crafts and Needlework	£1.50
Sunday 23 June	12.30 am	Jams, Pickles and Preserves	£1.50
Sunday 23 June	1.30 pm	Photography (Colour Section and Black and White Section)	£2.50
Sunday 23 June	2.30 pm	Poetry/Prose	£2.00

ENTRANT APPLICATIONS

COMPETITION TITLE	NAME	ADDRESS	POST CODE	PAYMENT METHOD
Flower arrangement	Sonjya Sheraton	2 Valley Way, Halifax	HX1 3TU	Cheque
Art –Portraits (Oils)	Tanya Davies	23 Merton Drive, Halifax	HX3 4BB	Cash
Crafts and Needlework	Alma Thorne	48a Wendle Road, Huddersfield	HD3 7RS	Cheque
Jams, Pickles and Preserves	Edith Vernon	12 Juniper Street, Huddersfield	HD2 8TV	Cash
Poetry	Allan Guildford	33 Watmough Street, Halifax	HX2 7HT	Access
Photography (Colour)	Miles Mitchell	26 Burns Crescent, Dewsbury	WF13 8BS	Cheque
Vegetable and Fruit	Mary Keene	177 Roxley Road, Huddersfield	HD4 4AC	Cheque
Art – Still Life (Acrylics)	Robert Adams	81 Garth Road, Halifax	HX2 9BW	Barclaycard
Art – Landscapes (Oils)	Adeline Roberts	19 Warrington Way, Dewsbury	WF12 7TN	Switch

LARRY'S MUSIC AND VIDEO STORE

STOCK CONTROLLER RESPONSIBILITES

MEDIUM	STOCK CONTROLLER	STORE LOCATION
Videos	Mike Denbury	Room 418, Racks 1-10, 18-30
CDs	Sharon Balmforth	Room 418, Racks 11-15, Room 417, Racks 2-6
Tapes	Rhonda Jones	Room 417, Racks 1, 7-12, Room 419, Racks 1-50
Headphones	Drew Montgomery	Room 418, Racks 16-17
Vinyl	Rhonda Jones	Room 419, Racks 51-65
Miscellaneous	Arshad Ahmed	Room 417, Racks 13-25

ADDITIONAL VIDEO TITLES

TITLE	REF	CATEGORY	PRICE (£)		NO IN STOCK	STORE LOCATION
			SELL	PURCHASE		
Meet Joe Black	43921	12	12.99	6.50	100	418/2
Shakespeare in Love	29117	15	13.99	8.00	12	418/3
Notting Hill	37762	15	12.99	6.50	25	418/29
Saving Private Ryan	28117	15	14.99	8.00	20	418/9
Jack Frost	20199	PG	9.99	4.50	30	418/22
Ransom	36185	18	13.99	7.00	16	418/19
There's Something About Mary	29935	15	9.99	4.50	10	418/4
The Full Monty	28137	15	14.99	7.50	130	418/25
Lost in Space	14339	PG	8.99	4.99	5	418/8
Pulp Fiction	05098	18	13.99	7.00	5	418/29

All new video titles to be added to our website
www.larrysvideos.co.uk

LEARN TO BECOME RICHER

PANACHE PERSONAL INVESTMENTS

Most of us would like to become wealthy overnight, or at least increase our buying power considerably. Our chances of winning the lottery or 'coming up on the pools' are very, very, very slim, but we carry on trying every week because we think 'someone has to win'.

At first sight, investing in stocks and shares may seem less exciting than taking a chance but it can be extremely interesting and profitable. Property, works of art, gold and precious jewels have all been considered to be good stores of wealth in the past but, as our society's values have changed, these may have become less predictable investments.

Networking and time-sharing of holiday properties have not proved to be the money-makers promised by many entrepreneurs. Fluctuations in the economy have less effect on the share market over a period of time than on disposable income, on which some other investment schemes are based.

PPIS/Mail/Jim Rennie

5

LEARN TO BECOME RICHER

Perhaps you are not happy to speculate. Panache Personal Investments will show you how to invest safely. Investing in the stock market is not as complex as it seems. Like all other institutions, it has its own jargon but the principles are reasonably simple.

Panache Personal Investments, a branch of the Panache Trading Ltd Group of companies, has designed a series of one-day seminars, conveniently timed on Saturdays, for would-be investors. The seminar programme aims to take the mystery out of the investment industry and make it accessible and, more importantly, profitable, for people who are interested but hesitate to take the plunge.

Just as no one house, car or job is right for everyone, so no one investment plan is appropriate for all potential investors. Our values differ and we have varying needs according to our age, occupation, life-style etc. The degree to which we are prepared to risk our hard-earned money is an important factor. The Panache Personal Investment Seminars could help you to decide on a strategy which is right for your circumstances and with which you feel comfortable.

In return for a small initial sum of approximately £1,500 per year and a few hours a week of your time, you could be earning up to £40,000. If that sounds unbelievable, simply come along and look at our statistics.

PPIS/Mail/Jim Rennie

6

LEARN TO BECOME RICHER

Successful investors who started off with Panache Seminars will be present at the first and subsequent seminars to assist you and to confirm the success of the programme. They will act as your tutors in the beginning and later as your mentors. Quite soon you will be friends and colleagues in this exciting new venture, assisting each other to continue to increase your wealth, and enjoying all the benefits this brings.

Complete the form on the reverse of this booklet to let us know that you are interested. We will forward full details of the programme of seminars to you, together with your preliminary lesson.

Details of venues, dates and times are enclosed separately for your reference. It is not obligatory to attend the same venue but the seminars should be attended in order as each one will build on the skills learned in the previous one.

Most of us would like to become wealthy overnight, or at least increase our buying power considerably.

Don't wait any longer – start making your fortune now!

PPIS/Mail/Jim Rennie

8

LEARN TO BECOME RICHER

Unlike most other seminars, the Panache programme is not linked to a financial institution and therefore does not promote particular products nor receive commission. The short-lived 'high' experienced with taking a gamble and anticipating the result, is not for everyone. If you would prefer researched facts and supported decision-making, the Panache Seminars may be just what you have been waiting for.

At the seminars, you will learn:

- the best time to start investing
- how to obtain your initial funds
- how to estimate risks
- how to avoid extra income tax
- how to make inflation work for you
- how to choose a reliable company
- how to avoid the usual pitfalls
- how to take full responsibility for your own wealth

THE FIRST SEMINAR IS FREE!

There is no need to pay out money in advance. You can test the product before you buy it. The hints and skills which you pick up in the first lesson will convince you that you are on to a winner and you will begin creating wealth immediately.

You will be given a simple but effective handbook which will support you through the first few days of your new wealth-creation activities.

PPIS/Mail/Jim Rennie

7

PANACHE INVESTMENT SEMINARS

DATE	SEMINAR	CITY	VENUE	TIMES	COORDINATOR
2 January	1 Getting Started	Glasgow	Western Hotel	9.30 – 4.30	Paula Sylvestre
9 January	1 Getting Started	Manchester	Carter Hotel	10.00 – 5.00	Frances Wood
16 January	1 Getting Started	Hull	Holland Hotel	9.30 – 4.30	Antony Collins
13 February	2 Moving On	Glasgow	Hunter Hall	10.00 – 5.00	Shaheen Kosar
20 February	2 Moving On	Manchester	Irwell Hotel	10.00 – 4.30	Robert Home
27 February	2 Moving On	Hull	Holland Hotel	10.00 – 5.00	Antony Collins
6 March	3 On the Launchpad	Glasgow	Hunter Hall	10.00 – 1.00	Chris Cooke
13 March	3 On the Launchpad	Manchester	Carter Hotel	9.30 – 12.30	Karl Hessen
20 March	3 On the Launchpad	Hull	Bridge Hotel	10.00 – 1.00	Rodney Lawton

SEMINAR FEES

SEMINAR	TITLE	DATES	FEE (£)
1	Getting Started	2 January, 9 January, 16 January	£100
2	Moving On	13 February, 20 February, 27 February	£90
3	On the Launchpad	6 March, 13 March, 20 March	£50

PANACHE DESIGN AND PRINT

Creative, reliable and speedy printing services
67 Firth Road
HUDDERSFIELD
HD12 7GT

DESIGN

❖ Brochures
❖ Greetings cards
❖ Leaflets
❖ Mailers
❖ Posters
❖ Presentation folders

SERVICE

❖ Superstar – maximum 1 week
❖ Quick – maximum 10 days
❖ Standard – maximum 3 weeks

COLOUR PRINTING

Colour printing is not as expensive as you may think. We have invested over £300,000 in new technology so that we can provide high quality colour work at a reasonable cost.

Selecting colours to give impact to your stationery and literature without losing clarity and legibility can be tricky. We will advise you on the best colour combinations and create a selection of samples for you to choose from. *(A small charge is made for this service.)*

PHOTOGRAPHY

You may supply your own pictures in print or transparency format, but please remember that the quality must be good.

If you would like our professional photographer to carry out this work, we would be pleased to arrange this for you.

Please telephone 01484 486753 for our full-colour brochure giving prices, product descriptions and examples, colour chart and typeface selector.

PANACHE DESIGN AND PRINT

Creative, reliable and speedy printing services
67 Firth Road
HUDDERSFIELD
HD12 7GT

Your printout may not be exactly the same as this one as you may have used different fonts and font sizes. However, the text should be the same as this.

Weekend Breaks

COME FOR A SHORT BREAK IN DARLOCK VALE

A guide to weekend breaks - Spring and Summer

HOTELS AND GUEST HOUSES

There is a wide selection of accommodation in this beautiful part of the West of England, ranging from modern hotels to rambling farmhouses, from historic houses to country inns. This information sheet will provide weekend visitors with a choice of places in which to stay in the Vale.

All the accommodation has been inspected and classified under the National Tourist Association Silver Triangle Scheme. Several of the hotels have won additional awards for their restaurants, wine lists or range of beers. All accommodation has en-suite bathrooms, colour TV, central heating and tea or coffee-making facilities in rooms.

Many visitors to Darlock Vale enjoy activities such as golfing, fishing, cycling, and horse-riding. Details of locations and organisers are to be found in the Darlock Vale Activities leaflet which can be obtained from local offices of the National Tourist Association.

NTA/DV/WB

1

WHERE TO STAY FOR A SHORT BREAK IN DARLOCK VALE
A guide to hotels and guest houses offering weekend breaks - Spring and Summer

There is a wide selection of accommodation in this beautiful part of the country, ranging from modern hotels to rambling farmhouses, from historic houses to country inns. This information sheet will provide prospective weekend visitors with a choice of places in which to stay in the Vale. All the accommodation has been inspected and classified under the National Tourist Authority Triangle Scheme. Several of the hotels have won additional awards for their restaurants, wine lists or range of beers. All accommodation has en-suite bathrooms, colour TV, central heating and tea or coffee-making facilities in rooms.

A visit to Darlock Vale could include activities such as golfing, fishing, cycling, and horse-riding. Details of locations and organisers are to be found in the Darlock Vale Activites leaflet which can be obtained from local offices of the National Tourist Authority.

The Good Food in Darlock Vale leaflet gives the visitor details of the many excellent restaurants, inns and hotels providing appetising and nourishing meals.

Visitors taking weekend breaks during May and June will be given free Pass to the Past Vouchers allowing up to 50% discounts on admissions charges to museums, art galleries and historic houses in the area. Please ask for details when booking.

White Wood Farm

Relax in front of a warm log fire, savouring the aroma of farmhouse cooking. The proprietor, Anna Morris, takes great pride in preparing meals from the fresh produce of her kitchen garden. Her bread and cakes have won many prizes at local agricultural shows. Situated just off the main road from Darlock to Telbridge and convenient for Telbridge Castle.

Glebe Villa

An early 19th century house approximately ¼ mile from the centre of Claybury on the East Minton road. Decorated by the owner, David Porter, in the Victorian style and containing many original features such as the magnificent oak staircase and stained glass windows. A friendly, family atmosphere where children are welcome. Residents' lounge and safe play garden for small children.

The Grove

A detached house in delightful gardens, offering a quiet and secluded haven on the outskirts of Darlock. Panoramic views across the Vale from most bedrooms. Meals taken in south-facing conservatory. A well-stocked library is open to all visitors. A non-smoking residence. Sorry, no pets.

Weekend Breaks

SELF-CATERING

If you prefer the informal, relaxed type of break where you can come and go as you please, try one of our self-catering cottages or log cabins. The leaflet Self-Catering in Darlock Vale gives full details.

The Good Food in Darlock Vale leaflet gives the visitor details of the many excellent restaurants, inns and hotels providing appetising and nourishing meals to non-residents.

> Visitors taking weekend breaks during May and June will be given free Pass to the Past Vouchers allowing up to 50% discounts on admissions charges to museums, art galleries and historic houses in the area. Please ask for details when booking your accommodation.

White Wood Farm

Relax in front of a warm log fire, savouring the aroma of farmhouse cooking. The proprietor, Anna Morris, takes great pride in preparing meals from the fresh produce of her kitchen garden. Her bread and cakes have won many prizes at local agricultural shows. Situated just off the main road from Darlock to Telbridge and convenient for Telbridge Castle.

Glebe Villa

An early 19th century house approximately ¼ mile from the centre of Claybury on the East Minton road. Decorated by the owner, David Parker, in the Victorian style and containing many original features such as the magnificent oak staircase and stained glass windows. A friendly, family atmosphere where children are welcome. Residents' lounge and safe play garden for small children.

Weekend Breaks

The Lilac Grove

A detached house in delightful gardens, offering a quiet and secluded haven on the outskirts of Darlock. Panoramic views across the Vale from most bedrooms. Meals taken in south-facing conservatory. A well-stocked library is open to all visitors. A non-smoking residence. Sorry, no pets. Vegetarian cuisine is offered by the owner, Jayne Green.

The Corn Dolly Inn

Character village inn dating back to the 17th century where, as you would expect, the walls have been decorated with fine examples of this ancient craft. Superb food, oak beams, patio garden.

Spring Mount Hall

Large, comfortable Georgian house in the quiet village of Mittenford. Antiques and paintings by local artists in public rooms. Award-winning cuisine.

PANACHE TRADING LTD

67 Firth Road
HUDDERSFIELD
HD12 7GT

Tel no: 01484 489472   Fox no: 01484 489315
Internet: www.panache.co.uk   e-mail: sales@panache.co.uk

Our ref LP/Enq/2001

Date of typing

Mr D Parker
Glebe Villa
210 East Minton Road
Claybury
DV8 9FG

Dear Mr Parker

HEALTH AND LEISURE EQUIPMENT

Thank you for your telephone enquiry regarding our range of equipment. We specialise in the planning and installation of 'Leisure Suites' for small hotels and we have 10 years' experience in this field. We purchase equipment and machinery from the best manufacturers throughout Europe. All products supplied by our company are rigorously tested and meet European standards.

Our service begins with a visit by our Planning and Design Engineers who will discuss your requirements with you in detail and carry out a full survey of the premises and/or rooms to be adapted.

It has come to my attention that Lower Hallburn Farm near to Darlock, who purchased a range of equipment from us about a year ago, is only a few miles from Claybury. I have contacted the proprietor, Mr Ben Oates, and he has kindly agreed to allow you to visit his Hotel and to discuss your proposals and our services with you. The address and telephone number are as follows: Lower Hallburn Farm, North Road, Hallburn, DV8 6HY. Telephone 01565-865906.

I have pleasure in enclosing our latest catalogue and price list and I will ask our Sales Department to telephone you in the near future to follow up your enquiry.

Yours faithfully

Amelia Byrom
Customer Liaison Unit

Encs

Copy: Sales Department
        File

4

Weekend Breaks

Lower Hallburn Farm

Riverside setting and only 2 miles from Hallburn, local market town, and the site of a Roman villa. Newly-constructed leisure suite with sauna, sunbed, mini-gymnasium and conservatory. Special diets catered for.

32 High Street

Georgian town-house in Darlock centre. Convenient for museums, riverside walks and shops. Wine bar and bistro on ground floor.

The Good Food in Darlock Vale leaflet gives the visitor details of the many excellent restaurants, inns and hotels providing appetising and nourishing meals to non-residents.

3 NIGHTS FOR THE PRICE OF 2

If you stay on Friday and Saturday nights during September, you may continue your break for an extra night (Sunday) at no extra cost. *This offer applies to bed and breakfast bookings at establishments with 2 or 3 Silver Triangles only.*

NTA/DV/WB

- Did you remember to indicate routing by ticking or highlighting the copies?
- If you reduced the pitch or margins for your letter, it may fit on one page like this example. This is acceptable provided that the pitch is not so small that the text is difficult to read.
- You may have used a ragged right margin. If no instruction is given, you may use the right alignment style of your choice.

WEEKEND BREAKS – HOTELS & GUEST HOUSES

NAME OF HOTEL/ GUEST HOUSE	CONTACT NAME	ADDRESS	TEL NO	PRICE PER PERSON (£)
32 High Street	Helen Miller	32 High Street, Darlock, DV1 8JH	01565-883423	£38.00
Glebe Villa	David Parker	210 East Minton Road, Claybury, DV8 9FG	01565-874523	£39.00/£75.00
Lower Hallburn Farm	Ben Oates	North Road, Hallburn, DV8 6HY	01565-865906	£37.00/£82.00
Spring Mount Hall	Alistair Mackie	Spring Mount, Mittenford, Darlock, DV3 9AS	01565-896589	£42.00/£90.00
The Corn Dolly Inn	William Hughes	The Green, East Minton, DV7 2CV	01565-878681	£40.00
The Lilac Grove	Jayne Green	WoodbridgeWay, Darlock, DV2 5DE	01565-882231	£80.00
White Wood Farm	Anna Morris	Darlock Road, Telbridge, DV10 7JU	01565-876548	£70.00

3 NIGHTS FOR THE PRICE OF 2 OFFER

NAME OF HOTEL/GUEST HOUSE	TEL NO	SILVER TRIANGLE AWARD	BB PRICE PER PERSON (£)
32 High Street	01565-883423	2	£38.00
Glebe Villa	01565-874523	2	£39.00
Lower Hallburn Farm	01565-865906	3	£37.00
The Corn Dolly Inn	01565-878681	2	£40.00

WHERE TO STAY

SHORT BREAKS IN DARLOCK VALE

Hotels and guest houses

Spring and Summer

The selection of accommodation in this beautiful part of the country ranges from modern hotels to rambling farmhouses, and from historic houses to country inns. This information sheet will provide prospective weekend visitors with a choice of places in which to stay in the Vale.

All the accommodation has been inspected and classified under the National Tourist Association Silver Triangle Scheme. Several of the hotels have won additional awards for their restaurants, wine lists or range of beers.

All accommodation has en-suite bathrooms, colour TV, central heating and tea or coffee-making facilities in rooms.

The Good Food in Darlock Vale leaflet gives the visitor details of the many excellent restaurants, inns and hotels providing appetising and nourishing meals.

Quality Cuisine

Anna Morris at White Wood Farm has won many prizes for her excellent English country fare. Spring Mount Hall's manager and chef, Alistair Mackie, has gained 4 Silver Triangles for his fresh and innovative creations.

Comfortable Surroundings

Look no further than the following for pleasant, warm and attractive décor and furnishings:

Glebe Villa
Lower Hallburn Farm
Spring Mount Hall
The Corn Dolly Inn
The Lilac Grove

A visit to Darlock Vale could include activities such as golfing, fishing, cycling, and horse-riding. Details are to be found in the Darlock Vale Activities leaflet from local offices of the National Tourist Association.

Visitors taking weekend breaks during May and June will be given free Pass to the Past Vouchers allowing up to 50% discounts on admissions charges to museums, art galleries and historic houses in the area. Please ask for details when booking.

Unit 11
Exercise 11B

THE SCOTTISH HIGHLANDS

LOCHS, GLENS and NATURE RESERVES

The glens and hills near Balquidder, where the notorious outlaw Rob Roy spent his last days, celebrate the beginning of the Highlands. Within the central Grampian Highlands lies the tree-fringed Loch Tummel, once so admired by Queen Victoria that it became known as the Queen's View. The Caledonian Canal, which connects Scotland's east and west coasts, passes through the infamous Loch Ness, alleged habitat of the legendary monster. Over in the forest-clad slopes of the Trossachs lie the vast 23-mile long bonnie banks of Loch Lomond that inspired many of the poems and novels of Sir Walter Scott.

SEA, SEALIFE, SEABIRDS and FARMLAND

Thousands of seabirds flock together on the steep red-sandstone cliffs that sweep down to sheltered sandy coves along the Moray Firth. The bustling fishing port of Lossiemouth, birthplace of James Ramsay MacDonald who became Prime Minister in 1924, hosts the Fisheries and Community Museum. Strathmore's fertile farmland by the sea hosts a mixture of cattle farms, steep braes and splendid beaches. The rocky headland across the West Voe of Sumburgh boasts a huge variety of wildlife and visitors looking out towards the Fair Isle can sometimes catch glimpses of dolphins and killer whales. The milder climate of the Ayrshire coast sees holiday resorts dotted amongst rocky coves and sandy beaches. In the farmland of the Shetlands Islands, there are more sheep and Shetland ponies than people and the islands are home to wildlife including:

- Gulls
- Skuas
- Puffins
- Seals

St Andrews, named after Scotland's patron saint, is situated within one of Britain's finest stretches of coastline, bordered on three sides by the Firth of Forth, the Firth of Tay and the North Sea.

CASTLES, MANSIONS and DISTILLERIES

Castles of Scotland have a lasting fascination. Eilean Donan, set on a rocky islet in Loch Duich, is an admirable reconstruction of a MacKenzie fortress. Deeside and Donside have a wealth of historic castles including Balmoral, Highland home of the Royal Family. In the region of Perth and Dundee, Guinevere, King Arthur's Queen, was incarcerated at Barry Hill and ghosts are still said to haunt the corridors of Glamis Castle. Travel back 300 years in time tasting the aromas and sound effects of Edinburgh's Scottish Whisky Heritage Centre.

Unit 11
Exercise 11B continued

Alternatively, Scotland offers a multitude of whisky distilleries where visitors can sample the delights of time-honoured techniques and processes. A few to try would be:

a) The famous Glenfiddich distillery founded in 1887
b) Clynelish – one of Scotland's finest malt whisky distilleries
c) Glenmurret distillery, established in 1775, displaying traditional methods

SKI SLOPES, CLIFFS and MOUNTAINS

Britain's highest mountain, the giant Ben Nevis, rises 4406 feet, from a sea loch to a bleak plateau, in the Great Glen. The jagged mountains of the Isle of Skye offer a serious challenge for the most experienced climbers. The tiny village of Torredon is set against a backdrop of magnificent, sculptured sandstone peaks. Spectacular cliff-top walks around Banff and Buchan allow breathtaking views of Highland scenery and dramatic sunsets. Winter sports abound on the northern snow-covered slopes of the sub-arctic plateaus of the Cairngorm Mountains where Aviemore, in particular, is renowned as a popular skiing resort.

CITIES, VILLAGES and ISLES

Dubbed 'The Athens of the North', Scotland's proud capital Edinburgh balances its high, dark buildings of the medieval Old Town with the classical architecture of the Georgian New Town. Edinburgh Castle, home of Scottish Kings and Queens down the centuries, dominates the city from its perch of volcanic rock. Scattered villages, surrounded by moors of red deer, still tell the tales of murder and treachery from days gone by. Ruined strongholds, wooded valleys, and heather-clad hamlets surround the villages and towns of Ayr and Kilmarnock, once the inspiration of Scotland's national poet, Robert Burns. The Inner Hebrides Isles form landscapes of wild beauty steeped in history including the 1775 Jacobite rebellion led by Bonnie Prince Charlie. The rugged moorlands of prehistoric standing stones, graves and brochs of the Outer Hebrides stretch in a 130-mile chain against Atlantic storms. The Orkney Isles take the traveller back in time to Stone Age tombs and Iron Age underground earth houses.

SEAFARERS SAILING CLUB
Special Events

EARLY EVENING BOAT CRUISES

Aboard the Princess Guinevere
Every Saturday and Sunday evening: July and August
6.30-9.30 pm
Adults: £5.50
Children and OAPs: £3.00

Cruise along the Breedale River between Derrin Valley and Guildbury Bridge, stopping for drinks at the Fox & Partridge

SUNDAY LUNCH SPECIALS

Aboard the Rembrandt or the Michelangelo
Traditional 3-Course Sunday Lunch
Extensive choice of menu
Every Sunday: June-September
12.00 noon - 2.30 pm
Adults: £12.50
Children and OAPs: £8.00

Relax and enjoy the sights and sounds of the surrounding countryside whilst listening to the gentle melodies of our own on-board music quartet

AFTERNOON TEA ON THE BONNY BREE

Aboard the Bonny Bree Breeze
Afternoon tea, scones with
strawberries and fresh cream
Every Sunday afternoon
throughout the season
2.00-4.30 pm

Adults: £5.50
Children and OAPs: £3.00

Enjoy a short 45-minute stop-off
at Breedale Crafts Centre

Seafarers Sailing Club, Briedale Riverbank, Derrin Valley, DA3 7GY
Tel no: 01459 348891

TREES AND SHRUBS

PLANTING

Generally, deciduous trees and shrubs are best planted between November and March whilst in a leafless state. Evergreens are usually planted in September and October, or preferably April when they start to make new growth. However, if plants are put out from pots, exceptions can be made since this does not disturb the roots, but no plants should ever be moved when the soil is icy or covered in snow. Plant in deeply dug and manured soil in a suitable situation for the species, ensuring that the planting hole is large enough to take the roots comfortably, leaving the soil slightly higher than the surrounding land to allow for normal levelling later. Young standard trees may need the support of a stake for several years until they become firmly established.

AFTER CARE

Soak the tree well if the ground seems dry at planting time. During the first summer, it is wise to spray the foliage of evergreens occasionally. Remove pernicious weeds, and apply a mulch (eg peat, bracken, leaves) to retain moisture and provide humus. Be careful not to dig too close to the shrubs to avoid damaging any feeding roots near to the surface. Very tender plants can benefit from a screen to protect them from the wind in their first year.

PROPAGATION

There are various methods of increasing stock such as seed, cuttings, layering, air layering, grafting, budding and division. Cuttings tend to be the most widely used method of propagation. There are two different techniques – half-ripe cuttings that are taken during the summer and hard-wood cuttings that are taken during the autumn. Growing from seed can be great fun and also very cheap. The best time to sow seeds is in early spring, about March.

Division simply involves lifting a tree or shrub and splitting it into several parts, making sure that each has some fibrous roots attached. The separated portions are then replanted. Division is best attempted in early spring before new growth begins.

GENERAL PRUNING

Pruning is vital for ensuring the maximum amount of good quality blooms, berries and fruits, and also to achieve balance, safety and shapeliness. As well as cutting back or removing sound branches, it is also essential to take out any dead or diseased wood. Methods of pruning vary, so it is wise to consult a good gardening book to become familiar with the habits of growth and flowering of particular species. Using incorrect techniques can lead to disease or infection setting in.

USE IN THE GARDEN

A carefully positioned tree or shrub can be used to mask of any unsightly aspects which detract from the beauty of the garden. They are also useful for forming windbreaks from any areas subject to prevailing winds, or to provide privacy from passers-by. Trees can be features in their own right, particularly those with attractively shaped or coloured leaves, flowering or berry trees, and those with coloured bark. Trees can also provide varying height levels to create balance and avoid the garden from becoming too flat-looking.

Unit 13
Exercise 13A

PANACHE TRADING LTD

MEMORANDUM

PERSONAL

From: Kim Redknapp, Marketing Manager
To: Heads of Departments
Ref: KR/009/34
Date: today's

LOCAL INDUSTRY INNOVATION FAIR

May I draw your attention to the attached letter which sets out some proposals for a Local Industry Innovation Fair.

I would appreciate it if you could forward your ideas and suggestions as to how we could benefit from participating in such an event. I believe that the event would provide us with an ideal opportunity to promote our business services to both current and prospective clients. We would also be able to network with other companies in the area who may be able to open up new opportunities for us through sub-contracting arrangements.

If there is anyone who would be interested in working with me on this initiative, I would be grateful if you could let me know on your reply. As you are aware, two of my key staff are on long-term sickness, so even a few hours from you or your staff would be very much appreciated. It will be necessary to have names of people who would be willing to 'staff' the event on a rota basis, although I am currently awaiting confirmation of dates when this will take place.

Please could you send your comments to Sue Bridges, Marketing Officer, by Friday *(date of Friday of next week)* so that she can co-ordinate them in readiness for my first planning meeting.

Enc

Copy: Sue Bridges
            File

Copy: **Sue Bridges** ✓
            File

Copy: **Sue Bridges**
            File ✓

Unit 12
Exercise 12D

GLORIES OF SCOTLAND

Alternatively, Scotland offers a multitude of whisky distilleries where visitors can sample the delights of time-honoured techniques and processes. A few to try would be:

a) The famous Glenfiddich distillery founded in 1887
b) Clynelish – one of Scotland's finest malt whisky distilleries
c) Glenturret distillery, established in 1775, displaying traditional methods

SKI SLOPES, CLIFFS and MOUNTAINS

Britain's highest mountain, the giant Ben Nevis, rises 4406 feet, from a sea loch to a bleak plateau, in the Great Glen. The jagged mountains of the Isle of Skye offer a serious challenge for the most experienced climbers. The tiny village of Torredon is set against a backdrop of magnificent, sculptured sandstone peaks. Spectacular cliff-top walks around Banff and Buchan allow breathtaking views of Highland scenery and dramatic sunsets. Winter sports abound on the northern snow-covered slopes of the sub-arctic plateaus of the Cairngorm Mountains where Aviemore, in particular, is renowned as a popular skiing resort.

CITIES, VILLAGES and ISLES

Dubbed 'The Athens of the North', Scotland's proud capital Edinburgh balances its high, dark buildings of the medieval Old Town with the classical architecture of the Georgian New Town. Edinburgh Castle, home of Scottish Kings and Queens down the centuries, dominates the city from its perch of volcanic rock. Scattered villages, surrounded by moors of red deer, still tell the tales of murder and treachery from days gone by. Ruined strongholds, wooded valleys, and heather-clad hamlets surround the villages and towns of Ayr and Kilmarnock, once the inspiration of Scotland's national poet, Robert Burns. The Inner Hebrides Isles form landscapes of wild beauty steeped in history including the 1775 Jacobite rebellion led by Bonnie Prince Charlie. The rugged moorlands of prehistoric standing stones, graves and brochs of the Outer Hebrides stretch in a 130-mile chain against Atlantic storms. The Orkney Isles take the traveller back in time to Stone Age tombs and Iron Age underground earth houses.

2

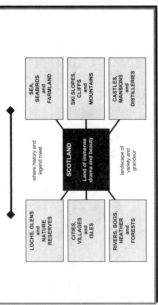

TOURIST ATTRACTIONS

TREES AND SHRUBS

PLANTING

Generally, deciduous trees and shrubs are best planted between November and March whilst in a leafless state. Evergreens are usually planted in September and October, or preferably April when they start to make new growth. However, if plants are put out from pots, exceptions can be made since this does not disturb the roots, but no plants should ever be moved when the soil is icy or covered in snow. Plant in deeply dug and manured soil in a suitable situation for the species, ensuring that the planting hole is large enough to take the roots comfortably. Tread down periodically, leaving the soil slightly higher than the surrounding land to allow for normal levelling later. Young standard trees may need the support of a stake for several years until they become firmly established.

AFTER CARE

Soak the tree well if the ground seems dry at planting time. During the first summer, it is wise to spray the foliage of evergreens occasionally. Remove pernicious weeds, and apply a mulch (eg peat, bracken, leaves) to retain moisture and provide humus. Be careful not to dig too close to the shrubs to avoid damaging any feeding roots near to the surface. Very tender plants can benefit from a screen to protect them from the wind in their first year.

PROPAGATION

There are various methods of increasing stock such as seed, cuttings, layering, grafting, budding and division. Cuttings tend to be the most widely used method of propagation. There are two different techniques – half-ripe cuttings that are taken during the summer and hard-wood cuttings that are taken during the autumn. Growing from seed can be great fun and also very cheap. The best time to sow seeds is in early spring, about March.

Division simply involves lifting a tree or shrub and splitting it into several parts, making sure that each has some fibrous roots attached. The separated portions are then replanted. Division is best attempted in early spring before new growth begins.

GENERAL PRUNING

Pruning is vital for ensuring the maximum amount of good quality blooms, berries and fruits, and also to achieve balance, safety and shapeliness. As well as cutting back or removing sound branches, it is also essential to take out any dead or diseased wood. Methods of pruning vary, so it is wise to consult a good gardening book to become familiar with the habits of growth and flowering of particular species. Using incorrect techniques can lead to disease or infection setting in.

USE IN THE GARDEN

A carefully positioned tree or shrub can be used to mask off any unsightly aspects which detract from the beauty of the garden. They are also useful for forming windbreaks from any areas subject to prevailing winds, or to provide privacy from passers-by. Trees can be features in their own right, particularly those with attractively shaped or coloured leaves, flowering or berry trees, and those with coloured bark. Trees can also provide varying height levels to create balance and avoid the garden from becoming too flat-looking.

SEAFARERS SAILING CLUB
Special Events

EARLY EVENING BOAT CRUISES

Aboard the Princess Guinevere
Every Saturday and Sunday evening: July and August
6.30–9.30 pm
Adults: £5.50
Children and OAPs: £3.00

Cruise along the Breedale River between Derrin Valley and Guildbury Bridge, stopping for drinks at the Fox & Partridge

SUNDAY LUNCH SPECIALS

Aboard the Rembrandt or the Michelangelo
Traditional 3-Course Sunday Lunch
Extensive choice of menu
Every Sunday: June-September
12.00 noon - 2.30 pm
Adults: £12.50
Children and OAPs: £8.00

Relax and enjoy the sights and sounds of the surrounding countryside whilst listening to the gentle melodies of our own on-board music quartet

AFTERNOON TEA ON THE BONNY BREE

Aboard the Bonny Bree Breeze
Afternoon tea, scones with strawberries and fresh cream
Every Sunday afternoon throughout the season
2.00-4.30 pm

Adults: £5.50
Children and OAPs: £3.00

Enjoy a short 45-minute stop-off at Breedale Crafts Centre

Seafarers Sailing Club, Breedale Riverbank, Derrin Valley, DA3 7GY
☎ *01459 348891*

PARTIES FOR SPECIAL OCCASIONS

CREATING THE RIGHT ATMOSPHERE

There is no magic formula for creating the right atmosphere to suit the occasion. However, with careful preparation and attention to details such as the nature of the invitation, displaying appropriate decorations, and serving special foods associated with the occasion, the atmosphere can be influenced.

SAINT VALENTINE'S DAY

Traditionally, this is the day when love blossoms, particularly among young people. Hearts, cupids and posies cut from pink card or paper, and small heart-shaped cakes and sandwiches, will help to set a romantic party mood.

HALLOWEEN

For the night traditionally associated with witches and mischief, decorations can be made to represent black cats, spiders, owls, witches and lanterns. Lanterns can be made from hollowed out turnips or pumpkins, or even jam jars covered with black paper silhouettes. Traditional foods are roasted chestnuts, various different nuts and fruit, especially apples. Ducking apples is the traditional game for parties on this day.

EASTER

Easter eggs, lambs, chickens and the famous Easter rabbit are all symbolic of this springtime celebration. Names of guests can be written or painted on to hard-boiled eggs. Small prizes such as little chocolate eggs, or small bags of sugar eggs, can be attractive for both adults and children. An attractive table centrepiece would be a small farmyard filled with small plastic animals. Amusing little egg figures can also be made from eggs and eggshells using pipe cleaners for arms and legs, wool or cotton for hair and pieces of felt for clothing.

PANACHE TRADING LTD

A meeting of the Executive Management Team of Panache Trading Ltd will be held on Friday 22 August in the Renaissance Conference Room, 67 Firth Road, Huddersfield, at 3.30 pm.

AGENDA

1) Apologies for absence

2) Minutes of the last meeting

3) Matters arising from the minutes

4) Financial analysis of assets and stock

5) Review of marketing strategy

6) Review of health and safety policy

7) Any other business

8) Date and time of next meeting

B RIDGEWAY
Honorary Secretary

Unit 14
Exercise 14B

MINUTES OF THE EXECUTIVE MANAGEMENT TEAM MEETING OF PANACHE TRADING LTD FRIDAY 22 AUGUST AT 3.30 PM IN THE RENAISSANCE CONFERENCE ROOM

PRESENT   Kellem Jordan (Chair)
Redknapp Kim
Richardson Gina
Normanton Alvin
Arif Surayah
Deneuve Estelle
Feathers Victor

1   APOLOGIES FOR ABSENCE – Hélène de Courcy, John Fern.

2   MINUTES of previous meeting were approved and signed.

3   MATTERS ARISING
3.1   The Auditor's Report was satisfactory.
3.2   The review of management salaries was postponed until the Personnel Director returned from sick leave.

4   FINANCIAL ANALYSIS OF ASSETS AND STOCK
The financial report showed healthy ratios of assets and stock. It was agreed to conduct a more detailed analysis of frequency of stock turnover and to explore the benefits of 'just-in-time' stock control methods. (Action SA)

5   REVIEW OF MARKETING STRATEGY
The corporate Marketing Plan for the next 3 years was presented to the Executive Team by Kim Redknapp, Marketing Manager. Agreed that Jordan Kellem would present this to the next Board meeting for approval. (Action JK)

6   REVIEW OF HEALTH AND SAFETY POLICY
6.1   Following the recent appointment of Roger Whitely as the new Health and Safety Officer, it was agreed that the current policy should be reviewed immediately. (Action RW)
6.2   Several written complaints had been received by staff about a number of the procedures being impractical, and these would be considered within the review. It was agreed that the Quality Manager, Gina Richardson, would circulate a questionnaire to all staff to analyse any other areas of staff concern and feed this back to RW. (Action GR)

7   ANY OTHER BUSINESS
Following the interest shown at the Local Industry Innovation Fair, Alvin Normanton outlined plans for a 10% expansion of the Sales Team. The Marketing Manager, Kim Redknapp, was thanked for representing the company's interests at the Fair and coordinating departmental activities.

8   DATE OF NEXT MEETING
To be notified.

Unit 14
Exercise 14C

MINUTES OF THE EXECUTIVE MANAGEMENT TEAM MEETING OF PANACHE TRADING LTD FRIDAY 22 AUGUST AT 3.30 PM IN THE RENAISSANCE CONFERENCE ROOM

PRESENT

		ACTION
Arif Surayah	(Finance Manager)	
Deneuve Estelle	(Personnel Manager)	
Feathers Victor	(Technology Manager)	
Kellem Jordan	(Chair)	
Normanton Alvin	(Sales Manager)	
Rednape Kim	(Marketing Manager)	
Richardson Gina	(Quality Manager)	
Ridgeway Barry	(Honorary Secretary)	

1   APOLOGIES FOR ABSENCE – Hélène de Courcy, John Fern.

2   MINUTES of previous meeting were approved and signed.

3   MATTERS ARISING
3.1   The Auditor's Report was satisfactory.
3.2   The review of management salaries was postponed until the Personnel Director returned from sick leave.

4   FINANCIAL ANALYSIS OF ASSETS AND STOCK
4.1   The financial report showed healthy ratios of assets and stock although some stock items were slow moving. It was AGREED to conduct a more detailed analysis of frequency of stock turnover and to explore the benefits of 'just-in-time' stock control methods.   **SA**

5   REVIEW OF MARKETING STRATEGY
5.1   The corporate Marketing Plan for the next 5 years was presented to the Executive Team by Kim Rednape, Marketing Manager. AGREED that Jordan Kellem would table the Plan at the next Board meeting for approval.   **JK**
5.2   A short-term Marketing Plan, focusing on immediate issues and actions for the next year, was also presented. Questions were raised about the implications of new technologies on the marketing strategy and Victor Feathers was asked to make a detailed report at the next meeting.   **VF**

6   REVIEW OF HEALTH AND SAFETY PROCEDURES
6.1   It was noted that there had been a 7½% increase in the number of accidents on company premises over the last year.
6.2   Following the recent appointment of Roger Whitely as the new Health and Safety Officer, it was AGREED that the current policy should be reviewed before the end of next month.   **RW**

**MINUTES OF THE EXECUTIVE MANAGEMENT TEAM MEETING OF
PANACHE TRADING LTD FRIDAY 22 AUGUST AT 3.30 PM IN THE
RENAISSANCE CONFERENCE ROOM**

ACTION

PRESENT

Kellern Jordan	(Chairperson)
Arif Surayah	(Finance Manager)
Ridgeway Barry	(Honorary Secretary)
Rendap Kim	(Marketing Manager)
Deneuve Estelle	(Personnel Manager)
Richardson Gina	(Quality Manager)
Normanton Alvin	(Sales Manager)
Feathers Victor	(Technology Manager)

1   APOLOGIES FOR ABSENCE – Hélène de Courcy, John Fern.

2   MINUTES of previous meeting were approved and signed.

3   MATTERS ARISING

3.1   Correspondence on agenda items was now being marked ᵂ/₀ Barry Ridgeway, Honorary secretary" to aid coordination.

3.2   The Auditor's Report was satisfactory but there were several weak areas to be reviewed.

3.3   The review of management salaries was postponed until the Personnel Director returned from long-term sick leave.

4   FINANCIAL REPORT

4.1   The financial report showed healthy trading ratios of assets and stock. It was agreed to conduct a more detailed analysis of frequency of stock turnover and to explore the benefits of 'just-in-time' stock control methods.   SA

4.2   More information was requested on the Profit and Loss Account.   SA

5   REVIEW OF MARKETING STRATEGY

5.1   The corporate Marketing Plan for the next 3 years was outlined to the Executive Team by Kim Rendap, Marketing Manager. Agreed that Jordan Kellern would present this to the next Board meeting for approval.   JK

5.2   There were issues in the Marketing Plan that may affect the operation of the Sales Force. Agreed that Alvin Normanton should assess the impact of improved marketing on sales and report back at the next meeting.   AN

1

6.3   Several written complaints had been received by staff about a number of the procedures being impractical, and these would be addressed within the review. It was AGREED that the Quality Manager, Gina Richardson, would circulate a questionnaire to all staff to analyse any other areas of staff concern and feed this back to RW.   GR

7   ANY OTHER BUSINESS

7.1   Following the interest shown at the Local Industry Innovation Fair, Alvin Normanton outlined plans for a 10% expansion of the Sales Team. The Marketing Manager, Kim Rednape, was thanked for representing the company's interests at the Fair and coordinating departmental activities.

7.2   Kim Rednape was asked to circulate feedback on the outcomes of the company's participation in the Fair to all Heads of Department.   KR

8   DATE OF NEXT MEETING
Arranged for Monday 15 September at 2.30 pm in the Renaissance Conference Room.

2

6 REVIEW OF HEALTH AND SAFETY POLICY

6.1 Following the recent appointment of Roger Whitely as the new Health and Safety Officer, it was agreed that the current policy should be reviewed and updated immediately. **RW**

6.2 Several complaints had been received from staff about a number of the procedures being impractical, and these would be included in the review. It was agreed that the Quality Manager, Gina Richardson, would circulate a questionnaire to all staff to analyse any other areas of staff concern and feed this back to RW. **GR**

7 ANY OTHER BUSINESS

7.1 It was agreed that the new Staff Appraisal Scheme was working well. Estelle Deneuve to advise on any Departments where the new scheme had not been implemented. **ED**

7.2 Following the interest shown at the Local Industry Innovation Fair, Alvin Normanton outlined plans for a 12½% expansion of the Sales Force. The Marketing Manager, Kim Rendap, was thanked for representing the company's interests at the Fair and coordinating departmental activities.

8 DATE OF NEXT MEETING

Arranged for Wednesday 17 September at 3.30 pm in the Georgian Conference room.

The meeting ended at 4.30 pm.

2

SIMPLE PARTY GAMES

CARDS IN THE BUCKET

Place a bucket or large basin about ten feet in front of a line and give each player ten playing cards. The object of the game is to flick as many cards as possible into the bucket. The one who gets the most in is the winner. The game can be played with corks, small paper airplanes or ping-pong balls.

COINS IN THE HAT

Players stand in a circle and are either given a coin by the host or asked to use one of their own. As music is played, the hat is passed around the circle from player to player. When the music stops, the person left holding the hat places their coin in the hat and then leaves the game. The music restarts and play resumes. The winner is the person left holding the hat, the prize being the hat full of coins. The value of the coin used sometimes affects the levels of cheating which players of this game tend to adopt!

TARGET BOUNCE

All you need for this game is an egg carton and some ping-pong balls. The aim is to bounce the ping-pong balls into the egg box compartments. The compartments may be numbered so that some score more than others. A target is set and the first person, or team, to reach that score is the winner.

PAPER STEPPING STONES

Each competitor is given two half pages of newspaper on which to 'run' a course. Standing on the first piece, he puts the other in front of him, steps on it, picks up the first piece and lays that in front of him, steps on it and so on until he completes the course. If the game is played by individuals, the person completing the race in the fastest time is the winner. If the game is played in relay teams, the first team to finish wins.

> Try to persuade your guests to participate in games you have arranged, but try not to embarrass a reluctant guest into doing something against their will.

Unit 15
Exercise 15C

TRAINING COURSES IN INFORMATION TECHNOLOGY

A number of short training courses in information technology will be available during the summer term. **We will be able to offer a limited number of places for participants to receive help with:**

- Free course fees

- Free examination fees

- Assistance with the cost of resources/materials

- Assistance with the cost of travel

- Assistance with the cost of childcare

For a personal interview, contact our training team on 01422 379789:

Janet Shearing
Suhail Akudi
Cleo Derrington

CODE	COURSE DETAILS	TUTOR
ADP7	Desk top publishing – all levels. Wednesday or Thursday afternoon: 2.30-4.00 pm. Monday or Wednesday evening: 6.00-8.30 pm.	Suhail Akudi
AIB2	Introduction to the Internet – beginners. Tuesday or Thursday morning: 9.30-11.00 am. Tuesday or Thursday evening: 7.00-8.30 pm.	Cleo Derrington
AWP12	Word processing - absolute beginners. Tuesday or Wednesday morning: 10.00-11.30 am. Monday or Thursday evening: 6.30-8.30 pm.	Janet Shearing
AWP18	Word processing - intermediate and advanced. Tuesday or Wednesday afternoon: 2.00-3.30 pm. Tuesday or Wednesday evening: 6.30-8.30 pm.	Janet Shearing
SDA3	Spreadsheets and databases – all levels. Monday or Wednesday morning: 9.30-11.00 am. Monday or Thursday evening: 7.00-8.30 pm.	Suhail Akudi

---

Unit 15
Exercise 15D

INSERTING SYMBOLS INTO A DOCUMENT

In the days when the typewriter was the only equipment available to prepare typed documents, spaces had to be left in the text so that any special symbols in the draft manuscript could be inserted afterwards by hand (using a pen). With the introduction of the computer, however, it became possible to insert symbols by keying in a single character or string of characters in the ANSI character set. For example, in the font Times New Roman the result of the field { SYMBOL 211 \f "Symbol" \s 12 } is the 12 point character: © (the copyright symbol). You can insert many common symbols by keying in the appropriate ANSI character code on the numeric keypad, such as typing ALT+0189 to insert ½.

INSERTING SYMBOLS WITH WORD 2000

One of the advantages of Word 2000 software is that it offers a much easier way of inserting symbols or special characters into a document. You can simply select **Symbol** from the **Insert** menu and then click on the preferred **Font**. When you click on a symbol, Word 2000 even allows you a close-up view before you insert it into your document. In the **Subset** list, there is also a list of extended language characters, such as Latin, Greek, Cyrillic (Russian), or Hebrew.

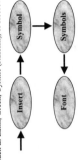

SYMBOL TYPES

The variety of symbols that can be inserted depends on which fonts are available on your particular computer. The default symbol font in Word 2000 is (**normal text**). This includes:

- Fractions or number forms such as ⅔, ½, ¾, ⅞. (Word 2000 will automatically insert fractions such as ½ as you key in.)

- International characters such as Ã, Œ, ë, Ɓ. These are particularly useful when keying in foreign names such as Françoise Viète.

- International monetary symbols such as £, F, ₧, ₫.

- General punctuation such as ‡, ‰, †, along with others not available on the standard keypad.

INSERTING SYMBOLS

SPECIAL CHARACTERS

By switching to the **Special Characters** tab of the **Insert, Symbol**

dialogue box, you can improve the appearance of text and insert

special characters into your document. A few examples of these

include ™ (Trademark), … (Ellipsis), ® (Registered), ¶ (Paragraph), §

(Section).

Although you may never need to use

many of these symbols it is useful to

know what is available for those that do

appear from time to time.

STIR FRY SUCCESS

WHY STIR FRY?

Stir frying has gained in popularity as a healthy way of cooking food, providing modest amounts of oil are used. Because it does not involve large quantities of liquid, it retains vitamins and minerals which are often lost when boiling or steaming. Apart from preserving nutrients, stir frying also tends to bring out the full flavour of complementary foods.

Firm fish fillets or chunks of fish are ideal for stir fry dishes. All poultry stir fries well, but must be cut into small pieces. Tough cuts of meat and poor quality mince should be avoided but minced steak, lamb or pork are suitable. Most vegetables, cooked or canned beans and pulses, cooked rice or pasta, can all be added to the stir fry.

FAST AND EASY

A boon for today's busy lifestyles, stir frying is fast and easy and does not require any special skills or techniques. It may be necessary to spend some time preparing some of the ingredients, but frozen and tinned ingredients may also be stir fried if time is precious.

EQUIPMENT

WOK   The traditional domed metal wok is the classic pan for stir frying. There is a wide choice of pans available, including non-stick, which offer various advantages, but deep sides and a well domed base are essential.

UTENSILS   A long handled stirring implement or spatula and a large scoop or draining spoon are useful. Remember that metal utensils should not be used on non-stick surfaces.

BASIC POINTS

Cut up the food fairly finely, and in similar sized pieces, so that it cooks quickly. (Food can be marinated in advance for extra flavour if preferred.) Trim any fat from meat and cut it across the grain as this gives the most tender results. Heat enough oil or other fat and evenly coat the pan before adding the ingredients. Add the ingredients in batches. Stir and turn the food, keeping it moving from the outside to the middle and vice versa. Cooked pieces can be pushed to one side of the pan. A small amount of liquid can be added to the pan to make a sauce just before the food is ready. Once the stir fry is ready, it should be served promptly.

Unit 16
Document 3

INSERTING SYMBOLS INTO A DOCUMENT

In the days when the typewriter was the only equipment available to prepare typed documents, spaces had to be left in the text so that any special symbols in the draft manuscript could be inserted afterwards by hand (using a pen).

With the introduction of the computer, however, it became possible to insert symbols by keying in a single character or string of characters in the ANSI character set. For example, in the font Times New Roman the result of the field { SYMBOL 211 \f "Symbol" \s 12 } is the 12 point character: © (the copyright symbol). You can insert many common symbols by keying in the appropriate ANSI character code on the numeric keypad, such as typing ALT+0189 to insert ½.

INSERTING SYMBOLS WITH WORD 2000

One of the advantages of Word 2000 software is that it offers a much easier way of inserting special characters or symbols into a document. You can simply select **Symbol** from the **Insert** menu and then click on the preferred **Font**. When you click on a symbol, Word 2000 even allows you a close-up view before you insert it into your document. In the **Subset** list, there is also a list of extended language characters, such as Latin, Greek, Cyrillic (Russian), or Hebrew.

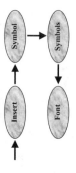

SYMBOL TYPES

There is a wide variety of symbols that can be inserted, depending on which fonts are installed on your particular computer. The default symbol font in Word 2000 is **(normal text)**. This includes:

- International monetary symbols such as £, ₣, **₧**, ₡.

- International characters such as Å, Œ, ė, ß. These are especially useful when keying in foreign names such as Françoise Viète.

- Fractions or number forms such as ⅔, ½, ¾, ⅛. (Word 2000 will automatically insert fractions such as ½ as you key in.)

- General punctuation such as ‡, ‰, †, and others that are not available on the standard keypad.

Unit 16
Document 2

STIR FRY SUCCESS

Stir frying is an ancient cooking technique which is ideal for contemporary living.

WHY STIR FRY?

Stir frying has gained in popularity as a healthy way of cooking food, providing modest amounts of oil are used. Because it does not involve large quantities of liquid, it retains vitamins and minerals which are often lost when boiling or steaming and tends to bring out the full flavour of complementary foods.

Chunks of fish or firm fish fillets are ideal for stir fry dishes. All poultry stir fries well, but must be cut into small pieces. Tough cuts of meat and poor quality mince should be avoided but minced steak, lamb or pork are suitable. Most vegetables, cooked or canned beans and pulses, cooked rice or pasta, can all be added to the stir fry.

QUICK AND EASY

Stir frying is a fast and easy method of lightly cooking food and does not require any special skills or techniques. It may be necessary to spend some time preparing some of the ingredients, but frozen and tinned ingredients may also be stir fried if time is precious.

EQUIPMENT

WOK The traditional domed metal wok is the classic cooking pan for stir frying. There is a wide choice of pans available, including non-stick, which offer various advantages, but deep sides and a well domed base are essential.

UTENSILS A long handled stirring implement or spatula and a large scoop or draining spoon are useful. Remember that metal utensils should not be used on non-stick surfaces.

BASIC POINTS

Cut up the food fairly finely into similar sized slices or cubes, so that it cooks quickly. (Food can be marinated in advance for extra flavour if preferred.) Trim any fat from meat and cut it across the grain as this gives the most tender results. Heat enough oil or other fat and evenly coat the pan before adding the ingredients. Add the ingredients in batches. Stir and turn the food, keeping it moving from the outside to the middle and vice versa. Cooked pieces can be pushed to one side of the pan. A small amount of liquid can be added to the pan to make a sauce just before the food is cooked. Once the stir fry is ready, it should be served promptly.

Add the slowest-cooking ingredients to the wok first. Fry the food until it becomes tender but still remains crisp.

CORONA CRAFTSHOP RESIDENTIALS

Learn a new craft and make new friends at one of our weekend craftshop residentials.

Situated in the heart of the Yorkshire Dales, Corona Cottage offers visitors a unique experience. Not only can you 'get away from it all' to sample the delights of the surrounding countryside, you can experience the satisfaction of learning a new skill and discovering hidden talents you never knew you had. Unlike the 'workshop' approach, our craftshops place the emphasis on:

- *FUN*
- *FRIENDSHIP*
- *RELAXATION*
- *ENJOYMENT OF LEARNING NEW SKILLS*

As part of our package, we offer high quality accommodation with TV and tea/coffee making facilities in all rooms. Accommodation is on a full board basis.

Prices to be added to the craftshop fee are:

- Single room with shared bathroom/toilet facilities: £45pp/pn
- Single room with en suite facilities: £55pp/pn
- Double room with shared bathroom/toilet facilities: £35pp/pn
- Double room with en suite facilities: £45pp/pn

All our craftshop residentials are staffed by professional instructors who have a wealth of experience and expertise in their chosen specialism.

1

SYMBOLS AND SPECIAL CHARACTERS

ADDITIONAL DEFAULT FONT SYMBOLS

In addition there are bullets, arrows, mathematical and scientific symbols. You may find more symbol fonts, such as Botanical or Wingdings, which include a range of decorative symbols. Fonts such as Math A or Math C include a wider range of mathematical fonts, which would be very useful if you were preparing documents for a statistician, or a teacher of mathematics.

SPECIAL CHARACTERS

By switching to the **Special Characters** tab of the **Insert, Symbol** dialogue box, you can improve the appearance of text and insert special characters into your document. A few examples of these include:

- ™ (Trademark)
- … (Ellipsis)
- ® (Registered)
- ¶ (Paragraph)
- § (Section).

THE EURO CURRENCY SYMBOL

Word 2000 allows you to display the euro currency symbol €. The fonts needed to display the euro currency symbol should have been installed when the Word 2000 software was installed. However, if the euro symbol prints out as a box you will need to check that your printer has the euro symbol in its resident fonts. If not, you will need to check with your printer salesperson how to update your printer fonts to include the euro currency symbol.

Although you may never need to use some of these symbols it is useful to know what is available for those that do appear from time to time.

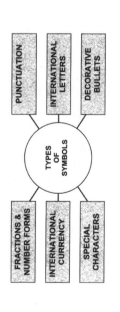

INSERT SYMBOL FACILITY

13

ACTIVITY		COST
COUNTRY CRAFTS	Basket and corn dolly making, dough modelling, pressed flower pictures, 3-D decoupage, china painting, candle making, glass painting.	£105.00
PAINT EFFECTS	Stippling, sponging, stencilling, clouding, rag-rolling, marbling, wood graining, liming, crackle-glaze, dragging, verdigris, bronzing and gold leaf.	£110.00
	Please bring overalls or other suitable clothing.	
PAPER CRAFTS	Calligraphy, papier-mâché, origami, quilling, Chinese lantern making, paper flower making, fancy dress masks, bookbinding.	£75.00
	Kite making will be offered as an alternative option to bookbinding.	
STONE & WOOD CRAFTS	Part of the craftshop day will take place at a nearby pottery in the local village (transport will be provided). Pottery, ceramics, stone carving, coal carving, plaster casting, mosaics, marquetry, woodturning, pyrography (poker work), garden ornaments.	£95.00
TEXTILE CRAFTS	Silk screen-printing, tie dying, cross-stitch, collage, embroidery (hand and machine), patchwork, lace making, quilting.	£85.00
	Silk painting techniques may also be available on the day for no extra charge.	